The Developing Countries in World Trade

The
Developing Countries
in World Trade

Policies and Bargaining Strategies

edited by
Diana Tussie and David Glover

Lynne Rienner Publishers ∎ Boulder
International Development Research Centre ∎ Ottawa

Published in the United States of America in 1993 by
Lynne Rienner Publishers, Inc.
1800 30th Street, Boulder, Colorado 80301

and in the United Kingdom by
Lynne Rienner Publishers, Inc.
3 Henrietta Street, Covent Garden, London WC2E 8LU

Published in Canada by the International Development Research Centre
PO Box 8500
Ottawa K1G 3H9 Canada
  Canadian ISBN 0-88936-668-3
  Canadian ISBN 0-88936-669-1 (pbk)

Library of Congress Cataloging-in-Publication Data
The Developing countries in world trade: policies and bargaining
  strategies / edited by Diana Tussie and David Glover.
      p. cm.
    Includes bibliographical references and index.
    ISBN 1-55587-384-7 (alk. paper)
    ISBN 1-55587-398-7 (pbk. : alk. paper)
    1. Developing countries—Commercial policy. 2. Free trade—
  Developing countries. 3. International trade. 4. International
  economic integration. I. Tussie, Diana. II. Glover, David, 1953-.
HF1413.D483   1993   92-34291
382'.3'091724—dc20   CIP

British Cataloguing in Publication Data
A Cataloguing in Publication record for this book
is available from the British Library.

Printed and bound in the United States of America

The paper used in this publication meets the requirements
of the American National Standard for Permanence of
Paper for Printed Library Materials Z39.48-1984.

To Erica, Natalia, and Ximena

Contents

Tables

Acknowledgments

This book would not have been possible without the contributions of a large number of people and organizations. We are particularly indebted to those trade negotiators who were so generous with their time and experience during lengthy interviews. We benefited greatly from the comments of those who participated in the project workshops, particularly Manuel Agosin, Patrick Low, John Odell, and Susan Strange. Celsa Domínguez and Marleny Tanaka provided valuable administrative support; Cristina Simone and María Wagner provided substantial input at various stages. We would like to thank the staffs of the North-South Institute in Ottawa, SELA in Caracas, and CASIN in Geneva for organizing our project meetings. Finally, we are grateful to Canada's International Development Research Centre and the Facultad Latinoamericana de Ciencias Sociales in Buenos Aires for financing and hosting the project. The views expressed are those of the authors and not necessarily those of IDRC.

Introduction

DAVID GLOVER & DIANA TUSSIE

Trade relations are undergoing more fundamental change than at any time since the immediate post–World War II era. The changes under way are crucial for the relations between developing and developed countries. The multilateral trading system is today facing its most severe test, with an apparent tilting of preferences of its major players in favor of subglobal arrangements. By contrast, a growing number of developing countries are embracing unilateral trade liberalization. The significance of these developments is worth emphasizing.

The 1980s were marked by a widespread balance-of-payments crisis that for many countries included a severe debt problem. This increased their need for export revenues. It also increased the influence of the World Bank and the International Monetary Fund (IMF) on policymaking in developing countries. Loans provided by these institutions to cover balance-of-payments deficits and restructure recipients' economies carried with them strict conditions, some of them related to trade policy. The Bank's policy-based loans—in particular structural adjustment and trade policy loans—were of great importance in moving developing countries to reduce barriers to imports; combined with currency devaluations required under Bank/Fund programs, the result was more open, export-dependent trade regimes.

External pressure was clearly important in provoking the initial movement to liberalization in most countries, and it continues to play a role in some today. Yet for a growing number of countries, including most of those in Latin America, there is now a government belief in the benefits of liberalization. This change in attitude has been one of the most remarkable developments of the early 1980s. As a result of these external and internal influences, developing countries have undergone significant trade liberalization. Between 1986 and 1991, thirty developing countries undertook unilateral liberalizations (GATT, 1991). Today a number of developing countries have more open trade policies, as measured by the level and dispersion of tariffs and the prevalence of quantitative restrictions, than the United States or the European Economic Community.

Along with this shift, developing countries have taken another step toward what developed countries have long demanded: active participation in trade negotiations in the General Agreement on Tariffs and Trade (GATT). Trade reforms have heightened the need for market access in a new range of products and increased their stakes in the system. To further these interests, developing countries have committed themselves, both individually and as members of coalitions, to the round of negotiations that began in Punta del Este in 1986, the Uruguay Round.

This reversal of attitudes and practice is at variance with trends in developed countries, where protectionism persists and is particularly pervasive for products exported from developing countries. These are not conditions conducive to trade reform. The shape of trade restrictions creates even more serious hazards. The broad postwar commitment to multilateralism has been losing considerable ground in both the policies and beliefs of major industrial countries. The United States, the major guarantor of the multilateral system, has been prone to "aggressive unilateralism" (Bhagwati, 1991). "Aggression" comes mainly in the form of sanctions applied to extract concessions from weaker trading partners. This has been done through Section 301 of U.S. trade legislation and the "Super 301" and "Special 301" mechanisms of the 1988 Omnibus Trade and Competitiveness Act.[1] Such a right to unilateral action has long been latent in U.S. law, but until the 1980s it was little exploited. In Western Europe the inclination toward managed trade has become pronounced. To the extent that major industrialized countries have shown interest in freer trade, it is through regional free trade agreements (FTAs).

At the same time, multilateral trade negotiations (MTNs) carried out under the GATT have become more ambitious and, correspondingly, more cumbersome. The Uruguay Round included a great many new issues as well as much unfinished business from earlier rounds. The new issues, including services, investment, and intellectual property rights, were numerous and complex to interpret and negotiate. In many cases, they also opened sensitive policy questions by touching on areas previously considered to fall within the discretion of domestic policymakers. Trade negotiations have begun to affect sovereignty as well as the historical and institutional fabric of societies. As new issues were added to older, intractable ones like agriculture, textiles, tariff escalation, and safeguards, the agenda became overloaded; the difficulty of reaching agreement was compounded and deadlines were repeatedly missed.

The slow and uncertain pace of progress in the GATT has led to frustration among the major powers and increasing resort to the bilateral and plurilateral measures discussed above. This, in turn, further undermines the effectiveness of the GATT. At the same time, there has been a decline in the multilateral instruments traditionally promoted by developing countries. International commodity agreements to stabilize and/or increase prices for primary exports have attracted less interest and support than they did in the 1970s, and few are operating effectively today.

These changes accumulated gradually over the 1980s and early 1990s, and their effects on developing countries have not yet been fully appreciated. The purpose of this book is to explore the implications of an altered world trading system for the developing countries, looking at two general areas. First, we describe how these changes affected trade policy and trade performance. Second, we analyze the effects on the bargaining positions and bargaining options of developing countries in the trade sphere. Among the research questions we have posed for ourselves are the following:

- What is the new context in which developing countries must bargain? In what direction is the world trading system headed, and what are its implications for developing countries?
- What were the effects of the balance-of-payments crises on the bargaining options of developing countries? How have conditionality and unilateral liberalization affected the bargaining options and power of developing countries?
- How were bargaining resources applied to improve the external environment in which developing countries are immersed? What factors influenced the effectiveness with which skills were applied?
- Was coalition bargaining by developing countries effective during the Uruguay Round? What were the factors impeding or promoting it?
- What are the interests of developing countries in uni-, bi-, and multilateral openings? What will the long-run impacts of their choices be?
- What results were achieved through bargaining?
- What are the future challenges? What can developing countries do to bargain with maximum effectiveness in the future?

We address these questions initially in a series of case studies of countries and coalitions and finally in a synthetic fashion in the concluding chapter. The case studies have been selected to highlight the bargaining issues raised by the policy reversals of previously inward-oriented countries. We have excluded the very poor and commodity-dependent least-developed countries since the problems and issues they confront are of a different nature. In all our case studies, problems of access predominate over problems of supply.

This book is the product of a two-year research project coordinated by the editors and carried out by the chapter authors. It forms the third phase in an ongoing investigation of international bargaining by developing countries. The initial phase examined the factors influencing the effectiveness of bargaining over external debt in the early to mid-1980s. It included questions that parallel many of those posed in the present study, such as coalition formation, the differing interests of small and large countries, and the development and application of bargaining resources. The results were published in Stephany Griffith-Jones, ed., *Managing World Debt* (Wheatsheaf, 1988).

The second phase looked at two aspects of debt bargaining revealed during the previous exercise. These were cross-conditionality (the relationship among conditions simultaneously imposed on loan recipients by multiple creditors) and banking and tax regulation. In theory cross-conditionality could decrease the bargaining power of debtors facing a de facto cartel of creditors or increase it if the conditions improve the consistency of the policy packages to which debtors must react. Empirically, we found the former tendency to predominate. The research on banking regulation attempted to find ways in which laws in creditor countries could be modified to increase the opportunity and incentives for commercial banks to reduce debt. Recommendations from this study were conveyed through parliamentary committees in Britain, the Netherlands, and Canada and achieved a degree of acceptance. The results of this phase of research were published in Ennio Rodríguez and Stephany Griffith-Jones, eds, *Cross Conditionality, Banking Regulation and Third World Debt* (Macmillan, 1992).

The third phase of our project involved conference meetings in Ottawa, Caracas, and Geneva. The first conference served to establish a common research framework for the case studies, the second and third to solicit comments from experts on the draft manuscript and to engage in a dialogue with policymakers about our findings. The project was financed by Canada's International Development Research Centre and coordinated by the Facultad Latinoamericana de Ciencias Sociales, Buenos Aires. The case studies were carried out by residents of the countries in question and involved the collection of documentary evidence, interviews with parties to the trade negotiations, and personal knowledge of negotiations some authors had observed or participated in.

The book begins with an overview of bargaining by developing countries in the Uruguay Round. Alejandro Jara focuses on the shift away from loose principles such as special and differential treatment to more pragmatic approaches, and on the reversal of positions on the new issues. Jara makes the point that in an environment of aggressive unilateralism, the round can be regarded as a means of containment. Indeed, the incentive for developing countries to participate actively in the round came from the need to sustain liberalization in a climate of aggressive unilateralism.

The second part of the book contains two case studies of major players in the system. Both explore the current drift toward regionalism and what it holds in store for developing countries. Deepening (and extending) European integration and the formation of FTAs involving the United States, mark a watershed in the history of postwar trade relations. Stephany Griffith-Jones looks at the introspection of the EC and its implications for developing countries, pointing out opportunities as well as dangers in the changing trade patterns that are likely to occur. She also examines the broader systemic effects of intrabloc concerns as well as the bargaining issues involved for developing countries. Ann Weston then reviews the factors underlying the emphasis on regionalism in the United States and Canada. For the United States, in particular, regional initiatives are designed to reinforce its aggressive stance in trade matters. The reverse holds for Canada, which expects regionalism to provide security of market access in a way that is akin to that of some developing countries, especially those in Latin America.

The next part of the book looks at national responses to these developments. First, four authors from Latin America analyze the trade policies and bargaining strategies of their respective countries. Claudia Schatan's chapter on Mexico offers several points of comparison with Canada's experience in negotiating an FTA with its larger neighbor. Mexico's strategy, in turn, has impinged on the choices available to Costa Rica and other small Central American countries on the rim of the United States, as they must decide whether to emphasize collective or individual strategies. These options are explored by Ennio Rodríguez, who highlights the numerous bargaining tracks opened up by the changed geopolitical environment in Central America. Diana Tussie shifts our attention once again to the larger countries as she examines the political economy of Argentine bargaining, including its internal dimensions. Marcelo de Paiva Abreu continues in a similar vein with an account of import substitution in Brazil (Latin America's largest economy), its evolution through the debt crisis of the 1980s, and the dilemmas it has faced in a series of recent bargaining episodes.

The next two chapters draw on Asian experience. Rajiv Kumar highlights the costs that India has incurred in pursuing its traditional role as a spokesman for the Third World in a new international context dominated by pragmatism. He also shows the problems in store as the country belatedly begins to liberalize, having forgone some of the advantages an earlier adjustment process might have entailed. The country case studies finish with a brief look at the remarkable success the Asian newly industrialized countries (NICs) have achieved with a sophisticated, flexible, and pragmatic style of bilateral bargaining. David Glover offers some speculations on how suitable this approach might be for other less-developed countries (LDCs).

Part 4 reviews the experience of developing countries in coordinated bargaining during the Uruguay Round. GATT, unlike the UN Conference on Trade and Development (UNCTAD), has generally not provided a forum favorable to coalition bargaining. This appears to have changed during the Uruguay Round. Chapter 10 examines the Cairns Group, an issue-oriented coalition that has brought together developed and developing countries to press for reform of world agricultural markets. Tussie draws some parallels with her earlier work on coalition formation in debt bargaining.[2] Her chapter offers insights about the factors that led the Group to hold together through some of the most difficult moments of the Uruguay Round, allowing it to play a constructive role in the debate over agriculture. Another coalition, composed entirely of developing countries, had less staying power. A Group of Ten (G10)[3] emerged during the prelaunch period of the Uruguay Round and then disbanded during the course of the negotiations. Kumar's study of the rise and fall of the G10 highlights the danger of overpoliticization. It provides a contrast between this traditional southern grouping, with its emphasis on principles and the pursuit of a resolution to the unfinished business in the GATT, and the mixed North-South membership of Cairns, which has taken a more pragmatic approach toward agricultural reform.

As more and more developing countries embrace open trade policies, a range of untried bargaining possibilities is created. At the same time, the drift toward regionalism in major markets poses new challenges. Active bargaining has become an integral part of trade strategy. The editors' concluding chapter provides some comparisons across these case studies, offering answers to the principal questions posed by the project and suggesting some policy implications for trade negotiators and decisionmakers.

NOTES

1. The terms *Super 301* and *Special 301* are not actually used in the law but have been adopted as the common way to identify these new statutory mechanisms. The provisions grant the U. S. Trade Representative (USTR) the authority to demand negotiations on "priority" practices that the United States finds unacceptable, regardless of whether they are proscribed by the GATT or another international treaty, and to use sanctions to force acquiescence. In addition, Super 301 calls for identifying countries rather than just specific practices, as the original 301 of 1974 provided. Special 301, which targets countries with lax treatment of intellectual property rights, has been applied to five of the countries in our case studies: Argentina, Brazil, India, South Korea, and Canada.

2. See "The Coordination of the Latin American Debtors: What Is the Logic Behind the Story?" in Griffith-Jones, 1988.

3. There is, coincidentally, another, much more influential and better-known Group of Ten, that operates in the IMF and World Bank. This group is made up of

ten developed countries; it meets prior to each meeting of the interim and development committees and issues a joint communiqué in relation to financial and monetary issues.

PART I
THE URUGUAY ROUND

1

Bargaining Strategies of Developing Countries in the Uruguay Round

ALEJANDRO JARA

This chapter deals with bargaining strategies developing countries have followed in the framework of the multilateral trading system as embodied in the GATT and other ancillary instruments agreed upon under the auspices of its contracting parties. The Uruguay Round of MTNs provides a good scenario in which to observe the evolution of the trading system, the trends of national trade policies, and the participation of developing countries.

A few caveats are in order. First, profound economic and political changes have taken place in the world and are still under way. The end of the Cold War, the collapse of communism in Central and Eastern Europe and in the former Soviet Union, the globalization of the world economy, the creation and consolidation of economic groupings or blocs, the debt problem of many developing countries, and the ensuing adjustment policies applied are among the main changes. The conditions and situations that governments presently face are very different from those existing when the Uruguay Round was launched in September 1986. In fact, some positions and principles held then have evolved quite drastically.

Second, it has become increasingly difficult to speak of a developing country strategy because of the growing differences and specificities in the economies and policies of developing countries. While such countries may still pursue some broad concerted action, they have tended to rely increasingly on regional positions or sectoral coalitions such as textiles and clothing or agriculture.[1] Wide divergences in negotiating positions among the more active developing countries have also been apparent, mainly as a result of the drastic changes in their economic policies (see Chapter 11).

THE MULTILATERAL TRADING SYSTEM

As embodied in GATT, the multilateral trading system is based on four principles. The rules and disciplines seek to establish (1) market access conditions that offer opportunities for operators to compete, since the system does not define results or outcomes; (2) nondiscrimination among members; (3) trade liberalization promoted through reciprocal and mutually advantageous negotiations; (4) rule of law by means of multilateral surveillance and accountability and a dispute settlement system (Bhagwati, 1991).

The trading system has undergone many changes since its creation in 1947. Its membership has jumped from the original twenty-three to 103 in 1992 and is bound to increase as other countries—such as Russia, the People's Republic of China, Poland, Hungary, and the Czech and Slovak Republics—apply or renegotiate their terms of accession. The system will be almost universal by the end of the decade. Another further change has been the incorporation of language and principles to take into account the situation and concerns of developing countries, though such modifications and additions are of little present value.[2] In addition, there has been a marked trend toward the fragmentation of the system following the implementation of some of the Tokyo Round results in the form of codes or arrangements applied by the main participants, namely, industrialized countries and a relatively small number of developing countries. Formation and strengthening of regional blocs and groups could also contribute to further fragmentation.

The trade policies of the major trading nations in particular have led to persistent erosion of the system's main principles and disciplines, though the trade policies of other countries, including developing countries, have also accelerated this trend. There are two main reasons for the breakdown. On the one hand, the details of GATT were never clear, governments easily taking advantage of the many loopholes.[3] In the context of mounting domestic pressures, policymakers have resisted adjustment to new conditions of competition and have shown growing disregard for the rules and disciplines of the trading system. On the other hand, governments (particularly those of the major trading nations) have devised special arrangements or instruments for dealing with specific problems, either on a sectoral basis or under the guise of across-the-board policies. The Multifiber Arrangement (MFA), market sharing, voluntary export restraints, and orderly market arrangements are good examples.

The MTNs were launched as an attempt to solve long-standing trade problems, to further trade liberalization and to enlarge the competence of the trading system. To an important extent, however, the major trading nations deliberately tried to use the negotiations to modify the basic multilateral principles and disciplines in order to accommodate or legalize their trade policies and instruments. Thus such countries have in effect turned principles into negotiating points or issues, thereby eroding the system's foundations.

The United States' abdication of its traditional role in defending the system has created a vacuum. As will be seen later, the containment of U.S. trade-policy formulation and application has over the years become one of the most attractive but unwritten objectives of the Uruguay Round. In what follows, some of the main issues and problems confronting the multilateral trading system will be examined with reference to the MTNs and the trade-bargaining strategies.

MARKET ACCESS

During the 1980s no significant steps were made in the trading system to solve long-standing problems or issues related to market access conditions, such as high tariffs, tariff escalation, nontariff barriers (NTBs), effective protection, quantitative restrictions, gray-area measures, and so on. This is not to say that in some markets conditions actually improved as a result, for example, of the implementation of the Tokyo Round tariff cuts, wide-ranging unilateral trade liberalization measures applied by many developing countries (particularly in Latin America), and bilateral free trade agreements. The latter, however, by definition imply discrimination toward third parties.

At the same time, the trade policies of some countries, particularly the major trading nations, drifted toward greater protectionism and discrimination through changes in their legislation and administrative practices. In sectors such as textiles, agriculture, and steel, existing restrictions and distortions to competition were enhanced. In such cases, measures were applied in response to domestic producers' pressures or by way of retaliation against another country, sometimes for reasons unrelated to trade. In short, even though world trade grew, the quality of market access conditions deteriorated because they were increasingly defined in terms inconsistent with the principle of nondiscrimination and the objective of liberalizing trade. Thus an expanding share of world trade became subject to additional restrictions, bilateral agreements, or some form of managed trade.

The system first responded in 1982 by holding a ministerial meeting, which by all accounts failed to reverse such trends. Nevertheless, under the resulting work program, valuable technical work was begun and a broad agenda set for what was to become the Uruguay Round MTNs. Yet the structure of the Punta del Este declaration and the ensuing negotiations was not conducive to improving market access conditions or the capacity of the system to respond effectively. The declaration contained two "main" political commitments, those to a standstill and to the roll-back of GATT-inconsistent measures. Although the commitment to a standstill may have been instrumental in relieving domestic pressures, it has been violated many times, judging from the number of complaints brought to and adjudicated by the GATT's dispute settlement mechanism. Only some contracting parties have observed the rollback commitment either by reversing a measure a dispute settlement panel has found to be inconsistent with GATT disciplines or in the context of a unilateral trade liberalization program. In other words, very little has been done to reverse GATT-illegal measures. This is not surprising. What *is* surprising is that there was a commitment of this nature to begin with and that extensive negotiating capital and time went into it.

Three factors explain the commitment to a standstill and rollback and its failure. First, the parties mainly interested were developing countries. Though many took a firm position, insisting from the outset on full compliance with this commitment, only a few acted by notifying the surveillance body of the specific measures they believed had to be rolled back, even though there was no lack of information.[4] Second, many developed contracting parties firmly resisted the establishment of clear and efficient procedures to carry out the process leading from notification to action. Third, and perhaps most importantly, it is quite naive to await action under the rollback promise since no government could be expected to incriminate itself by reversing an illegal measure protested by another party or simply on a unilateral basis. In addition and in spite of language to the contrary in the Punta del Este declaration, to use GATT-illegal measures as bargaining chips clearly conspires against unrequited action.

The MTNs were initially organized into fifteen negotiating groups, services included, of which the following dealt with market access: tariffs, nontariff measures, tropical products, natural resource–based products (NRBPs), textiles and clothing, and agriculture.[5] To an important extent this structure was established at the behest of developing countries, particularly in the cases of tropical products, NRBPs, and textiles and clothing.

The nontariff measures group was in effect a catchall group because the more meaningful measures were already dealt with in other groups, such as those dealing with GATT articles, the Tokyo Round arrangements and agreements, subsidies, and countervailing measures and safeguards. Thus this group was left to deal with more marginal measures on a bilateral basis (request and offer) or through a multilateral approach (rule making). This group was ideally suited to negotiate away GATT-inconsistent measures, thereby lending them a dangerous aura of legitimacy: it meant paying for the derogation of measures that—had GATT rules been abided by—should not have been applied in the first place.

Related to the structure of the negotiations is the issue of sectoralization. Thus while tariffs and nontariff measures can be dealt with across the board, tropical products, NRBPs, agriculture, and textiles and clothing respond to a sectoral approach. However, such sectors have all encountered problems of coverage mainly because of opposing product-specific interests of some industrial countries. Although there is a rationale for negotiating on agriculture and textiles and clothing on a sectoral basis, there is none for doing so on tropical products or NRBPs. In effect, by isolating a particular sector in a negotiating group, where there is no discrimination in terms of the relevant multilateral disciplines, the demandeurs signaled to their counterparts the inadvertent willingness to pay a higher price than would have been the case had market access problems, that is, tariffs and nontariff measures, been dealt with in horizontal negotiations. At the same time, a sectoral strategy has the pitfall of creating potential hostages to results in other areas; the United States, for example, has made its offer on tropical products conditional to the outcome of agricultural negotiations.

In the case of tropical products, some results were achieved at the 1988 Montreal midterm review, including unprecedented concessions granted by some developing countries. NRBPs were the result of concerted action by Canada, Chile, and Peru at the 1982 ministerial meeting of contracting parties. Coverage problems[6] and absence of wide support have virtually depleted NRBP negotiations of any meaning.

Tariff negotiations posed a problem of their own. Tariff cuts had traditionally been negotiated on a bilateral basis, involving the importing country and the main supplier of the product in question. Such a system is inherently biased against small suppliers. If a country, typically a developing country, has an export structure that lacks diversity or has a relatively small production capacity, it will qualify as a main supplier for a only small number of products, usually commodities that more often than not are subject to low or no duties in importing developed countries, whether these have most-favored-nation (MFN) or preferential status. Even though in the Tokyo Round a formula cut was applied to manufactures generally, in the Uruguay Round strong U.S. opposition prevented an agreement on a similar negotiating modality. At the midterm review a compromise of sorts was achieved with agreements on a target for tariff cuts of not less than the average Tokyo Round reductions (approximately 33 percent).

The U.S. position was based on the premise that a formula approach would have favored the so-called free riders, countries that take advantage of concessions exchanged by others pursuant to the MFN rule. Greater competition, enhanced competitiveness of other economies, and shifts in exchange rates, among other factors, have changed the supplying position of countries to a given market in many products. The U.S. stance is revealing in that it seeks to deny the possibility of changes in patterns of production and trade and favors instead an attempt to maximize bilateral reciprocity. Moreover, seeking to liberalize trade in certain sectors such as steel, chemicals, petrochemicals, pharmaceuticals, nonferrous metals, wood, and paper—most of which generate problems of agreement on coverage—the United States also proposed sectoral reciprocity (zero for zero, whereby all trade is free of duties, nontariff measures, and subsidies) . On both counts the attitude of the United States is based on a strategy to seek reciprocity of results and managed trade, thus undermining the foundations of the GATT system.

The product-by-product approach leaves a large number of developing countries without the possibility of effectively participating in market access negotiations. This is particularly true for products they do not traditionally supply; the liberalization of these goods then depends largely on negotiations among the main exporters, usually industrialized countries.[7] The absence of a formula approach such as the one used in the Tokyo Round makes it more difficult to tackle tariff escalation and tariff peaks, thus leaving open one of the main problems developing countries confront. Tariff escalation and peaks are pervasive in sectors of paramount interest to developing countries, which highlights another fallacy of the free rider argument.

The United States' sectoral approach in fact places a higher priority on U.S. trading interests than on those sectors the Punta del Este declaration earmarks for fullest liberalization because of their importance to the trade of a large number of developing countries. Thus though the results of market access are still pending and a proper evaluation cannot be undertaken, negotiating on the basis of the modalities proposed by the United States means that developing countries are marginalized.

Nevertheless, many developing countries, particularly those of Latin America and the Caribbean, have unilaterally liberalized their trade by reducing tariffs and eliminating nontariff measures (see Chapters 4–6). Many such countries have made offers that include binding all their tariffs following the precedent Chile set during the Tokyo Round and Mexico's accession to GATT in 1986. In addition, several countries (Venezuela, Costa Rica, Bolivia, El Salvador, etc.) have acceded to GATT and bound their complete tariff schedules. Pursuant to language agreed upon at the midterm review, such countries have sought credit and recognition for unilateral trade liberalization—so far to no avail. Tariff offers by some developing countries (again, especially Latin American nations) include bindings across the board, something no industrialized country has yet done or offered. Even though such "ceiling bindings" place a top limit on tariffs and represent a radical departure from previous high levels of restrictions, because the applied rate in some countries is much lower, the United States in particular holds that such offers are not worth much and do not appear to be improving present market access conditions.

The extent to which developing countries bind their trade liberalization under GATT will depend both on the market access incentives they are able to get in return in the MTNs and the improvement of multilateral rules and disciplines. In other words, while developed countries have been demanding that developing countries "graduate," that is, assume greater and more fully obligations under GATT, this will depend on whether the latter reverse the slide toward protectionism and discriminatory managed trade.

It would seem that, on the one hand developing countries have pursued a self-defeating strategy first by seeking the establishment of negotiating groups for sectors of high importance to them and, second, by placing too much initial emphasis on loose principles and commitments such as special and differential treatment and rollback. In contrast, they had the opportunity and moral authority to insist on reciprocity, particularly in terms of the scope of bindings and the elimination of nontariff barriers. Some countries pursued this strategy only belatedly and were neither overt nor forceful enough. On the other hand, the negotiating modalities imposed clearly conspired against developing countries' legitimate and reasonable expectations.

SECTORAL ISSUES:
AGRICULTURE AND TEXTILES AND CLOTHING

The negotiations on agriculture and textiles and clothing deal not only with market access but also with rules and disciplines, since trade in both sectors is regulated by special arrangements. There is thus a need to isolate the negotiations with specific mandates and negotiating groups. The objectives set out in the Punta del Este declaration are important as the first meaningful attempt in GATT to address head on the root of the problems and to initiate a process of reform of trade policies consistent with new or reinforced GATT disciplines. On agriculture this was largely possible because of the strong position taken by both the United States and the Cairns Group. The mandate for textiles and clothing, in contrast, was sought by exporting developing countries, though the main developed contracting parties could not oppose it in light of their attempt to include intellectual property rights, trade-related investment measures, and services—the so-called new areas—in the negotiations.

Both sectors are good examples of producers' resistance to adjustment and competition and therefore to attempts to liberalize trade. In both cases the resistance originated in the United States and was soon taken up in other industrialized countries, particularly those of Western Europe and Canada. What is certainly unique is how in both sectors domestic interests succeeded in institutionalizing protectionism through multilateral disciplines embodied in GATT (Articles 11.2 and 16.3 of the General Agreement in the case of agriculture) or by means of special instruments agreed upon under the auspices of GATT contracting parties (the Multifiber Arrangement for most textiles and clothing and the Dairy Arrangement negotiated in the Tokyo Round that inter alia sets minimum export prices).

The intricate web of bilateral quotas negotiated under the MFA cover may be negotiated away, even though this may take at least ten years to complete and new products and suppliers could be covered by the disciplines that will regulate trade during the transition period. The possible freeing of trade is due to a combination of factors. The quid pro quo with regards to the "new areas" has already been mentioned. Another factor is the increased competitiveness of many manufacturers in developed countries through specialization and improved technologies. In addition, suppliers of many developing countries have become very efficient in taking advantage of the quota rents derived from the MFA system and therefore have acquired a vested interest in either maintaining the present system or having a very gradual phaseout. Finally, mention must also be made of the influence developing countries exercise by in terms of both unity and coherence.

Agriculture was a stumbling block even before the negotiations were launched. Since the Tokyo Round failure in this sector, world markets for major crops deteriorated leading to further price and income support and export subsidies in the major industrialized countries. In addition to unfavorably affecting market access conditions and export competition, the disarray in agriculture triggered a trade war between the United States and the European Community (EC), particularly after the first put together a war chest to recover markets.

GATT disciplines on agriculture were weak and ill defined to start with, mainly to accommodate U.S. domestic policies. Following the 1955 waiver granted to the United States and the establishment of the Common Agriculture Policy (CAP), a basic foundation of the EC, by the 1960s the agriculture policies of industrialized countries were well on their way to becoming entrenched systems of price or income support to farmers that could not be applied without restrictions at the border and export subsidies to dispose of surpluses. The United States, however, changed its position in a radical way, particularly after the 1982 ministerial meeting. Along with the Cairns Group, the United States was successful in securing a far-reaching mandate at Punta del Este. The first U.S. agricultural proposal in the Uruguay Round was not only market oriented and trade liberalizing but radical in that it sought the complete elimination of border measures and export subsidies and tight restrictions on domestic support measures. Western Europe and Japan have resisted reform, even appealing to nontrade concerns such as security of food supplies.

Developing countries have been of two or three minds. Some joined the Cairns Group, a highly successful coalition and a decisive factor in the negotiations. Other countries, such as Jamaica, Egypt, Mexico, and Peru, coalesced in the net food-importing countries group, concerned that liberalization would raise prices for imported foodstuffs. This group gradually lost ground probably in recognition that they also have export interests best served by favoring liberalization. Because in all likelihood results will not liberalize trade significantly nor lead to an elimination of export subsidies, their initial concerns withered away. Still other developing countries have remained at the margin of the negotiations because their interests lie mainly with tropical products, a misguided tactic since any results are bound to include new or reinforced disciplines that will be applicable to all agricultural products, including tropical. Once again, the isolation of tropical products in one negotiating group would appear to be a self-defeating strategy.

The negotiations on agriculture remain the single most important and divisive issue of the MTNs. They reach beyond border protection and quite clearly imply reform of domestic policies, allocation of subsidies, and income or price support measures. The United States, the Cairns Group, and the Latin American and Caribbean countries have made clear that without a satisfactory outcome on agriculture, the whole package of results could fall through. The immediate results seem modest, but they would nevertheless initiate a long-term process of market-oriented reform. For the purposes of this chapter, it is important to note that a few but active participating developing countries, particularly the Latin American members of the Cairns Group,[8] undertook an aggressive strategy in a coalition with like-minded countries. Admittedly, such a drastic stance was possible because one of the two major powers, the United States, was on their side. Nevertheless, such action underscores the decisive role coalitions with a positive reform intent may have on the outcome.[9]

UNFAIR TRADE: IMPORT COMPETITION
AND THE SAFEGUARDS COMPLEX

Traditionally, unfair competition is used to describe trade that takes place under distorted conditions stemming either from price discrimination practiced by the exporter (dumping) or from subsidies granted by the exporting country. The Tokyo Round codes on antidumping and subsidies attempted to regulate the implementation of the very loose disciplines of

GATT's Article 6. However, following protectionist pressures in the early 1980s, domestic regulations on unfair competition were amended several times in both the United States and the EC (and in other countries as well), with the purpose of making it increasingly easy to initiate antidumping or countervailing complaints against imports.

It is worth recalling some of the new instruments resulting from such legislative amendments. Injury to domestic industry usually must be proven separately for each country or exporter investigated, with the consequence that there will seldom be a finding of injury in the case of small suppliers.[10] In order to secure protection against all suppliers, the practice of cumulatively assessing all parties subject to the complaint has been established and, worse, made practically mandatory. At the same time, the definitions of dumping and subsidization have been enlarged inter alia by extending to both upstream and downstream stages of production and by using methods of calculation that result in wider margins of unfair competition. Similarly, the right to initiate a complaint and have an investigation initiated has been made extensive to producers other than the manufacturer of the similar product, such as grape growers' requesting an investigation against wine imports. Yet another practice is anticircumvention, whereby the antidumping or countervailing measures applied to a finished product are extended to similar products that to some degree are assembled in the importing country, thus affecting domestic production and foreign investment.

At the same time, the more traditional means for contingent protection provided for by GATT (namely, safeguard measures) are infrequently resorted to. Such measures dealing with "fair" competition require an injury finding and compensation; otherwise, retaliation is provided for. Thus measures to offset the injurious effects of unfair competition have in practice become surrogate to safeguard measures. In addition, both the EC and the United States have frequently exercised their economic and political power to force supplying countries into so-called voluntary export restriction arrangements of one sort or another (gray areas). Consequently, protection is highly "selective," and no right to compensation or retaliation arises.

Article 19 and both the antidumping and subsidies codes have been renegotiated in the MTNs. Participants such as Japan, Hong Kong, Korea, Singapore, and Mexico have actively sought tighter disciplines. The United States and the EC in particular have advocated instead that rules be changed to accommodate or multilateralize their domestic practices.

Antidumping and countervailing measures along with Article 19 disciplines on safeguards constitute what is known as the "safeguards complex." It is highly probable that the results of the Uruguay Round with regard to antidumping and countervailing measures will be limited because of the resistance of the two major participants to negotiate improved disciplines. Such measures will then continue to be widely used not only against unfair competition but as a means of providing contingent protection to domestic industry. However, an agreement is likely with regard to Article 19, including the phasing out of existing gray-area measures.

The linkages among the three areas mentioned are quite obvious; it would seem that more active participation by developing countries, relating the technical details to both economic arguments and the basic principles of the system, could have produced better albeit still marginal results. Instead, following the conclusion of the MTNs, an uphill struggle will be necessary in order to initiate a process of multilateral trade disarmament.

UNFAIR TRADE:
EXPORT COMPETITION AND COMPETITION POLICY

The concept of unfair competition has spilled over into concerns over markets for exports and new areas with a moral or ethical dimension unrelated to economics. In the case of markets for exports, the traditional and still relevant concern has been over distortions arising from subsidization. However, unfairness has now also been used to look into actual trade results of competition in other markets, regardless of the existence of subsidies. This implies devising policies and actions geared to achieve intrasectoral reciprocity of trade barriers, whereby one party will regard as unfair competition access conditions in an export market that are inferior to those prevailing in its own market.

Likewise, the concept of unfairness has been extended to trade imbalances at the bilateral level (Japan most often singled out as the culprit) using arguments such as the difficulties of market penetration because of alleged trade barriers or government or intraindustry informal arrangements. In the words of J. Bhagwati, "The question of fairness is now considered important enough to justify actions that can only be described as reopening the terms of earlier trade negotiations in view of 'ex-post' realities" (Bhagwati, 1991, 19–20).

Action on domestic competition regulation has also been labeled unfair. For example, this charge is behind the U.S. action under the Structural Impediments Initiative (SII) to negotiate bilaterally with Japan over questions such as retail distribution, antitrust regulations, and share of public work contracts. The concern over labor rights and subsequent U.S. action on this count further illustrate the expansion of the notion of unfair trade.[11] Likewise, under the 1988 Omnibus Trade and Competitiveness Act, the secretary of the treasury is mandated to hold consultations with other governments if there is a management or manipulation of exchange rates giving those countries an unfair trade advantage. Concerns over the burden of environmental policies and how this affects competitive advantage have also entered into the definition of fair trade.

In its search for "fairness," the United States has resorted to aggressive instruments—in the form of unilateral retaliation or threats of such retaliation—to force changes in the policies of trading partners, particularly under Section 301 of its trade legislation.[12] Though power politics is a permanent feature of international relations, the United States had generally practiced it only within the rules and procedures of the multilateral trading system—until Special 301 and Super 301 were unleashed under the Omnibus Trade and Competitiveness Act of 1988. By unilaterally imposing or attempting to impose its standards of fairness (also referred to as reciprocity or level playing field) and disregarding due multilateral process, the United States not only contributed to the erosion of the GATT system in the midst of the Uruguay Round (unilateral trade sanctions are illegal under GATT) but also discredited its commitment to the MTNs, since the changes sought in those countries singled out were unrelated to a multilaterally negotiated quid pro quo. (See the cases of Argentina, Brazil, and India in Chapters 6, 7, and 8.)

Unfairness in export competition was dealt with in the subsidies code resulting from the Tokyo Round. Early on, the code proved to be an ineffective discipline with regard to subsidies granted to exports of agricultural products. Two complaints brought by the United States against the EC are outstanding. The panel that examined the first complaint, on wheat flour, was unable to conclude that the EC's export subsidies had allowed it to acquire a more than equitable share of the world market.[13] The second complaint raised a more clear-cut issue. Under the code, export subsidies can be granted to primary products only in their natural form or processed if processing is normally required for the product to be sold in important quantities in international markets (for example, liquid milk must be turned into powder). Though the majority of the panel (four out of five) ruled that export subsidies the EC granted to the wheat component of pasta did not meet the code standard, the code committee was split between European countries and the rest of the signatories.[14]

The United States' implementation of the code vis-à-vis developing countries became a major stumbling block for accession by the latter. While the rules provided for autonomous commitments by developing countries to restrict or eliminate export subsidies, the United States made the application of the injury test to other countries conditional on securing such a commitment either on a bilateral or multilateral basis. Thus despite the code's special and differential treatment in favor of developing countries, the U.S. policy encouraged a few developing countries to join reluctantly but alienated the majority.

Furthermore, developed countries granted themselves an exception to the prohibition of export subsidies to manufactures. Indeed, in an annex containing the illustrative list of export subsidies, the code provided that official credits granted to exports by governments party to an Organization for Economic Cooperation and Development (OECD) arrangement will not be deemed to be prohibited in the code.

The issue of agricultural export subsidies is dealt with separately in the negotiations on agriculture. Though the outcome is unknown, it is likely to provide for some reduction but not elimination of such subsidies. Welcome as this may be, the problem of special rules to favor farmers of the major industrial countries will persist. This imbalance is furthered by the probability of improved rules and disciplines for nonagricultural products and provisions for developing countries to eliminate export subsidies.

As stated before, one of the main concerns of participants in the Uruguay Round has been how to bring the United States back into the fold of GATT rules and procedures. Pressure has mounted to secure a commitment to cease the use of unilateral trade retaliation and could become one of the main trade-offs other countries would seek as a condition of accepting the final package of results. By and large, developing countries have forcefully complained against unilateralism but have not acted collectively to propose practical ways to achieve agreement or to make it a condition of the acceptance of the final package. Developed countries such as the EC members and Canada have played a much larger role in this respect.

THE FRAGMENTATION OF THE SYSTEM: CODES AND ECONOMIC GROUPINGS

The Kennedy Round antidumping code set an example for the Tokyo Round that resulted in nine separate agreements of a less-than-universal membership, giving rise to the so-called GATT-plus system. Though the codes are largely open to accession by all, only a few LDCs have subscribed to some of them, as they were negotiated among a handful of industrialized countries with little or no participation of developing countries. Throughout the 1980s a multitiered system with different levels of rights and obligations was in place. Most industrialized and developing countries have expressed dissatisfaction with this situation. The standards set by the codes are almost inevitably applied to or imposed on nonsignatory developing countries. Thus the latter assume increasing obligations with no rights or have their trade subject to disciplines to which they are not parties.

Though the codes will be amended in the Uruguay Round, there has been no serious and concerted effort to convert them into truly multilateral instruments. A universal adoption of such instruments could, though, be forthcoming. Indeed, the Punta del Este declaration was conceived as a "single undertaking," which some countries such as the United States and the EC have interpreted to mean that the final package of results must be accepted in its entirety,[15] presumably in order to discourage alleged free riders. This would in fact mean that results, particularly those concerning market access, could be applied on a conditional MFN basis, a radical departure from GATT rules and practices.[16] If so, the practical effect would be to have an almost universal membership of the codes and other arrangements, thereby avoiding—perhaps inadvertently—further fragmentation of the system. This issue is also linked to the question of the institutional framework with the legal and administrative capacity required to cover agreements on trade in goods, services, and intellectual property rights.

Developing countries have failed to address the question of the single undertaking from a systemic point of view and to elaborate conceptually on all its linkages and consequences. Some of their general statements reveal the caution that results from the failure of defining national positions. Besides leaving the initiative largely in the hands of the major trading nations, developing countries have allowed this question to be decided upon at the last minute, when their bargaining power would be weakened by the need to use their negotiating capital on more pressing and immediate concerns such as market access generally.

The formation or consolidation of economic groupings has also been a concern of the multilateral trading system (see Chapters 2 and 3 in this volume). For developing countries, trade relations with the United States, the EC, and Japan are all of relatively equal importance. Therefore trade blocs and regional fortresses would be against their interests. GATT rules thus become of paramount importance. Article 24 governs the formation of free trade zones and customs unions. Experience with numerous arrangements, particularly those subscribed to by European countries, shows that such disciplines have been unilaterally interpreted and distorted beyond recognition. Only a handful of countries (such as Japan, Australia, New Zealand, and India) have tried to bring more precision and discipline to the provisions of the article, with limited success. In all probability, the results of the Uruguay Round review of Article 24 will be an improvement that will, however, require further and increasing attention in the future.

THE NEW ISSUES: SERVICES, INVESTMENT MEASURES, AND INTELLECTUAL PROPERTY RIGHTS

The triad of new issues brought into the negotiations by the major developed countries provoked initial strong resistance by developing countries generally.[17] Though services had already been the subject of much technical work since the 1982 GATT ministerial meeting, by 1986 it still remained largely uncharted territory. Lack of statistics on and information about the economics of services sectors in domestic economies, as well as the fact that they are regulated by different departments (unlike agriculture and manufacturing, each of which has a ministry of its own), made governments fearful of negotiations to establish multilateral, GATT-like obligations and to open up their domestic markets.

As the negotiations developed, a Multilateral General Agreement on Trade in Services (GATS) became a distinct possibility, if not an unavoidable outcome. Concurrently, and mainly because of technical assistance provided by UNCTAD and other organizations such as the Latin American Economic System (SELA), authorities in capitals and Geneva negotiators progressed in the learning curve. Both domestic interests and objectives were more clearly identified in the context of the Uruguay Round. For their part, industrialized countries, particularly the United States and the EC, became more and more defensive as they realized the effects that an agreement would have on certain sectors (such as audiovisual, telecommunications, financial, and maritime and air transport.) Thus they sought either to open up their markets on a conditional MFN basis (among other exceptions), to exclude entire sectors from the coverage of the agreement, or both.

The positions were thus reversed. While most developing countries saw the services negotiations as meaning little gain for them, they took the offensive and strongly defended an effective multilateral and nondiscriminatory agreement. As early as February 1990, when the structure of the agreement was under consideration, eleven Latin American countries, coordinated under SELA, made a formal proposal of a complete text for a Multilateral General Agreement on Trade in Services. This brought some balance to the discussions, which at the time had only one full but not entirely coherent proposal on the table, that of the United States. The Latin American and Caribbean proposal became a rallying point for many, and the text negotiated so far in many respects follows both its structure and language. This action clearly illustrated that interests can be secured by medium and small countries, if joint action is applied positively. By taking a constructive initiative, they gained the upper hand and an important and perhaps decisive place in the negotiations.

Intellectual property was also at the outset a North-South issue. Until the midterm review, most developing countries continued to maintain that the crux of the matter—such as exclusion from patentability—could not be negotiated because it was not within the competence of GATT but rather within that of the World Intellectual Property Organization (WIPO). At the same time, they began to raise lines of defense, such as the need for exceptions for development and public interest. While technically correct, this strategy left those countries out of the mainstream of the negotiations. However, surprisingly, important agreements were reached at the midterm review that laid the basis for the ensuing discussions and placed developing countries back into the negotiations. The decisions did not formally prejudge the question of the international implementation of the results, i.e., whether they should be part of an enlarged GATT system or instead be referred to WIPO, but the point was in fact largely conceded in favor of the former.

The shift toward a more positive stance on the part of many developing countries was made possible by a combination of factors: changes in domestic legislation—for example, allowing patents for pharmaceuticals—brought about largely under pressure of foreign transnational corporations with the strong support of (and threats of retaliation by) the U.S. government; greater involvement by domestic experts on intellectual property; and the awareness that resistance to engage in negotiations would leave them outside of an outcome that would nevertheless be imposed on them. Thus the North-South confrontation became less and less relevant to the result of the negotiations.

The negotiations on trade-related investment measures (TRIMs) are worth only a brief mention. All participants were quite confused and confusing as to what the measures should entail. Many proposals by both developed and developing countries involved disciplines based on effects because experience has shown that such an approach renders obligations unworkable. In the end, the results merely pointed to an agreement prohibiting what is already prohibited by Articles 3 and 11 of the GATT.

CONCLUSIONS

The ministerial meeting held in Brussels in December 1990 was a failure of proportions, a monument to mismanagement and lack of positive leadership. Before it took place, no observer or participant thought of it as the final meeting of the round. Instead of a breakthrough, Brussels was a setback on many issues and for the MTNs as a whole. A year later, on December 20, 1991, the GATT director general, with the acquiescence of governments, tabled a draft of the Final Act with the complete and bracket-free texts in all areas of the negotiations. He thus arbitrated on the issues governments had been unable to reach a consensus on. By mid-January 1992, it became clear that while not fully satisfied, the great majority of participants, including notably most developing countries and the United States, were willing to support the act. However, the EC (particularly French farmers) and other European countries as well as Japan effectively blocked approval because of the proposed text on agriculture.[18]

The negotiations, both in substance and procedure, have shown the extent to which relative power has shifted. While the United States had been the undisputed power and exercised strong leadership, it has now opted out of its responsibilities. Its trade-policy formulation process has increasingly become captive to sectoral domestic interests. Though these interests had prevailed to some degree in securing protection in the past, the extent to which they currently predominate and the disregard of multilateral disciplines have changed the overall direction and thrust of U.S. trade policy, with worldwide effects.[19] Other industrial powers, such as the EC or Japan, lack either the cohesion or the clout to exercise such leadership. This vacuum cannot be fully filled by developing countries, although many are increasingly committed to multilateralism. Whether acting jointly or individually, developing countries have become more active and constructive than in the past, aided by more transparent though still imperfect and lackluster procedures.

In sum, most developing countries now find themselves in the position of using the system's principles and procedures to protect and further their economic interests. In order to do so, across-the-board disciplines and the willingness to use a strong dispute settlement must be privileged in shaping strategies. Sectoral approaches and exceptions in the name of development but lacking a sound economic basis should be discouraged. Coalitions seem to better serve their purpose when built around well-defined interests of like-minded countries, whether developed or developing. In addition, it has become apparent that developing countries also need to approach negotiations with a clear view of how and where the multilateral system should evolve in order to meet their interests, thereby defining a position on future questions such as competition policy, environment and trade, and regionalism. The suggested "systemic" approach begs the question of the use and promise the multilateral trading system holds for the bulk of developing countries. Assuming a result of the Uruguay Round, a reinforced system will emerge. The benefits thereof will depend on the willingness of governments to use the disciplines and procedures to enforce rights and obligations. It will also be essential to envisage a new round of trade negotiations, to take the initiative in defining its agenda, and to promote and undertake the necessary groundwork.

NOTES

Views expressed in this chapter are the author's and do not necessarily represent the position of either SELA or the government of Chile. The author is grateful to Esperanza Durán and Diana Tussie and to Marcelo de Paiva Abreu and Patrick Low for their comments and insights.

1. Developing countries act jointly in GATT and in the MTNs through an informal group; the Latin American and Caribbean countries act as a regional bloc within the framework of SELA, as do the Southeast Asian countries under the Association of Southeast Asian Nations (ASEAN). For an account of action

by the main exporting developing countries of textiles and clothing, see Chapter 11 in this volume. On agriculture, see Chapter 10 on the Cairns Group.

2. Such is the case with the incorporation of Part 4 into the General Agreement in 1965 (which exempted developing countries from providing reciprocity) and the Decision on Special and More Favorable Treatment for Developing Countries adopted as part of the Tokyo Round results in 1979.

3. For example, the provisions of Article 24 governing the establishment of free trade zones and customs unions have not been fully complied with in the great majority of actual economic integration arrangements. Similarly, the major trading nations have resorted to voluntary export restrictions, thus circumventing the application of nondiscriminatory safeguard measures.

4. For example, see the catalog (over 1,000 pages) of most quantitative restrictions and other similar measures applied by contracting parties, produced by the Working Group on Quantitative Restrictions established in pursuance of the 1982 work program. Another source of information is UNCTAD's data base on nontariff measures.

5. At the beginning of 1991 and following the failure of the Brussels meeting, a single negotiating group was established for market access comprising the negotiations on tariffs, nontariff measures, tropical products, and NRBPs.

6. For example, the EC has insisted that market access negotiations on fisheries be complemented by arrangements concerning access to supplies to overcome the restrictions pursuant to the almost universal rule of the 200-mile exclusive economic zone, and the United States has pursued the inclusion of energy products. Similarly, there has been wide disagreement between some European countries and Chile over the inclusion of wood pulp and paper under the coverage of this group.

7. This can best be appreciated in light of the increasing importance of manufactures in the trade of many developing countries. For example, while the growth rate for total exports of Latin American countries during the 1980s was zero, the export of manufactures had the highest annual growth rate, double that of other exports by the region and higher than the corresponding rate of the rest of the world. In 1955, manufactures accounted for only 3.1 percent of total exports by Latin America, yet toward the end of the 1980s they constituted more than 33 percent (based on data of UN, *Monthly Bulletin of Statistics*, and UNCTAD, *Handbook of International Trade and Development Statistics*).

8. Argentina, Brazil, Chile, Colombia, and Uruguay.

9. For a full account of the Cairns Group, see Chapter 10 in this volume.

10. The United States applies the injury test only in countervailing (subsidies) cases to imports from countries that have acceded to the subsidies code and in the case of developing countries only if they have undertaken a multilateral or bilateral commitment to reduce or eliminate export subsidies, whether or not they are signatories of the code. Under GATT Article 6, the injury test is mandatory, but the United States argues that it has legal cover under GATT's grandfather clause, which allows a contracting party to maintain GATT-inconsistent measures, provided they are applied pursuant to mandatory legislation predating that country's accession to the General Agreement.

11. See Section 503 of the 1984 trade act. The United States has suspended some developing countries from its Generalized System of Preferences (GSP) because of labor rights. The United States has also brought this issue to the GATT, requesting the establishment of a working party.

12. For a full account of the evolution of both U.S. and Canadian trade policies, see Chapter 3 in this volume.

13. The outcome was hardly surprising since the code only elaborated Article 16.3 of GATT concerning primary products, pursuant to which a favorable ruling of violation is possible only after injury has occurred and is demonstrated, while account must be taken of the special circumstances that affect or may have affected the trade flows in question. This is one more piece of evidence in the argument that rules based on effects are useless.

14. The code allows the subsidization to export of any agricultural, forestry, and fishery commodity. If the EC's interpretation were taken to its logical conclusion, virtually any manufactured product having a primary component could be subsidized upon exportation, thereby opening a huge loophole and defeating the purpose of the code.

15. The government procurement code is an exception since it provides for national treatment for certain governmental purchases, while GATT Article 17:2 exempts them from such an obligation. The civil aircraft agreement and the arrangements for dairy products and bovine meat also constitute exceptions.

16. Under the current proposal to create the Multilateral Trade Organization (MTO), acceding countries must accept all the instruments, and the resulting GATT is declared to be legally distinct from the General Agreement of 1947. Thus the results of the market access negotiations would only be extended to those countries accepting and implementing the entirety of the final package of results of the Uruguay Round.

17. For a detailed account, see Chapter 11 in this volume.

18. Most observers and participants believed there was little chance of finalizing the MTNs by the end of 1992, so the real deadline has become February 1993, after the U.S. elections and before the fast-track authority lapses. Without fast-track authority any agreement signed by the administration can be unravelled by Congress. Foreign governments cannot risk negotiating with a powerless administration.

19. This is not to say that the position of the United States in the Uruguay Round has been of a protectionist and discriminatory nature in all areas. For example, on agriculture the United States has proposed a complete liberalization and elimination of export subsidies, a rather unrealistic negotiating position.

2

Economic Integration in Europe: Implications for Developing Countries

STEPHANY GRIFFITH-JONES

This chapter examines the changes occurring in intra-European trade relations and the implications for different categories of developing countries. It stresses how the volume, complexity, and simultaneity of changes in Europe distract the attention of European policymakers from multilateral trading issues (like the Uruguay Round), which are of such growing importance to developing countries. The chapter concludes with suggestions for strategic responses available to developing countries in the context of European integration so as to ensure maximum access to those markets and a brief examination of the implications of changes in Europe for the multilateral trading system.

EC TRADE POLICY

The EC, much more than the United States or Japan, has always divided the rest of the world into groups in the design of its trade policy: its own members, the European Free Trade Association (EFTA); the Mediterranean; the former colonies in Africa, the Caribbean, and Pacific (ACP); the Mahgreb.[1] The EC has a complex multitiered system of trade preferences and import restrictions for developing countries. Preferences vary among regions and countries as well as for products. The ACP countries benefit from both. Successive Lomé conventions have guaranteed duty-free access manufactures and for most agricultural goods not covered by the CAP. Haiti and the Dominican Republic signed the convention for the first time in 1989, bringing the number of ACP countries to sixty-eight under Lomé IV. The second group of developing countries subject to preferential trade agreement consists of twelve Mediterranean countries that have free access for most manufactures and semimanufactures, with restrictions in textiles and clothing. Agricultural products not covered by the CAP benefit from reduced tariff duties.

A lower preferential status applies to Asia and Latin America; these countries benefit from tariff preferences under the EC's GSP. However, a considerable number of "sensitive" products are subject to tariff quotas or ceilings. Many of these quotas or ceilings (especially in textile and clothing) are still divided into subquotas among member states. Certain subquotas remain underutilized, but there are restrictions on the transfer of an unused portion to a member whose quota is filled; this increases the effective restriction on the textile and clothing exports of developing countries.

The main policy instrument to reinforce EC quantitative restrictions such as MFA has been Article 115 of the Treaty of Rome, which allows member states to suspend free circulation of goods within the EC when outside suppliers are circumventing or threatening to circumvent national subquotas by transshipping goods through another member state. However, if border customs checks are fully removed, the article will become irrelevant. Article 115 has been used to reinforce quantitative restrictions imposed by individual member countries against third countries. With the completion of the single market, the EC is compelled to adopt a uniform trade policy towards third countries. This means that national restrictions have to be either totally eliminated or adopted at EC level. Although the first solution would be in the spirit of enhanced competition inherent in the single market initiative and compatible with an open international trading system, it might not be politically feasible.

EC member countries with a relatively high level of quantitative restrictions have been demanding EC-wide restrictions to replace their own protective measures in "sensitive" areas. Some member countries are seeking compensation for the protection they now enjoy. Such compensation could be in the form of higher tariffs (i.e., tariff equivalents of quantitative restrictions) or of import quotas set at EC level.

The adoption of a liberal trade policy will be more feasible should the completion of a single market prove to be a success. However, even an overall liberal trade policy might be accompanied by selective imposition or prolongation of protectionist measures at sectoral level. This would aim at "mature" and "weak demand" industries including clothing, textile, iron, and steel, which are of particular interest to developing-country exporters.[2]

EC trade policy in the 1970s and 1980s was characterized by growing recourse to nontariff intervention. As Jara (Chapter 1) points out, especially during the 1980s major developed nations tended towards greater protectionism and discrimination through changes in their legislation and administrative practices. EC protectionist measures in agriculture are based on the CAP, which entails restrictions at the border and subsidies to domestic producers. In other sectors the EC has also increasingly used nontariff intervention by mechanisms such as quantitative restrictions

(QRs), including voluntary export restraints (VERs), orderly marketing arrangements, and basic price systems imposed both at EC and member state levels. Should the single market lead to abolition of national sub-quotas, this would mean some liberalization, since each exporting country could exploit its EC quotas more fully, given the restrictions on the extent to which an unused portion can be transferred to a member whose quota is filled. The EC has also been abusing countervailing duties (CVDs) and antidumping duties (ADDs). ADDs are increasingly directed at a wide range of heterogeneous products, most notably electronic consumer goods. In addition to Japan, the main targets are South Korea, Taiwan, Hong Kong, Brazil, and Mexico.

Developing countries as a whole would gain from trade creation if there is a reduction in nontariff barriers after 1992, although there would be some redistribution of gains among developing countries, given the highly segmented EC policy toward different groups of countries. The liberalization process might have particularly adverse effects on ACP exporters of manufacturing exports, such as clothing, and of agricultural products, such as bananas, as in the latter case they will compete with lower-cost Latin American producers.

POLICY DEVELOPMENTS IN EUROPE

Rapid progress in economic integration (especially but not only in the EC) may eventually lead to a Greater European Market or European Economic Space. The transformation of the EC into a true common market within which goods, services, and factors of production are able to move freely is on course and should be completed by the end of 1992. Full integration of Spain and Portugal into the EC is due to be completed by January 1993 for nonindustrial products and by January 1996 for industrial products. Negotiations between the EC and EFTA for a European Economic Area (EEA) have been finalized. The objective of the EEA is to extend the provisions of the Single European Market (SEM) to EFTA countries by ensuring the free movement of goods, services, persons, and capital throughout the EC and EFTA countries. It is expected to bring major benefits to EFTA, although it involves a considerable loss of autonomy. Partly for this reason, Austria and Sweden have applied for membership in the EC, and other countries may follow suit.

Trade restrictions on Eastern European exports to Western European countries have been eased. Moreover, three countries in central and Eastern Europe (Czechoslovakia, Hungary, and Poland) are finalizing negotiations on association agreements that would gradually extend to them access to the SEM over a period of ten years. The agreements also call for the three countries' "ultimate, though not automatic," membership in EC. The full details of these agreements are still to be worked out. Ties are also becoming closer between the countries in central and Eastern Europe and EFTA. In late 1990 the EFTA countries began negotiations with Czechoslovakia, Hungary, and Poland aimed at signing free trade agreements. Both the free trade agreements with EFTA countries and the association agreements with the EC are asymmetric in the sense that trade liberalization and the removal of obstacles will be reciprocal but timetables will differ, being slower for the Central and East European countries.

IMPACTS ON DEVELOPING COUNTRIES

During the late 1990s an essentially integrated market covering a large portion of Europe will emerge. The trade of developing countries with Europe is bound to be affected, and groups of developing countries will be affected in different ways, depending not only on the composition of their exports to Europe but also on the position they are able to negotiate within Europe's scale of preferences. The efforts of carrying out all these major changes simultaneously will distract European attention from multilateral negotiations and from trade with developing countries.

Most of the quantifiable short- and medium-term effects on developing countries will be the result of the growth of demand and the evolution of market access conditions. The expansion of the 1992 program to EFTA will have lesser consequences for non-European trading partners because it involves a much smaller market than that of the EC. The effects of European integration on central and Eastern Europe will be of a long-term nature, largely because the current economic dislocation in these countries rules out any significant increases in imports, especially from developing countries. Special trading relationships with Western European countries could in the long run contribute to recovery in Eastern Europe, and to the extent that this is so, demand for tropical beverages, raw materials, simple manufactures, and capital equipment will rise. If trade policies toward non-European partners remain open, developing countries could eventually be in a good position to increase their exports to Central and Eastern Europe.

The SEM is expected to have fairly quick impacts on developing countries. In fact, many of the effects may have already occurred. Most of the European Commission's proposals to the Council of Ministers have already been adopted, and firms within the EC took action in anticipation of 1992. A wave of mergers and takeovers has swept Europe since the launching of the SEM program in 1985. There has also been a sharp increase in domestic and foreign investment in the EC, partly induced by the SEM. These trends will continue. Other impacts will be of a longer-term nature and will depend interalia on how trade policies in Europe evolve in response to adjustment pressures.

The SEM is expected both to create trade for and divert trade from developing countries. Increases in income in the EC as a result of the SEM will raise demand for imports from developing countries. Improved productivity caused by the SEM, however, leads to trade-diverting effects. Davenport and Page (1991) provide recent estimates of quantifiable effects of the SEM on developing-country exports, which are summarized in Table 2.1.

The total impact of the SEM, estimated at around 7 billion European currency units (ECUs), was slightly above 5 percent of exports from developing countries to the EC in 1987. This would imply a rather modest

Table 2.1   Estimates of the Impact of 1992 (based on 1987 data)

	EC Imports from LDCs (in millions of ECUs)	Effects of 1992 (in millions of ECUs)
Merchandise trade		
Creation, primary goods	60,864	3,223
Creation, manufactures	45,842	4,434
Diversion, manufactures		-4,651
Terms-of-trade effects		733
Subtotal		**3,739**
Horticultural, fishery products, if member state quotas abolished	1,344	350
Textiles, if member state quotas abolished	10,571	439
Elimination of excise taxes, 5 percent VAT:		
Coffee	4,646	253
Cocoa	645	52
Tea	1,457	6
Harmonization of taxes:		
Tobacco	1,969	-63
Bananas	1,563	142
Services		
Trade expansion effects	22,705	1,227
Price of EC services		636
Total	131,974	6,781

Source: Davenport and Page, 1991.

total effect from the SEM, especially as the volume of exports from developing countries to the EC in the second half of the 1980s grew about 8 percent in volume terms. The estimated net effects of the SEM would therefore imply a boost to developing countries' exports of less than one year's worth of growth. In proportion to existing levels of exports, trade expansion effects, according to Davenport and Page, would be important mainly in manufactures (and to a lesser extent in services, especially tourism) and primary goods. However, manufacturing trade diversion is likely to exceed trade creation in that sector. Terms-of-trade effects, both in merchandise and in services, are expected to be favorable both because of higher EC demand for commodities, which will increase their prices, and lower EC export prices for manufactures and services due to efficiency gains.

Estimates are by necessity crude, given that so many assumptions need to be made, but they point to the likely scale of the impact, which will probably be both positive and limited. The above estimates for effects of elimination of national quotas assume that there will be not more protectionism; however, there is a danger of a protectionist reaction to the adjustment problems caused by the SEM, especially given the recent bad record on VERs, antidumping, and other discriminatory practices discussed above. Should such protectionism emerge, the positive effects of national quota abolition could be significantly reduced. Further relatively important diversionary effects can be expected from the rapid finalization of the integration of Spain and Portugal into the EC, especially as these countries compete more directly with imports from developing countries than do other EC producers (Davenport and Page, 1991, 21).

UNCTAD (1991) expects somewhat higher net trade creation effects than do Davenport and Page, mainly because predictions are based on rather high income elasticities, which may overestimate trade-creation effects; according to UNCTAD's estimates, net trade creation (excluding effects from terms of trade, abolition of national quotas, and tax changes) would reach around 7 percent of developing-country exports in 1988. The basic conclusion that net growth of these exports as a result of 1992 is likely to be positive and limited, through, still holds.

UNCTAD (1991) also provides an interesting decomposition of net trade-creation effects by categories of developing countries. The biggest gainers are reportedly the oil exporters of western Asia and northern Africa and the economies of Southeast Asia, which export predominantly manufactures. The estimated net trade-creation effects for ACP and Latin American countries is far smaller.[3]

Other effects of the SEM could shift import demand from one group of developing countries to others. The abolition of national trade restrictions would be detrimental to producers from ACP countries and EC overseas territories, who at present enjoy preferential access to specific EC countries in commodities such as bananas, rum, and sugar. The abolition of national quotas would probably be accompanied by a shift in demand to lower-cost suppliers among developing countries, which now face national trade restraints.

The effects of the SEM on developing-country exports are therefore likely to be tangible, positive, but relatively small, assuming that EC external trade policy remains unchanged. The evolution of policy toward non-EC countries will be a fundamental determinant of the size, and even the sign, of its effects on developing countries (UNCTAD, 1991). The handling of national QRs—whether they will simply be eliminated or replaced by EC QRs, and how restrictive the latter are—will be crucial. At present, there are two kinds of national QRs: those on horticultural and fishery products applied mainly by France, Italy, Greece, and Belgium and Luxembourg on imports from countries such as Mexico, Argentina, Chile, Brazil, Egypt, Kenya, Israel, Côte d'Ivoire, Mauritius, Fiji, Thailand, Morocco, Cyprus, and Cuba; and those applied under Article 115 of the Treaty of Rome by several EC countries mainly on the more industrialized developing economies of Asia and on China.

It is not clear how these restrictions will be handled in the post-1992 EC. The optimal solution would be their elimination, but that outcome is far from certain, particularly in the current trading environment. In this connection, resort to increased EC-wide VERs in sectors experiencing adjustment assistance and the upsurge of antidumping actions are a cause for serious concern. As Davenport and Page (1991) show, the number of antidumping actions by the EC has risen significantly, suggesting that the 1992 project may already have intensified resort to this instrument. In the early 1980s, EC actions against firms affected mainly Latin American countries; in the late 1980s, these actions were concentrated on high-tech products, mainly exported by the Asian NICs.

The extension of the SEM to EFTA could have some trade-diversion impacts on developing countries, since an EEA agreement would extend the cost-reducing benefits of the program to EFTA producers of manufactures. Potential trade diversion would fall mostly on non-European developed countries, which are EFTA's major competitors in the EC. The exports of only a few developing countries overlap with those of EFTA. As regards trade creation in EFTA itself, even if incomes in EFTA are given a boost by European integration, the small size of the EFTA market suggests that the positive trade impact on developing countries will be minor.[4]

The effects of the incorporation of Central and Eastern Europe will be felt as trade with Western Europe increases. Trade flows between Eastern European countries and Western Europe are already important, the latter region taking almost 90 percent of the former's exports to developed market economies in the late 1980s.[5] Furthermore, since the beginning of 1990, exports to Western Europe have risen sharply, and they are expected to continue expanding at a fast pace throughout the 1990s.

No comprehensive assessment of the impact of the recent trade liberalization measures in favor of Eastern European countries is presently available. Preliminary estimates show meaningful though small gains. For example, the EC's concessions on textiles are estimated to be worth approximately 80 million ECUs to Poland and 50 million ECUs to Hungary. More broadly, Hungarian economists have attributed about one-third of the rather rapid growth of exports to the EC in the first half of 1990 to the EC's liberalization of trade.[6]

In the short to medium term, however, the response of Central and Eastern European exporters to their newly granted trade preferences and to the even closer ties with Western European countries likely to be developed in the late 1990s will be severely limited by supply constraints. Developing-country exports of manufactures are therefore unlikely to face any significant competition from Eastern Europe for some time to come. However, the selective preferential access the EC is beginning to give to Eastern European restricted products (agricultural goods, steel, and especially footwear) could lead to same-trade diversion for developing countries.

The extent to which exports from Central and Eastern Europe will compete with exports from developing countries in European markets (and particularly in the EC) does not depend solely on their climb in the preferential hierarchy of the EC. The policies (e.g., on exchange rates, wages, and other factors that affect competitiveness) the Central and Eastern Europe countries follow will be at least as influential; furthermore, in the short and medium term, the risk of trade diversion will be linked to similarities in export structures.

Table 2.2 ranks countries according to the similarity of their export structures to those of the Central and Eastern Europe to the EC. The countries of Central and Eastern Europe compete in the EC markets primarily with each other. They overlap much less with developing countries, and mainly with the Asian NICs and China. The single Latin American country with significant overlap is Brazil, which competes with Czechoslovakia and (to a lesser extent) with Poland, Hungary, Romania, and the former USSR.

A more detailed examination of the forty-six most important products imported by the EC (at levels above $7 million) from Central and Eastern Europe and their main developing-country competitors in 1989 shows a similar picture: Brazil again emerges as the country that has most to fear from potential competition in ten items, including automobiles, flat-rolled products of iron, unwrought aluminum, cyclic hydrocarbons, chemical wood pulp, footwear, semifinished products of iron and steel, pig iron, and ball bearings. The other countries that appear to compete most are, predictably, Turkey (in six products), Taiwan (five products), South Korea (four products), and Hong Kong (four products). Far less affected were other developing countries, with Mexico having to compete with only two products.

In the long term, preferential access to Western European markets, combined with the advantage of physical proximity, could well have an impact on export-oriented foreign investment in sectors in which Central and Eastern European countries have a comparative advantage. The high levels of educational attainment in Central and Eastern Europe, together with low wages, suggest that they could eventually gain competitiveness in technology-intensive manufactures and in some modern services. Foreign companies have already expressed an interest in investing in Czechoslovakia, Hungary, and Poland. So far, actual investment flows have been small, but they are expected to grow fairly sharply as some of the obstacles to private investment, such as uncertainty over property rights, are removed, and provided there is political and macroeconomic stability in these countries. Some fairly sizable foreign investments in Czechoslovakia and Hungary have been in high technology and automobiles, with the Western European markets largely in mind, especially in the context of 1992 and a broader European space. In other countries, the likelihood of foreign direct investment displacing developing countries exports seems far less likely.

In trade itself, the revolutionary changes occurring in central and Eastern Europe can provide new market opportunities for developing countries, particularly if and when economic reforms are successful and lead to sustained growth and if special efforts are made by entrepreneurs, governments, and international institutions to identify market opportunities rapidly, promote demand for exports, establish new trading links, and explore or develop sources for trade finance. In the short term, however, sharp declines in output and imports in central and Eastern Europe have led to overall rapid declines in imports from developing countries.

Should the current structure of trade links between developing and central and East European countries remain and the level of imports start rising, demand for developing countries' (and especially Latin American) products would mainly expand in the items of foodstuffs, beverages, and tobacco. This may be particularly true for nonessential tropical products (e.g., tropical fruit, coffee, and tea) but also for other food products (e.g., vegetables, seafood) where there is unsatisfied demand; income elasticities are therefore far higher than in Western Europe. However, sufficient foreign exchange to fund increased imports of consumer goods must be available.

To the extent that the countries of Central and Eastern Europe start to increase their industrial output, they will demand more raw materials.

Table 2.2 Rank of Countries in the EC According to the Similarity of Their Export Patterns with Those of East Europe, 1985–1987

Rank	Soviet Union Country	Index	Poland Country	Index	Romania Country	Index	Czechoslovakia Country	Index	Hungary Country	Index	Bulgaria Country	Index
1	Canada	38	Hungary	55	Hungary	52	Poland	54	Yugoslavia	57	Hungary	47
2	Czechoslovakia	37	Czechoslovakia	54	Poland	51	Hungary	52	Poland	55	Czechoslovakia	44
3	Sweden	36	Romania	51	Yugoslavia	49	Austria	51	Romania	52	Yugoslavia	42
4	Brazil	35	Yugoslavia	50	Italy	43	Italy	46	Czechoslovakia	52	Poland	42
5	South Africa	34	Austria	44	Czechoslovakia	41	Belgium/Lux.	45	Austria	47	Romania	40
6	Finland	32	Italy	43	Bulgaria	40	Bulgaria	44	Bulgaria	47	Venezuela	37
7	Chile	32	Bulgaria	42	Portugal	38	Yugoslavia	44	Italy	44	South Africa	35
8	Ghana	32	Brazil	42	Austria	35	Brazil	44	Denmark	39	Austria	35
9	Poland	31	Belgium/Lux.	40	China	35	Sweden	42	Switzerland	39	Italy	33
10	Côte d'Ivoire	31	Portugal	40	Thailand	34	France	42	Netherlands	37	Belgium/Lux.	32
11	France	31	Spain	39	Greece	34	Netherlands	41	Belgium/Lux.	37	Greece	32
12	Israel	31	France	39	Turkey	34	Romania	41	Turkey	36	Brazil	32
13	United Kingdom	30	Sweden	38	South Korea	33	Switzerland	39	China	36	Other Europe	32
14	Belgium/Lux.	30	South Korea	37	Belgium/Lux.	33	Norway	39	Greece	36	Colombia	31
15	Norway	29	Denmark	37	Tunisia	32	Spain	39	France	36	China	30
16	Spain	28	Norway	36	Spain	31	Denmark	38	Portugal	35	Switzerland	30
17	Netherlands	28	China	36	Taiwan	29	United Kingdom	37	South Korea	34	France	30
18	Mexico	28	Netherlands	35	Denmark	29	Soviet Union	37	United Kingdom	33	Turkey	29
19	Australia	27	Finland	33	Brazil	29	Finland	36	Israel	33	Algeria	29
20	Venezuela	27	Taiwan	33	France	28	GDR	35	Spain	32	Denmark	28

Source: Calculations of the Deutsches Institut für Weltwirtschaft (DIW), Berlin, based on OECD foreign trade data; table taken from U. Mobius and D. Schumacher, "Eastern Europe and the EC, Trade Relations and Trade Policy with Regard to Industrial Products" (Berlin: DIW, 1990).

Note: 0 Implies completely different structures and 100 completely identical ones.

Furthermore, since reforms will be accompanied by restructuring, there will be an important increase in imports of machinery, transport equipment, and telecommunications (provided there is sufficient domestically generated or external foreign exchange to finance it). Most of these increased imports will be provided by the developed market economies, with some share possibly coming from the Asian NICs. Developing countries may benefit indirectly because of increased demand for their raw materials. As in the case of 1992, there would be a favorable terms-of-trade effect for developing countries.

Furthermore, to the extent that industrial restructuring in Central and Eastern Europe results in the closing down of internationally uncompetitive factories in traditional sectors such as steel, iron, and coal, this may increase opportunities for developing-country exports.

IMPLICATIONS FOR BARGAINING

Regional issues have increasingly dominated the time, efforts, and focus of West European policymakers. There are already significant efforts to complete the SEM and the parallel initiatives encapsulated in the post-Maastricht package, including a sizable expansion of the EC's budgetary allocation, which involves an important internal debate about the size, structure, and financing of such a large budgetary increase. Taking place simultaneously are the efforts of integrating Spain and Portugal, as well as negotiating with EFTA countries for closer links (via the EEA and individual applications to join the EC). To this already expansive but mainly predictable West European agenda is added the large, complex, and broadly unpredictable agenda opened by the revolutions in Central and Eastern Europe and the disintegration of the Soviet Union. Trade policy is involved as well as aid and technical assistance in trying to prevent civil war, as illustrated for example by the role of the EC peacekeeping force and peacemaking political efforts during the civil war in Yugoslavia.

In the short run, not only policy efforts but also the evolution of the Western European economy will be dependent on events in the former Soviet bloc. The German economy is suffering because of massive financial transfers, especially to the former GDR, and from inflationary pressures linked to increased budget deficits. A stringent monetary policy is being pursued to counteract such pressures, which leads to higher interest rates and lower growth in the largest and previously most dynamic West European economy. High German interest rates create upward pressure on interest rates in EC member countries, linked to the deutsche mark by the exchange rate mechanism (ERM), thus disseminating deflationary effects through the region. This slowdown of growth coinciding with the completion of the SEM in 1992 is unfortunate, as it could accentuate a somewhat more protectionist outcome toward developing countries than would have otherwise occurred.

The complexity of all these changes makes the EC's policy priorities more inward looking. The EC has not had the clear positive objectives in the Uruguay Round that developing countries and the United States have for agriculture and other sectors (see Chapters 10 and 1). Its objectives have been more defensive, retaining elements of CAP in exchange for MFA modifications, for example. Therefore, as Davenport and Page (1991) argue, the GATT is clearly not the most important international trade forum for EC policy. In early April 1992, the EC was reported to be the only member of the GATT not to have agreed even in principle to support the Final Act, drawn up by Arthur Dunkel in December 1991 as a compromise reform package to break the deadlock of the Uruguay Round; though other GATT signatory countries expressed reservations with elements of this package, they have at least in principle supported it. As is well known, differences over farm trade, particularly over the CAP, as well as protection of U.S. farmers have become a major issue at best delaying and at worst blocking finalization of the Uruguay Round. It is thus even less likely that the EC could take up the leadership—which the United States has to an important extent abandoned (see Chapter 3)—of promoting progress in, and supporting discipline of, the multilateral trading system. This is particularly true given that the EC's history of trade relations with developing countries has always stressed special (rather than multilateral) arrangements. Though 1992 seems not to have accentuated this trend, it has encouraged groupings like the ACP to adapt their own trade policies to the SEM and to seek more preferential arrangements. The developing countries have suffered from the delay of the Uruguay Round as EC attention was drawn to 1992 and other European concerns seen as more relevant and more pressing. Like the United States, (see Chapter 3) the EC can afford to be aggressive within the GATT because of its pursuit of alternative regional strategies. Developing countries are especially hard hit by this change of attitude, given their clear interest in furthering multilateral trade liberalization, as they have invested so many resources and so much effort in an export-led model. Indeed, the distracting effect of European integration, as it taps energy that might otherwise go into multilateralist efforts, seems more important for developing countries than the quantitative effects of trade creation and diversion of European integration discussed above.

The overlap of the run-up to 1992 and the Uruguay Round has, however, had some positive effects; as Davenport and Page (1991) point out, the simultaneity of both processes has inhibited the European Commission from more protectionist, 1992-related actions on textiles and clothing and probably on shoes and bananas. Furthermore, concerns about

EC use of antidumping mechanisms have increased in the run-up to 1992, leading some developing countries headed by Hong Kong to form a group in the GATT to try to change arbitrary and biased EC regulations (see Chapter 1).

Though the SEM has potential positive effects for both developing countries and the GATT process (such as introducing new areas of competence), there is a concern that the EC's new self-confidence and the need to make 1992 work effectively could encourage the EC to broaden the areas of protection and trade negotiation. The EC can try to set rules of origin or local contents to restrict access. The EC's more lucrative position and growing relative weight in the world economy raise legitimate fears that it might attempt measures similar to the U.S. Super 301 actions (see Chapter 3), which the GATT has been powerless to stop or regulate.

As regards trade-diversion effects resulting from the SEM, it would seem desirable for developing countries (or for international and regional organizations concerned with their access to markets) to attempt to develop an appropriate methodology and evaluate ex post facto the magnitude of those trade-diversion effects. Such evaluation serve as a basis for assessing possible compensation by the EC for such trade diversion.

There seems to be a genuine concern that the international trading system will become increasingly dominated by a group of three participants: greater Europe, the United States, and Japan. A clear example of how the EC has begun to use its expanded power is reflected in its demands for "reciprocity" (from developing and developed market economies) in return for continued access to EC markets, a position that seems inconsistent with the MFN principle. Indeed, the Single European Act (SEA) did not reaffirm the obligation in the EC treaty to promote trade between the EC and third countries. On the contrary, the European Commission argues in its white paper that third countries should not benefit from the advantages of a larger market after 1992 unless they make concessions. An illustration of how the EC could potentially use the principle of reciprocity as a bargaining chip is given by the EC's submission of July 1989 to the GATT negotiating group on textiles and clothing; here the EC sets *itself* up (and *not* a multilateral arbitrator) to determine whether other countries are providing sufficient market access to its products and refers this access not just to textiles and clothing but to all markets in other countries, a practice rather reminiscent of Super 301.

The liberalization of developing countries can only bear full fruit if developed markets maintain or increase their openness. Furthermore, developing countries must point to the new forms of protectionist risk that the institutional changes resulting from the SEM and greater Europe, as well as the growth of nontariff barriers (particularly in the EC) pose for them; they should request that these trends are compensated for or abolished. As long as this does not occur, any EC demand for reciprocity does not seem at all justified.[7]

The success of an open market economy requires *not only* adequate trade policies but also effective and firm bargaining at all appropriate fora as well as bilaterally, so that the developed economies keep their markets open. In this respect, interesting lessons can be learned from the Asian countries, who in addition to opening up their economies (albeit often selectively), have been very successful in the key complementary bargaining tactics for maintaining market access and circumventing barriers they could not bargain away (see Chapter 9).

The first response to an action such as antidumping is to support its discussion and clarification at a general level in the GATT, further strengthening the group led by Hong Kong. Although developing countries have been very active in aspects such as antidumping and safeguards more broadly, they still restrict themselves mainly to general statements; as Jara stresses in Chapter 1, they need to negotiate in greater detail and with more precision the complex technical issues involved. The experience of the Cairns Group (see Chapter 10) shows that considerable negotiating skill and expertise are required, especially in light of strong EC and U.S. resistance to make formal commitments in this area. More generally, on this and other issues of market access, developing countries should seek active support from international institutions that encourage free trade; in particular, institutions like the World Bank that have done so much to encourage developing countries to open their economies unilaterally should be equally active in helping the same developing countries have access to free markets. The valuable appraisals on trade policies produced at the GATT via the trade policy review mechanism, should be used as a lever for putting pressure on developed countries to remove protection.

A second possible response is to use publicity and seek public opinion support (for example, by mobilizing European NGOs) to combat any specific limitation to market access. Bangladesh successfully applied such lobbying tactics a couple of years ago to stop a limitation to its UK market access. Effective lobbying can either focus on how protection could damage the exporting country (or particular groups—e.g., the poor—within it) or target consumer interests (and its organizations) by showing how protection could harm EC consumers via higher prices. Lobbying of this kind requires professional lobbyists based in Brussels and Geneva as well as active use of embassy staff for these and related purposes. Japanese and ASEAN lobbying experiences provide important lessons; the use of lobbying as a means of achieving policy objectives is also well developed in the United States, where former senior policymakers (with good access to politicians) are hired for such purposes.

A third possibility implies actions using parallel issues (via either persuasion or threat) of roughly an equivalent magnitude. The type of counterpressure actions that can be undertaken are the threat to ban imports of an EC influential company (which will then lobby the European Commission on behalf of the developing countries in question, so as to ensure its own market access), the threat to limit more generally (or to buy last) the products from the EC, and the threat of antidumping action. Asian countries seem to have a successful record in this type of action. For example, in the early 1980s Thailand reportedly faced the possibility of a restriction of its EC quota for manioc, one of its most important exports; it threatened immediately to reduce imports by the same amount of the additional limitation that its exports would have faced. As a result, the EC withdrew the quota reduction. Indonesia and Malaysia used similar tactics to block restraints on their exports. Some countries like Thailand apparently even use approval or renewal of key licenses for foreign investors in their countries to ask for concessions in exchange, which in some cases implies requests to lobby on behalf of the country in trade matters.[8]

Finally, developing countries can also resort to antidumping actions themselves, partly to counteract genuine dumping but even as a bargaining chip to avoid or achieve withdrawal of antidumping measures against them. South Korea applied ADDs for the first time in April 1991. It is important to emphasize that either for potential antidumping actions by developing countries or to help combat such practices, EC antidumping actions are based on rather strange calculations; Davenport (1988) reports that 94 percent of the cases against developing countries were investigated on the basis of "constructed prices" rather than estimating the cost of production, as is implied by the GATT rules. Furthermore, the onus of proof is on the exporter, who must demonstrate that the injury was caused by other factors; this procedure makes antidumping easy to prove. Antidumping threats would have to be carefully picked to make them credible and also to prevent significant loss of relatively cheap trade. More broadly, the antidumping instruments would have to be used in a selective, clearly targeted way so as to avoid any risk of generating an undesirable confrontation with powerful trading partners.

In these as well as in other issues relating to broader aspects of EC trade policy, it is essential for developing countries to have timely and detailed information. It would seem advisable for countries (individually or in groups) to hire lawyers and other specialists who can analyze EC directives as they are being prepared and as they go through the legal procedures and tell whether the directives have potentially adverse effects. By detecting these in time, pressure can be brought to bear to alter the policies. In this context, it is important to know the steps whereby EC directives are approved. First, the European Commission proposes a directive to the Council of Ministers; the amended directives are presented to the European Parliament and then go before national parliaments for ratification. Appeals can also be made to the European Court of Justice.

Besides bargaining for ensuring access to open markets, developing countries must act at a more technical level to ensure that their products meet the harmonized standards adopted as part of the 1992 program. These standards, which create serious information problems for even the most advanced European suppliers, are particularly problematic for small countries, as the fixed information costs are relatively higher as a proportion of actual or potential trade flows. So a first strategic effort must be to acquire relevant information about new standards; this can be done by developing countries at a national or regional level. Davenport and Page (1991) report that the main sectors in which harmonized technical standards can create problems are plants and flowers (which will require "plant passports" and/or pre-export inspection), meat products, and especially fish and fish products; as regards the latter, the Commission may establish a list of processing plants and factory vessels authorized to export to the EC. Satisfying the new rules may take considerable and timely investment in constructing new sewage plants or improving existing ones. Furthermore, it is important to use public relations so as to reassure European countries and relevant authorities of the quality of products.

Large changes in Europe and European integration pose both important opportunities and new problems for developing countries. Strategies need to be designed that allow these countries to maximize use of new market opportunities and overcome problems of market access; collective actions by groups of developing countries may be valuable to augment their bargaining power, especially in a world of increasing regionalism. The real nature of the GATT must be fully understood in both recent multilateral and regional terms. Though developing countries need to continue their commitment to strengthen the multilateral trading system, they may also need to diversify their bargaining strategy to emphasize regional and bilateral bargaining, even if they rightly believe this to be second best (see Chapters 4 and 5).

When the debt crises exploded in the early 1980s, indebted developing-country governments made incredible efforts by servicing their debts to safeguard the stability of the international banking system, even to the extent of sacrificing output and growth of their economies. Thus they took more than their share of responsibility in managing this international issue. In the 1990s the governments of developing countries are again among the strongest defenders of the interest of the international system, this time on the trading front. Even more than in the case of debt, the burden of maintaining an open multilateral trading system cannot, however, be carried mainly by developing countries; to be successful, the system requires the support of the major industrial economies. Should the major industrialized countries fail to provide increasingly free access to their markets—especially multilaterally, through the Uruguay Round, but also in the context of important regional groupings like the EC—developing countries may reluctantly be forced to rethink their enthusiasm for their own trade liberalization. This would be unfortunate.

NOTES

This chapter draws on research done for UNCTAD with Parvin Alizadeh, to whom special thanks must go for providing the study of trade creation and diversion for UNCTAD. I am very grateful to Diana Tussie and Manuel Agosin for their stimulating and detailed comments. I wish to thank Judita Stouracova for providing statistics; I am also extremely grateful to Sheila Page, Chris Stevens, Gary Hufbauer, and Michael Davenport for their valuable information and thoughtful suggestions.

1. This section draws heavily on P. Alizadeh and S. Griffith-Jones, 1992, and especially on Chapter 3, Part A of UNCTAD, 1990.

2. I thank Chris Stevens for this point.

3. For more detailed estimates by country and by sector, see UNCTAD, 1991, and Alizadeh and Griffith-Jones, 1992.

4. For more detailed analysis, see Alizadeh and Griffith-Jones, 1992.

5. United Nations, *Monthly Bulletin of Statistics,* several issues.

6. See Kadar, 1990.

7. I thank Gary Hufbauer and Vicente Donoso for insightful suggestions on this point.

8. Interview material.

Canada and the United States: Drifting Toward Regionalism

ANN WESTON

The U.S. now has a multi–track policy but with no clearly defined set of objectives and policy instruments: the new direction has an uncertain destination, but the journey has commenced.
—S. Ostry, "Anti-Dumping: The Tip of the Iceberg," p. 25

This chapter reviews recent trends in Canadian and U.S. trade policy, focusing on issues of interest to developing-country negotiators. In particular it seeks to explain the factors underlying the current emphasis on regionalism. In Canada the focus has been on the Canada–U.S. Free Trade Agreement (CUSFTA), with the government participating somewhat reluctantly in the U.S. negotiations with Mexico over a North American Free Trade Agreement (NAFTA). The U.S. interest in regionalism has been more extensive, as reflected in the Enterprise for the Americas Initiative (EAI).

The chapter begins with an exploration of the political and economic context of trade bargaining. In both countries trade-policy making has become increasingly politicized. In the United States especially, this has constrained the administration's bargaining flexibility. The second half of the chapter examines the merits of the regional trade bargaining strategies emerging in the United States and Canada and their implications for developing countries. For the United States, the CUSFTA, NAFTA, and EAI are designed to reinforce its aggressive stance in the GATT and unilaterally, as well as to serve immediate regional objectives. For Canada, interest in the NAFTA and EAI is limited to defending its preferential status in the U.S. market and to developing longer–term trade links with the rest of the hemisphere.

The chapter concludes by examining the widespread skepticism about the United States' multitrack trade policy and its compatibility with a strengthened GATT. The emergence of a Western Hemisphere trade arrangement may offer some benefits to developing countries in the region, but these will be concentrated and uncertain, with a price to pay in concessions to the United States, trade and investment diversion from third countries, diluted South-South regional integration, and a diminished role for the GATT.

KEY DETERMINANTS OF NATIONAL OBJECTIVES

While they differ in some respects, there are a number of similarities between the economic objectives of the U.S. and Canadian governments. A priority for both governments has been reduction of the fiscal deficit, which reached 9 percent of gross domestic product (GDP) in Canada in 1985 and 6 percent of GDP in the United States in 1983 (see Table 3.1). The emphasis on public spending restraints has limited the scope for government to deal with unemployment or to promote economic restructuring. It has not, however, deterred the governments from reducing tariffs, though it may have encouraged the use of other trade barriers (e.g., ADDs or agricultural import quotas) as fiscally cheaper tools for domestic protection.

Reducing inflation from the double-digit levels recorded in the early part of the 1980s (shown in Table 3.1) has been another target, and especially in Canada this led to a policy of high interest rates (with a significant spread above U.S. rates toward the end of the decade). This has tended to attract foreign capital and keep the Canadian exchange rate high, depressing exports.

The fiscal deficit has been a key component in the decline in U.S. domestic savings in the 1980s and the widening gap with investment. This has been matched by a substantial current account imbalance. A similar gap arose in Canada in the 1980s, with the growth in investment outstripping savings, contributing to a decline in the traditional merchandise trade surplus. While there is some debate about the relative contribution of macroeconomic variables and the exchange rate in resolving this imbalance, many in the United States continue to emphasize the importance of trade policy.

Even though trade accounts for a small share of U.S. GDP, the need to service the rise in debt owed to nonresidents (see Table 3.1) has focused attention on the trade imbalance. A key objective, therefore, is to reduce the trade deficit or even achieve a trade surplus, whether by export promotion or import restriction.

Bilateral trade imbalances in the United States (shown in Table 3.2) have been used to justify concerns about "unfair trade" and to legitimize both import relief and market-opening measures. Two particular targets

Table 3.1 Economic Indicators for Canada and the United States
(in billions of Canadian and U.S. dollars, respectively, unless otherwise indicated)

	1980	1981	1982	1983	1984	1985	1986	1987	1988	1989	1990
Canada											
Real growth rate (%)	1.5	3.7	-3.2	3.2	6.3	4.8	3.3	4.0	4.4	3.0	0.9
Unemployment rate (%)	7.5	7.5	11.0	11.8	11.2	10.5	9.5	8.8	7.8	7.5	8.1
Inflation rate (CPI) (%)	10.2	12.4	10.9	5.7	4.4	3.9	4.2	4.4	4.0	5.0	4.8
Fiscal deficit	-11.5	-14.3	-15.5	-28.7	-32.7	-38.5	-34.5	-30.7	-28.2	-29.0	-29.0
Deficit as a % of GDP	4.2	4.6	4.4	7.7	8.1	8.7	7.2	6.1	5.1	4.8	4.5
Federal debt	53.4	64.5	83.2	103.0	129.8	163.0	178.7	202.4	228.7	249.4	271.0
Debt as a % of GDP	19.3	20.8	23.4	27.5	32.0	36.7	37.4	40.0	41.5	41.3	41.6
Merchandise trade balance	8.8	7.3	17.7	17.5	19.8	16.4	9.9	11.1	10.1	7.6	10.8
Current account balance	-1.1	-6.1	2.8	3.1	2.7	-2.0	-10.2	-9.2	-10.2	-16.7	-16.0
United States											
Real growth rate (%)	-0.2	1.9	-2.5	3.5	6.5	3.0	2.8	3.4	4.4	2.5	1.0
Unemployment rate (%)	7.2	7.6	9.7	9.6	7.5	7.2	7.0	6.2	5.5	5.3	5.3
Inflation rate (CPI) (%)	13.5	10.4	6.1	3.2	4.4	3.5	1.9	3.7	4.0	4.8	5.4
Fiscal deficit	-76.2	-78.7	-125.7	-202.5	-178.3	-212.1	-212.6	-147.5	-155.5	-143.8	-219.4
Deficit as a % of GDP	2.8	2.6	4.0	6.0	4.8	5.3	5.1	3.3	3.2	2.8	4.0
National debt	737.7	825.4	987.7	1,174.5	1,373.4	1,598.5	1,813.3	1,953.9	2,096.9	2,244.2	2,548.1
Debt as a % of GDP	27.5	27.5	31.7	35.1	36.9	40.2	43.1	43.4	43.3	43.5	47.0
Debt owed to nonresidents	129.7	136.6	149.5	166.3	205.9	224.8	263.4	299.7	362.2	392.9	na
Merchandise trade balance	-25.5	-28.0	-36.5	-67.3	-112.5	-122.2	-145.1	-159.5	-127.0	-114.9	-108.7
Current account balance	1.8	6.4	-8.0	-47.0	-99.0	-122.6	-145.4	-162.2	-129.0	-110.0	-99.6

Sources: *Bank of Canada Review*, Bank of Canada: Ottawa, June 1991; *International Financial Statistics*, 1986 and 1991, International Monetary Fund: Washington, D.C., 1986 and 1991; *World Economic Outlook*, International Monetary Fund: Washington, D.C., April 1987.

have been Japan and the NICs, which accounted for 36 percent and 23 percent, respectively, of the U.S. trade deficit in 1990, whereas in 1980 the United States had a trade surplus with the latter. The Canadian deficit with the NICs is much smaller and is offset by the surplus with other countries.

Heavy dependence on the U.S. market is a critical factor in any discussion of Canadian trade bargaining. Canada is a leading trading nation, ranking eighth in the world in 1990, but more than two-thirds of its trade is with the United States, as indicated in Table 3.3. Another issue in both Canada and the United States is the changing composition of trade (see Table 3.4) and the growing manufactures trade imbalance, which in the United States was a major contributor to the deterioration in the merchandise trade account. The U.S. manufactures surplus of $15.5 billion in 1981 turned into a deficit of $119.1 billion by 1988, with a related decline in manufacturing employment. These trends are often viewed as symptoms of declining competitiveness.

There has been a major debate on how to reverse this trend by macroeconomic, trade, or industrial policies. Because there are only small surpluses in agriculture and services, some have argued that improvements must come primarily in manufactures trade, implying "significant structural adjustment challenges for some trading partners who have come to rely on ever-expanding manufactures trade surpluses [with the United States] as a major source of their economic growth" (U.S. Department of Commerce, 1989, 18).

Apart from its large exports of cars to the United States, Canada's trade remains highly dependent on its agriculture and natural resource industries (see Table 3.4). This explains Canada's priority in the Uruguay Round to resolution of the EC-U.S. agricultural subsidy trade war and the reduction of tariff escalation on processed products.

Finally, in both countries, increasing attention has been given to the flows of private foreign investment (PFI), both inward and outward. An interesting feature of the 1980s was the sharp influx of PFI into the United States (including from Canada), responding to concern about access to the U.S. market as well as the depreciation of the dollar (after 1985) and an increase in the global movements of capital. This has influenced trade policy. In Canada the desire to be a competitive site for investment was an important driving force behind both the CUSFTA and the decision to join the NAFTA negotiations. U.S. corporations have also sought changes in Canadian and Mexican investment and trade regulations to ease their location decisions.

To summarize, improving trade performance through trade policy initiatives has been a key U.S. objective. The United States has emphasized manufactures and bilateral trade balances with several countries. Canada has had a narrower bilateral focus, principally securing access to the U.S. market.

Table 3.2 Direction of U.S. Exports and Imports
(in millions of dollars and in percentages)

	Exports				Distribution of Total X			
	1960	1970	1980	1989	1960	1970	1980	1989
World	14,840	39,050	220,781	363,807	100.0	100.0	100.0	100.0
Developed Countries	8,800	28,690	125,353	230,078	59.3	73.5	56.8	63.2
W. Europe	3,850	10,360	n.a.	n.a.	25.9	26.5	n.a.	n.a.
EC	n.a.	n.a.	58,861	86,570	n.a.	n.a.	26.7	23.8
UK	1,000	2,150	12,695	20,866	6.7	5.5	5.8	5.7
Canada	3,140	10,580	35,395	78,266	21.2	27.1	16.0	21.5
Japan	1,110	6,020	20,790	44,584	7.5	15.4	9.4	12.3
Developing Countries	5,960	10,140	87,629	128,716	40.2	26.0	39.7	35.4
Latin America	4,020	5,620	38,745	49,055	27.1	14.4	17.5	13.5
Mexico	n.a.	n.a.	15,146	24,969	n.a.	n.a.	6.9	6.9
Brazil	n.a.	n.a.	4,352	4,799	n.a.	n.a.	2.0	1.3
Asia	1,510	3,650	23,330	57,403	10.2	9.3	10.6	15.8
Korea	n.a.	n.a.	4,685	13,478	n.a.	n.a.	2.1	3.7
China	n.a.	n.a.	3,755	5,807	n.a.	n.a.	1.7	1.6
Africa	420	810	6,520	5,104	2.8	2.1	3.0	1.4

	Imports				Distribution of Total M			
	1960	1970	1980	1989	1960	1970	1980	1989
World	20,410	42,590	256,959	493,652	100.0	100.0	100.0	100.0
Developed Countries	13,030	29,630	126,311	295,954	63.8	69.6	49.2	60.0
W. Europe	6,360	12,730			31.2	29.9	0.0	0.0
EC			39,988	88,821	0.0	0.0	15.6	18.0
UK	1,460	2,480	10,273	18,881	7.2	5.8	4.0	3.8
Canada	3,740	8,810	41,999	89,550	18.3	20.7	16.3	18.1
Japan	1,440	4,610	32,973	97,110	7.1	10.8	12.8	19.7
Developing Countries	7,090	12,600	122,585	196,294	34.7	29.6	47.7	39.8
Latin America	3,870	6,480	38,915	60,100	19.0	15.2	15.1	12.2
Mexico			12,835	27,590	0.0	0.0	5.0	5.6
Brazil			4,000	9,001	0.0	0.0	1.6	1.8
Asia	2,730	5,070	25,845	101,368	13.4	11.9	10.1	20.5
Korea			4,434	20,543	0.0	0.0	1.7	4.2
China			1,164	12,901	0.0	0.0	0.5	2.6
Africa	490	990	26,318	14,756	2.4	2.3	10.2	3.0

Sources: Derived from UN, *Handbook of International Trade and Development Statistics,* 1976, and *Direction of Trade,* International Monetary Fund: Washington, D.C., 1983 and 1990.

Table 3.3 Direction of Canadian Exports and Imports (in millions of U.S. dollars and in percentages)

	Exports				Distribution of Total Exports				Distribution of Non-U.S. Exports			
	1960	1970	1980	1989	1960	1970	1980	1989	1960	1970	1980	1989
World	5,420	12,420	67,730	120,673	100.0	100.0	100.0	100.0				
Developed Countries	4,900	11,330	54,742	105,300	90.4	91.2	80.8	87.3				
W. Europe	990	1,680	n.a.	n.a.	18.3	13.5	n.a.	n.a.	58.9	46.5	n.a.	n.a.
EC	n.a.	n.a.	8,416	9,819	n.a.	n.a.	12.4	8.1	n.a.	n.a.	31.6	27.8
UK	600	660	2,713	2,984	11.1	5.3	4.0	2.5	35.7	18.3	10.2	8.4
United States	3,740	8,810	41,068	85,305	69.0	70.9	60.6	70.7				
Japan	120	560	4,238	7,429	2.2	4.5	6.3	6.2	7.1	15.5	15.9	21.0
Developing Countries	490	1,000	7,619	9,819	9.0	8.1	11.2	8.1	29.2	27.7	28.6	27.8
Latin America	265	580	2,900	2,043	4.9	4.7	4.3	1.7	15.8	16.1	10.9	5.8
Mexico	n.a.	n.a.	419	525	n.a.	n.a.	0.6	0.4	n.a.	n.a.	1.6	1.5
Brazil	n.a.	n.a.	736	447	n.a.	n.a.	1.1	0.4	n.a.	n.a.	2.8	1.3
Asia	210	317	2,305	5,571	3.9	2.6	3.4	4.6	12.5	8.8	8.6	15.8
Korea	n.a.	n.a.	355	1,354	n.a.	n.a.	0.5	1.1	n.a.	n.a.	1.3	3.8
China	n.a.	n.a.	742	967	n.a.	n.a.	1.1	0.8	n.a.	n.a.	2.8	2.7
Africa	20	77	918	803	0.4	0.6	1.4	0.7	1.2	2.1	3.4	2.3
Excl. U.S.	1,680	3,610	26,662	35,368	31.0	29.1	39.4	29.3	100.0	100.0	100.0	100.0

(continues)

	Imports				Distribution of Total Imports				Distribution of Non-U.S. Imports			
	1960	1970	1980	1989	1960	1970	1980	1989	1960	1970	1980	1989
World	5,550	16,180	61,004	117,146	100.0	100.0	100.0	100.0				
Developed Countries	5,090	14,720	50,031	99,371	91.7	91.0	82.0	84.8				
W. Europe	1,540	2,890	n.a.	n.a.	27.7	17.9	n.a.	n.a.	63.9	51.6	n.a.	n.a.
EC	n.a.	n.a.	4,940	13,272	n.a.	n.a.	8.1	11.3	n.a.	n.a.	24.9	31.2
UK	960	1,440	1,782	3,856	17.3	8.9	2.9	3.3	39.8	25.7	9.0	9.1
United States	3,140	10,580	41,201	74,556	56.6	65.4	67.5	63.6				
Japan	185	760	5,496	8,066	3.3	4.7	9.0	6.9	7.7	13.6	27.8	18.9
Developing Countries	420	1,200	7,874	14,101	7.6	7.4	12.9	12.0	17.4	21.4	39.8	33.1
Latin America	260	690	3,196	4,113	4.7	4.3	5.2	3.5	10.8	12.3	16.1	9.7
Mexico	n.a.	n.a.	295	1,434	n.a.	n.a.	0.5	1.2	n.a.	n.a.	1.5	3.4
Brazil	n.a.	n.a.	296	954	n.a.	n.a.	0.5	0.8	n.a.	n.a.	1.5	2.2
Asia	136	395	1,460	7,877	2.5	2.4	2.4	6.7	5.6	7.1	7.4	18.5
Korea	n.a.	n.a.	354	2,079	n.a.	n.a.	0.6	1.8	n.a.	n.a.	1.8	4.9
China	n.a.	n.a.	132	999	n.a.	n.a.	0.2	0.9	n.a.	n.a.	0.7	2.3
Africa[a]	27	110	458	1,100	0.5	0.7	0.8	0.9	1.1	2.0	2.3	2.6
Excl. U.S.	2,410	5,600	19,803	42,590	43.4	34.6	32.5	36.4	100.0	100.0	100.0	100.0

Sources: Derived from UN, Handbook of International Trade and Development Statistics, 1976, and Direction of Trade, International Monetary Fund: Washington, D.C., 1983 and 1990.

Note: a. Includes South Africa.

**Table 3.4   Composition of Canadian and U.S. Trade
(in billions of U.S. dollars)**

| | 1980 | | | 1989 | | |
	Exports	Imports	Balance	Exports	Imports	Balance
Canada						
Total	64.93	59.98	5.95	116.00	113.97	2.03
Primary Products	32.91	15.62	17.29	42.61	17.75	24.86
Manufactures	29.98	41.21	-11.23	69.05	92.61	-23.56
United States						
Total	225.64	253.00	-27.36	363.63	493.01	-129.38
Primary products	71.17	121.88	-50.71	81.28	111.63	-30.35
Manufactures	145.91	124.23	21.68	264.71	366.43	-101.72

Source: Derived from GATT, *International Trade 1988–90*, vol. 2, 1990.
Note: Commodities not classified according to kind are included in total.

TRADE BARGAINING AS A POLITICAL PROCESS

Trade bargaining in the United States and Canada has become increasingly politicized, partly as a result of the growing dependence of both economies on trade. Also, trade is no longer seen as a narrow technical matter but one touching a wide array of issues relating to sovereignty and social welfare.

For instance, the debate in Canada over the CUSFTA became very heated as the agreement went beyond traditional border measures to include sensitive subjects like investment, energy, and culture. In addition, there was widespread concern that given the predominance of the United States, a bilateral agreement would lead to the erosion of Canadian standards for health care and working conditions. With the proposed NAFTA, the focus in both countries has broadened further to include environmental standards and labor rights.

The process of trade-policy making in the United States has been diffuse, shared by Congress, the administration, and the private sector. Recent changes in trade legislation, however, have diminished the administration's authority. According to the U.S. Constitution, Congress is responsible for making and executing U.S. trade policy. But for several decades it has delegated negotiating and executive authority to the administration (e.g., under the fast-track authority), primarily to reduce political pressure from narrow interest groups. Nonetheless, Congress, notably through the House Ways and Means Committee and the Senate Finance Committee, retains substantial influence, both through the formulation of trade legislation and through frequent scrutiny of the administration's performance (e.g., briefings from the USTR on the progress of disputes).

The 1988 Omnibus Trade and Competitiveness Act incorporated several changes reflecting congressional concern that the administration was giving inadequate attention to domestic interests compared to diplomatic priorities (Bhagwati and Patrick, 1990). For example, Congress believed the growing importance of the USTR would reduce the influence of other departments and their capacity to bring a broader perspective to U.S. trade policies. Some observers have even suggested that the White House has lost initiative on trade to Congress, with the result that U.S. trade policy is now essentially made in Congress.

The debate in early 1991 over the extension of the administration's fast-track authority for the Uruguay Round and the NAFTA negotiations underlines the fragility of the process. More and more congresspeople are expressing opinions on trade policy, while labor, environmental, and church groups fear that the expansion of trade will erode social standards in the United States rather than raise them in Mexico. These special interests have joined with like-minded groups in Mexico and Canada to form a cross-border coalition opposed to NAFTA.

Besides consultations with Congress and the various government agencies, the president through the USTR draws upon a network of private-sector advisory committees. A large number of private-sector groups have also been set up to monitor and lobby the administration and Congress. Their efforts to influence both legislation and executive decisions have grown with their interest in trade. Complexity of U.S. trade policy is another factor; as UNECLAC (1990, 18) notes, monitoring has become important with the very detailed calendars for policy implementation in the 1988 trade act.

These private-sector groups cover a considerable range in perspective and influence, from small, industry-specific groups such as the Flower Retailers' Association to large ones like the U.S. Chamber of Commerce and Consumers for World Trade (Destler and Odell, 1987). Banks have typically maintained a low profile in discussions of U.S. import policy, despite their interest in developing-country capacity to service their debts. On banking and financial services they have been strong supporters of the U.S. policies of reciprocity and market opening under the threat of retaliation.Foreign lobbying efforts have increased in parallel. According to U.S. government figures, expenditures by registered foreign lobbyists amounted to $451 million in 1989, though this is likely an underestimate (UNECLAC, 1990, 5).

While several authors have commented on a growth in protrade groups, including the large service corporations, it is not clear that these groups necessarily oppose import-competing interests. An important fallout from the 1988 trade act, in particular the toughened 301 provision, is the weakening of the protrade/antiprotection coalition (Finger, 1991, 20). Exporters no longer need to support import liberalization in the United States to improve their access to other markets. In essence, the 1988 act offers maintenance of existing access to the U.S. market (rather than new import concessions) in return for better access to foreign markets. Failure by foreigners to open up will lead to restrictive retaliation.

In Canada, by contrast, Parliament's role in trade-policy making is minor. This changed somewhat in 1987–1988 with the negotiation of the CUSFTA, which was a major issue of parliamentary debate. The proposed extension of this agreement to include Mexico has also provoked controversy. Most of Parliament's involvement in trade policy is manifested through two committees: the Commons' Standing Committee on External Affairs and International Trade (SCEAIT) and the Senate Standing Committee on Foreign Affairs. But neither body has much influence. As a recent SCEAIT report noted, "The Canadian tradition and system, unlike the American, gives Parliament only a very marginal role in the making of trade policy, confining its participation to bringing Canadian law into conformity with treaty obligations" (1991, 24).

There is little political accountability, since majority governments are able to pass trade agreements routinely. They are presented for approval, not for advice or amendment. SCEAIT's cross–country hearings on the CUSFTA were held without a full and final text being available for review and with limited time for discussion. When the trade minister sought SCEAIT's advice on Canada's role in the NAFTA negotiations, the decision to negotiate was taken before SCEAIT's deliberations had concluded. SCEAIT has called for this process to change: "This tradition is now dangerously obsolete because the rapidly changing nature of the international system is blurring the old distinctions between what are strictly domestic and international concerns. In these new circumstances, political debate of international trade policy is inevitable and political consensus desirable if not essential" (1991, 24). By contrast, the government has held regular consultations with the private sector during negotiations on the Uruguay Round, the CUSFTA, and now the NAFTA through fifteen sectoral advisory groups on international trade (SAGITs) and an overview committee (the International Trade Advisory Committee, or ITAC).

Changes in trade law in the 1980s in both Canada and the United States have granted the private sector greater access to trade remedies and thus resulted in the "privatization of trade policy" (Ostry, in Trebilcock and York, 1990, 17). For example, in the U.S. trade act of 1988, injury no longer has to be proven for relief against patent infringements under Section 337; new criteria make it more likely injury will be found in CVD cases; and the grounds for dumping have been extended.

In Canada the Special Import Measures Act of 1985 extended the right to bring safeguard complaints to any producers (provided they constitute a major share of their industry); this "direct access" provision had previously been limited to textile and clothing producers. One positive aspect of the act, however, was the introduction of a public interest provision under which the benefits of import relief are to be weighed against the costs to consumers, retailers, and others (though this is to be applied with discretion, and the findings are not binding). Another was a five-year sunset clause requiring antidumping and CVD cases to be reviewed before extension. A third positive development was the creation of the Canadian International Trade Tribunal in 1988. This replaced inter alia the Textiles and Clothing Board, which had been closely associated with the domestic industry. Besides its judicial functions, it may, at the government's request, undertake general trade inquiries, and this may eventually lead to more transparency in trade-policy making.

A final dimension to be taken into account is the division of responsibilities between the federal government and the provinces or states. In Canada the constitutional crisis triggered by the failure to accommodate Quebec's demands for special status has led to a review of federal–provincial relations. Trade bargaining is being affected as the negotiations move into areas of provincial responsibility, and some observers doubt the provinces will implement international agreements. Similar concerns have arisen in the United States for example, over trade-related environmental regulations.

TRADE AND INDUSTRIAL POLICY

Driven by concerns about industrial competitiveness, considerable discussion has taken place in Canada and the United States over the role of trade and industrial policy in economic management. In the past, both countries attempted to resist pressures for protection and managed trade, appealing to the GATT principles of trade liberalization, multilateralism, and nondiscrimination.

But while recognizing the importance of underlying macroeconomic factors, both Canada and the United States have attempted to deal with sectoral trade problems through the maintenance of high effective tariffs, quotas or VERs, ADDs, or CVDs (GATT, 1990a and 1990b). These have typically involved the labor-intensive, low-technology industries (clothing, footwear ,etc.). For example, both Canada and the United States have negotiated increasingly restrictive VERs for clothing under the Multifiber arrangement, going against the trend in other importing countries. While there are no longer any QRs against footwear, there continue to be high tariffs supplemented by various ADD and CVDs.

A patchwork of policies has also been introduced, sometimes on strategic grounds, to support higher-tech industries in the United States by restricting access to the domestic market; these include VERs on steel, cars, and machine tools. More generally, changes in U.S. trade law (notably the 1988 trade act) provide an aggressive response to foreign exporters in that they aim to curb practices that give the United States' competitors "unfair" advantages.

Backing up these border measures have been various industrial support programs. In the United States support has come in the form of defense contracts, other public procurement policies, and exemptions from antitrust laws to allow companies to do collaborative research. Such an array of ad hoc, reactive measures has satisfied neither those in favor of nonintervention and liberal trade nor supporters of a more coherent and comprehensive strategic trade and industrial policy.[1] The latter argue that U.S. trade policy is ineffective in restricting imports and in opening export markets, while industrial policy needs to be strengthened, for example, through more public support to research and training. In this view, it is the failure to develop a coherent industrial policy that has led the government to fall back on the aggressive use of ADDs. Furthermore, the fragmentation of trade policy powers has undermined the formulation of strategic trade policies.

Neither the CUSFTA nor the proposed NAFTA was initially perceived to be central to U.S. industrial policy—certainly neither was initiated by the United States But both have important implications for U.S. industry and especially that growing share of U.S. corporations with global linkages. The CUSFTA provided these firms with the opportunity to rationalize production between their Canadian and U.S. plants. (It also provided other benefits, such as more secure access to Canadian energy and to investment in Canada.) Despite a few unresolved and sensitive issues (such as subsidies and binding U.S. trade practice to settlement by a bilateral panel), the CUSFTA was not controversial, and it won congressional support.

In contrast, the heated debate over NAFTA suggests that this agreement is of much greater strategic interest. Even though the bilateral trade and investment links are as yet much smaller, they are growing rapidly (see Table 3.5). Besides the opportunities for increased exports and investment, many are concerned about the possible negative impact on employment in labor-intensive and even some high-tech, import-competing industries in the United States—an issue that did not emerge in the CUSFTA given the much smaller differentials in labor costs between Canada and the United States. One issue is the effect of competition with lower Mexican wage costs on efforts to shift U.S. industry to a high-tech, knowledge-intensive growth path.

Developments in Canada have been somewhat different, dictated partly by the smaller domestic market. Until the late 1970s, federal indus-

Table 3.5   U.S. Trade and Investment Links with Canada and Mexico

	Canada			Mexico		
	1985	**1989**	**Growth (% per year)**	**1985**	**1989**	**Growth (% per year)**
U.S. exports ($millions)	47,251	78,266	13.4	13,635	24,969	16.3
U.S. imports ($millions)	69,427	89,550	6.6	19,392	27,590	9.2
FDI (stock)	C$77.4 bn[a]	C$119 bn	7.4	$14.6 bn	$26.6 bn	16.2
U.S. share in FDI	75%	68%		n.a. (72% in 1989 flow)	62.8%	

Sources: Derived from *Direction of Trade Statistics,* International Monetary Fund: Washington, D.C.: 1987 and 1991; *The Likely Impact on the United States of a Free Trade Agreement with Mexico,* United States International Trade Commission: Washington, D.C., February 1991; *The Opportunities and Challenges of North American Free Trade: A Canadian Perspective,* Investment Canada: Ottawa, April 1991.
Note: a. 1983.

trial policy involved the maintenance of relatively high effective tariffs, and some nontariff barriers, amid an array of other policies designed to promote industrial output and reduce dependence on the export of semi- or unprocessed natural resource products. An important dimension was the promotion of regional development. Trade policy, besides maintaining protection of certain sensitive industries, was designed to promote trade with third countries and so lower dependence on the U.S. market, primarily through the GATT.

Since the mid–1980s, the federal Conservative government has introduced a series of radical changes in keeping with its noninterventionist ideology and its attempts to reduce the fiscal deficit. The trade, industrial and regional assistance programs, considered by some to have been a failure,[2] have gradually been cut back. The Western and Atlantic Canada programs have been separated from industrial support, while the latter has shifted from being grants-oriented to service- and knowledge-oriented and non-firm specific. According to Doern, this resulted from "a lingering fear, only partly addressed in the CUSFTA, that many Canadian industrial policy actions used in the past will be subject to countervail challenges under American trade law on the grounds that they are trade distorting" (1990, 56).

Instead, the CUSFTA has become a key tool of industrial as well as trade policy. It was designed to promote rationalization of Canadian industry and to increase productivity through economies of scale, offered by more secure access to the large U.S. market. This in turn was expected to attract PFI to Canada (while provisions to protect growing Canadian investment in the United States from nascent nationalism were also important). At the same time the CUSFTA was intended to "lock in" policy reforms and prevent a return to previous interventionist policies. Precisely for this reason, the CUSFTA was seen as a threat by Canadians who favored a more active industrial strategy involving training and research.

Further industrial restructuring is likely with the NAFTA, though it is too early to conclude that the benefits will outweigh the costs.[3] In this case the stated strategic interest has essentially been a defensive one, that is, to secure for investors in Canada the same market access available to investors in the United States. Canada also wants to help develop the rules (e.g., of origin) and the timetable that will govern its competition with Mexican products in the U.S. market.

The efficacy of this emphasis on FTAs is an issue of more than domestic interest. Without complementary adjustment policies, concerns about free trade with Mexico may weaken support in Canada and the United States for closer economic links with developing countries. It has already been suggested in the United States that job losses in particular sectors arising from the NAFTA could be offset by stricter controls on third-country imports.

For developing countries, there is also the broader issue of the legitimacy of government intervention in managing economic change. Some may be concerned about the precedents set by the CUSFTA and NAFTA and fear pressure to extend this approach through the EAI, and even to other developing countries through the GATT.

TRADE-BARGAINING STRATEGY

The emergence of a regional dimension in U.S. and Canadian trade bargaining strategies can be traced to a number of factors. One of the most important is U.S. frustration with the GATT process. The GATT's day-to-day practices (such as dispute settlement) have proved too slow or its rules inadequate to deal with what many in the United States consider "unfair" trading practices (e.g., nonenforcement of workers' rights, currency undervaluation). These concerns have been reinforced by a perception that the U.S. market—which accounted for a major share of world import growth in recent years—has been the mainstay of the multilateral trading system. In the Uruguay Round negotiations the United States has therefore been a prime mover for more stringent rules as well as the addition of new subjects (like services) in which it has a strong export interest. But the slow pace of the negotiations and the difficulty of securing an acceptable consensus have led the United States to pursue a multitrack policy of unilateralism, bilateralism, and regionalism, alongside multilateralism. Another concern has been the strengthening of regional economic integration in other parts of the world, notably the EC and within the Asia-Pacific basin. Besides the issue of access for exporters, this raises questions about the ease of investment flows.

This is not to suggest that the GATT is no longer important to the United States. Indeed, the United States has continued to be actively involved in the GATT, for example, in terms of contributing proposals in the Uruguay Round and in bringing disputes for multilateral settlement (e.g., EC Airbus subsidies). Success in the GATT remains the priority to resolve major systemic problems like distortions in agriculture or new rules for services. But the U.S. stance within the GATT has become more aggressive, backed up by the pursuit of alternative strategies outside the GATT. These have various objectives: to achieve quick results, to act as a catalyst and lever in the GATT, and to obtain insurance against the spread of regional blocs.

Outside the GATT, the United States has pursued an increasingly aggressive and essentially unilateral trade strategy (Bhagwati and Patrick, 1990; GATT, 1990a). This has targeted a number of rapidly growing exporters such as Korea and Thailand as well as Japan. A number of elements illustrate the toughness of this new strategy. First, it is unilateral in that the United States has sought changes in other countries' practices without offering any new concessions in return. Bargaining has been limited, though some countries have been able to secure more lenient treatment, such as a slower timetable for compliance with U.S. demands. In several instances the United States has been prepared to accept VERs instead of proceeding with ADDs or other import relief measures. In response there has been greater recourse to the GATT to overturn U.S. trade actions, but the number of cases against the United States still represents a small fraction of the U.S. total.[4] Second, a new element in U.S. trade policy is the greater scope for the administration to initiate action against "unfair" traders in other countries rather than waiting for petitions from domestic industries. Third, the United States has focused on changing other countries' domestic regulations governing imports and other issues such as intellectual property, as well as their export practices. For example, following a Section 301 petition and a series of ADD proceedings, an agreement on semiconductors was signed with Japan to improve U.S. access to the Japanese market and to prevent dumping in third countries. In return the 301 and ADD proceedings were dropped.

Fourth, such U.S. practice often goes beyond the GATT in that some of these areas are as yet outside the GATT's competence—notably intellectual property, insurance, and workers' rights. There is also an emphasis on results rather than rules. In some cases the United States has introduced more restrictive interpretations than those written into the GATT, such as the rules governing CVDs. Under the 1989 SII with Japan, regular discussions are held on structural constraints facing U.S. business operations, such as *keiretsu* (cross-shareholding) and other practices the United States considers anticompetitive. Even where applying GATT rules, the tight timetable in the 1988 trade act allows for retaliatory action without prior sanctioning by the GATT council.

Another element of aggressive trade policy concerns agricultural export subsidies under the Export Enhancement Program. This war chest, amounting to $2.5 billion in 1988, has sought to win back market share from the EC, particularly for wheat, but exporters in third countries have been affected. The program has also supported such U.S. exports as rice and cotton, of which developing countries (e.g., Thailand and Egypt, respectively) are major suppliers.

The U.S. interest in discriminatory bilateral or regional agreements is recent; traditionally the United States has opposed them when instituted by other groups of countries. The 1980 Caribbean Basin Initiative (CBI) was its first step in this direction. The subsequent agreement with Israel, the CUSFTA, and the proposed NAFTA have been even more far-reaching.

In none of these agreements has the United States been the demandeur, though its positive response has reflected strong interests—both from a longer-term systemic perspective as well as immediate trade and investment objectives. As Treasury Secretary Baker reiterated on several occasions in 1988, "We are seeking a healthy dynamic linkage between bilateral and multilateral initiatives so as to prod and reinforce the GATT....The rewards of this agreement offer an incentive to other governments. If possible, we hope this follow-up liberalization will occur in the Uruguay Round. If not, we might be willing to explore a 'market liberalization club' approach, through minilateral arrangements or a series of bilateral agreements." In the case of Mexico, the United States has other important objectives—political, immigration, debt, and development. Many of these objectives also underlie the proposed extension of the NAFTA to the rest of the hemisphere.

Canadian trade strategy until the early 1980s could also be summarized as mainly multilateralist. Because Canada is a smaller nation heavily dependent on trade, the GATT offered it an effective means of preventing its larger trading partners (especially the United States) from introducing unilateral trade restrictions (Curtis, 1985; Stone, 1984). It also provided a means of reducing dependence on the U.S. market by promoting trade with third countries. Canada's shift to a "broadly bilateralist" path[5] reflected several factors, including skepticism about the effectiveness of efforts to diversify markets, concern about U.S. protectionism, recognition of U.S. unwillingness to deal in the GATT, and awareness of U.S. readiness to move quickly with like-minded countries.

Initially (in 1983), the Liberal government considered a sectoral approach to Canadian–U.S. trade liberalization, partly because most changes were predicted to be intrasectoral and also because it would have fewer negative implications for political sovereignty. But negotiations were extended to a broad range of sectors and nontrade issues, partly to meet the broader domestic objectives of the new Conservative government and partly to provide the side-payments sought by the United States.

Apart from its immediate objectives, CUSFTA was meant to change the dynamics of Canadian trade negotiations with other countries in the GATT, notably Japan and the EC, which would have to pay for entry to Canada on the same terms as the United States. Previously they had been able to secure the same treatment under the GATT's MFN rule.

The third and most recent phase of Canadian trade strategy, still in the making, can be characterized as reluctant regionalism. Canada has been involved in some loose regional initiatives, such as Pacific Basin Economic Cooperation, on the understanding that this should not undermine multilateralism but should be open to other members and should reinforce the GATT.

The suggestion of a free trade agreement between the United States and Mexico in early 1990 took many in Canada, including the government, by surprise. The government continued to be overtaken by the Mexican and U.S. political timetables that led to and earlier launching of negotiations than expected. The strategy that has been adopted is essentially defensive and reactive. There is no evidence that Canada would have sought a free trade agreement with Mexico had the United States not done so. It is also unlikely that Canada would enter into free trade discussions with South America and the Caribbean without the EAI.

A chief reason for participating in the NAFTA negotiations is to ensure that Canada offers the same advantages as a location for investment as does the United States, resulting in free access to all three North American markets. If the United States proceeds to negotiate a series of free trade agreements, first with Mexico and then with the rest of the hemisphere, a hub-and-spoke system could emerge, the United States, as the hub, having (ceteris paribus) the locational advantage over any of the spokes (Wonnacott, 1990).

Another of Canada's objectives is to protect its recently acquired interests in the U.S. market by becoming involved in the negotiations on the auto sector, the rules of origin, and the phasing of liberalization. Several studies have underlined the possibility of trade diversion, as Mexican products overlap with many Canadian ones (e.g., Magun, 1991; Trela and Whalley, 1991). Magun (1991), using an export similarity measure, shows that there is increasing overlap, with the index rising from 16 in 1971 to 34 in 1987, where 0 = dissimilar export distribution and 100 = identical export distribution. (This analysis is highly static and therefore inadequate for assessing the dynamic impacts of the NAFTA or even just the potential competition resulting from the restructuring of the Mexican economy.)

It is not clear, however, what bargaining chips Canada has to play, either with the United States or with Mexico. With the recent experience of U.S. objectives and bargaining techniques, Canada may be able to help Mexico on some issues. There may also be areas of mutual interest such as the strengthening of the dispute settlement provisions or discussions with the United States on subsidies and dumping, leading to more progress than either would be able to achieve independently (Hart, 1990, 129). But Mexico already appears to be moving further than Canada on culture and on intellectual property. And both Mexico and the United States have stated clearly that if Canada proves obstructive, it will be asked to leave the negotiations.

Aside from defensive considerations, the positive impacts of NAFTA for Canada do not appear to be that significant. Mexico is a minor market for Canada compared to many other countries, though it is the largest in the hemisphere after the United States. There is longer-term potential, but even this is limited compared to larger developing countries like China, India, or Brazil. Nor does Canada share the United States' geostrategic interest in the region. Though an important policy issue because of a growing number of immigrants from Mexico and further south, immigration is not as sensitive in Canada as in the United States.

There may be a stronger development rationale for Canada's assuming a role in the EAI: it already has preferential trade with several countries in the Caribbean, under the cooperation program known as CARIBCAN,[6] and wider bilateral aid interests in many parts of the region. However, these links are considerably weaker than those with many other extraregional countries, some of whom face the probability of trade diversion as a result of the EAI. (They are also weaker than U.S. trade and aid interests in the region.)

The GATT's importance for Canada has inevitably been diminished by the CUSFTA; the latter is to some extent a cushion against the failure of the former. But GATT still has a significant role to play in the promotion of Canadian trade interests. This is reflected in Canada's active participation in the current negotiations. Canada has three principal objectives: to strengthen GATT rules on agricultural export subsidies; to promote access to third markets in new and old areas; and to increase the efficacy of the GATT, especially the dispute settlement mechanism. The GATT mechanisms for dispute settlement and market liberalization are important for Canada's dealings with third countries: it does not have the same scope as does the United States for bilateral let alone unilateral bargains. The mechanisms also play a role in residual areas of bilateral disagreement, both in disputes on newly agreed-upon rules[7] and areas in which agreement on new rules could not be reached (such as subsidies).

RESULTS AND IMPLICATIONS
FOR DEVELOPING COUNTRIES

It is too early to draw firm conclusions about the benefits and costs of this new regionalist thread in Canadian and U.S. trade policy. As of mid-1992, the fate of the Uruguay Round was still uncertain. A key issue in the CUSFTA—subsidies—remained to be resolved, while the details of NAFTA, let alone the modalities of the EAI, still had to be finalized. Failure of the United States to get the NAFTA through Congress, for example, could lead to a major rethinking of the EAI. The comments that follow are therefore speculative. They focus first on the interests of the United States and Canada before turning to some implications for developing countries: Mexico, the rest of Latin America, and those outside the Western Hemisphere.

In several respects the U.S. policy of aggressive unilateralism appears successful. It secured several VERs and other trade-restricting concessions in eighteen of the twenty-six cases in which it threatened retaliation from 1985 to 1988 (Ostry, 1990b, 26). A number of countries have made market-opening commitments and agreed to modify their intellectual property laws in response to U.S. demands. Some have gone even further by disinvoking their right to use GATT Article 18b (allowing safeguards for balance-of-payments purposes).

It has been argued that these market-opening measures more than offset the trade-restricting commitments and thus U.S. trade policy on balance has contributed to world trade growth. But this begs a number of questions. First, some of these market-opening changes would have occurred anyway, with the present trend of liberalization and deregulation in many countries. Second, some of the commitments favor U.S. exporters, contributing to the evolution of a discriminatory, fragmented world trading system. Third, while this strategy has resolved some immediate irritants, it has not removed the major factor underlying the U.S. trade imbalance: domestic macroeconomic policy.

The success of the bilateral agreement with Canada lies partly in the terms the United States was able to secure for its exporters, investors, and buyers of Canadian energy. It has also spawned several other bilateral discussions under the EAI. By mid-1992, thirty-one out of thirty-four countries had signed framework agreements with the United States, the exceptions being Cuba, Haiti, and Suriname. Many expect to begin FTA negotiations with the United States once the NAFTA talks conclude.

There is reason for concern about the implications of a string of FTAs, whatever their individual merits: "proceeding piecemeal will result in a complex crazy-quilt system in which U.S. trade with different partners is subject to different regulatory regimes" (Lawrence and Schultze, 1990, 23). There is also likely to be less liberalization with piecemeal negotiations, with less scope for trade-offs. In the case of the EAI, these concerns may be addressed by a plurilateral approach, but the optimal approach may still be to work through the GATT.

The implications for the GATT, and for U.S. participation in the GATT, are mixed. Some aspects of the CUSFTA have been used as a model for the Uruguay Round texts; the CUSFTA has also illustrated to others the United States' priorities and limitations, (such as the exclusion of transport). On the negative side, it is possible that these unilateral, bilateral, and regional quick fixes may weaken domestic commitment to the GATT and the obligations that go with GATT membership. One example is the emerging U.S. preference for reciprocal deals on financial services rather than an arrangement based on the MFN principle. This trend would be a blow for many developing countries and the former Eastern bloc. Finally, FTAs carry the danger of trade diversion. A successful Uruguay Round (i.e., one that involves major cuts in U.S., Canadian, and Latin American protection) is needed to minimize the trade diverted from third countries.

In Canada the merits of the FTA with the United States continue to be hotly contested. In some respects its timing was unfortunate—being closely followed by the global recession and the appreciation of the Canadian dollar. It is too early for the full effect of the tariff and nontariff barrier liberalization to be known. But it has been unable to prevent a substantial drop in manufacturing output and employment and the closure of several U.S. subsidiaries; indeed, its critics argue it has been a major cause of these changes.

While the liberalization of access to the U.S. market is being phased in over ten years, the security provisions came into immediate effect and have been put to the test on several occasions, especially by Canadian exporters. Most of the panel cases have involved ADD and CVD cases and have gone in Canada's favor. A major shortcoming of the CUSFTA, however, was the failure to agree on a common approach to ADD and

CVD. The binational appeal process works within the domestic law of the importing country rather than a new set of common laws, and many smaller exporters consider it expensive and ineffective. In 1991 Canadian confidence was undermined by the U.S. decision to question a panel's ruling on Canadian pork, under the extraordinary appeals procedure, on grounds that appeared political—to win support for the renewal of the fast-track authority. Nor has the CUSFTA shielded Canada from sanctions in areas where no agreement was reached, such as intellectual property. (Canada has been "named" under Special 301, for its laws on pharmaceutical patents.)

Canadian participation in the NAFTA has been advocated as a damage limitation exercise, to minimize the dilution of its gains in the U.S. market by insisting on tough origin rules and a long phase-in period. But a strategy that is too self–centered will backfire, leading to Canada's expulsion from the talks. Canada's experience underlines one risk in a bilateral strategy: a country cannot count on the preferential margins it acquires as fixed, even though they have been paid for.[8] These will be diluted by the NAFTA and any subsequent FTAs signed by the United States in the context of the EAI. Canadian participation in the EAI may bring some compensation, however, such as increased access to regional markets, the possibility of collective leverage over the United States, and maybe a permanent secretariat to service these relationships.

But for Canada, the GATT will remain the principal means of applying multilateral pressure to curb U.S. protectionism. It is too early to determine how the CUSFTA has affected Canada's role in the GATT, let alone how it has affected the GATT itself. Determination to push several issues in the Uruguay Round coupled with active coalition building has increased Canada's authority and its ability to shape the new GATT rules. Unfortunately, in the key area of agricultural export subsidies, this combined effort has proved unable to draw the United States and the EC to a satisfactory compromise.

To discuss the implications for developing countries of this regionalist strand in U.S. and Canadian trade policy, it is necessary to distinguish between Mexico and the rest of Latin America and the Caribbean, and developing countries outside the hemisphere (see Chapters 4 and 5 in this volume). For Latin America and the Caribbean, entering into a free trade agreement with the United States would accelerate the economic liberalization many of them have already initiated. But there would be some key differences.

First, there would be a shift from multilateral to preferential liberalization. This would have domestic welfare costs, to the extent that it diverts trade and investment from third countries. Such effects would be diminished as barriers to third countries come down. But it cannot be presumed that this will happen with the same momentum, especially if the Uruguay Round collapses.

Second, Latin America would have to make major concessions to the United States on trade, investment, and other areas of economic intervention, in the hope of securing preferential access to the U.S. market. (In fact, according to Erzan and Yeats, 1991 the United States is likely to gain more from any FTAs, since its exports face higher barriers in Latin America than vice versa.) This would mark a break from the past, when the developing world made few binding concessions, under the GATT provisions of relative reciprocity. The range of measures to be liberalized would also go beyond the scope of those traditionally dealt with in the GATT. Some have questioned whether this would be a costly bargain. Is extensive liberalization appropriate if it compromises industrialization efforts? Will the United States meet its side of the bargain, given the recent Canadian experience?

Third, an FTA with the United States would increase Latin American exports by $2.9 billion, or 9 percent of current exports to the United States (Erzan and Yeats, 1991). The amounts are small because Latin American exports currently face fairly low barriers. Furthermore, the gains are likely to be relatively concentrated, with 90 percent going to Mexico, Brazil, and Paraguay. There would also be adjustments between the countries of the region. In particular some investment is likely to move from the Caribbean Basin countries as their preferential status in Canada and the United States is eroded.

Mechanisms for dealing with possible asymmetries in terms of adjustment have been raised in the discussions about NAFTA. The simplest option is a slower phase-in of liberalization in the less-advanced countries or for less-advanced sectors. This has been suggested for Mexican agriculture, where an end to the *ejido* system could displace large numbers of poor people. Phasing–in would refer not just to the elimination of border measures but also to other forms of government intervention (e.g., industrial development subsidies). A second option is the creation of a social fund to ease the process of adjustment, following the example of the EC. It could also address the issue of differentials in labor and environmental standards. (The environment fund proposed by the United States as part of the EAI may form a precedent.)

Fourth is the impact on regional integration within Latin America. Erzan and Yeats (1991) suggest that intra-Latin American trade would be adversely affected by a series of bilateral U.S.-Latin American deals (the hub-and-spoke model). Even with a plurilateral arrangement, the obligation to trade freely with the United States and Canada may undermine some efforts to develop regional industries. The current revival of the Caribbean Economic Community (or Common Market), for instance, depends in part on the adoption of a common external tariff. A potential conflict may be resolved, however, by a slow phase-in of trade liberalization with the United States.

Fifth, in trade volumes it is relatively unimportant whether or not Canada is part of this new hemispheric picture—Canada accounts for less than 2 percent of Latin American exports. But there may be strong political economic reasons for Latin America to favor Canadian partnership. In particular it would help to "plurilateralize" the relationship, diminishing the probability that the United States would pursue bilateral agreements and instead encouraging the formation of a free trade area with an ever-expanding membership to reduce U.S. dominance. Canada would then be able to share its experience of negotiations with the United States.

Finally, the GATT will continue to be important for many Latin American and Caribbean countries, and not just for resolving bilateral difficulties with the United States in the regional market. An important area is the extensive U.S. and EC use of agricultural export subsidies in third markets.

Turning to the rest of the developing world, there are two principal issues: trade and investment diversion and the broader systemic effects. The evidence emerging from various modeling exercises is suggestive rather than rigorous. A key problem is that most fail to distinguish between developed and developing countries in the rest of the world. Thus, for example, Cox and Harris (1991) estimate that NAFTA will lead to a very small drop in the rest of the world's share of U.S. imports, from 72.73 percent to 72.09 percent. Brown, Deardorff, and Stern (1991) forecast a small decline in exports from the rest of the world of $5.3 billion following a NAFTA, with zero tariffs and a 25 percent increase in quotas on Mexican exports of agriculture, food, and textile products to the United States. Erzan and Yeats (1991) estimate that a U.S.–Mexican deal including elimination of tariffs and NTBs would displace imports to the United States from Latin America by $28 million, and the rest of the world by $0.5 billion.

With respect to agricultural products, Hufbauer and Schott (1992) note that the United States could increase its imports of sugar, coffee, and various horticultural products from Mexico. In the case of sugar, this would require the maintenance of barriers against third countries. For coffee, where Mexico is a major world exporter, an indirect effect may be to diminish the already weakening U.S. support for the international coffee agreement.

Some analysts have estimated the impact of an inward-looking NAFTA in terms of raising trade barriers or just delaying trade liberalization. For instance, Cox and Harris (1991) predict that if the NAFTA introduced a tariff increase of 10 percent toward the rest of the world, it could lead to a significant decline of 10 percentage points in the rest of the world's share in U.S. imports. A recent study estimates that NAFTA could produce large U.S. job gains, in the order of 225,000 to 264,000, if the agreement allows North American goods to displace imports from third countries (cited in Hufbauer and Schott, 1992, 109). This is in contrast to the job losses otherwise forecast. Such analysis can become self–fulfilling: i.e. it may be accepted as essential to buying off domestic opposition to the NAFTA and fiscally cheaper than any form of adjustment assistance. But there would be a domestic welfare loss as well as the costs to third countries.

Trade diversion may be exacerbated by attempts to stiffen the rules of origin, as suggested in the case of autos in the NAFTA discussions. Raising the minimum domestic content to qualify for North American tariff treatment would particularly affect the Japanese and other "transplant" car factories in North America, which use sources from outside the region to supply a large proportion of parts.

Morici (1991) also mentions the possibility of other countries' being "crowded out" as a result of Article 1102 of the CUSFTA, which allows the United States, for example, to exempt Canada from global safeguard action (taken under GATT, Article 19) if Canada supplies less than 5 to 10 percent of U.S. imports. Where imports from Canada are still restrained, they must be allowed a certain amount of growth. Granting similar treatment to Mexico under NAFTA would aggravate this crowding out.

On the more general issue of global systemic change, NAFTA and possible subsequent extensions within the hemisphere have reinforced concerns in many developing countries about the future of the global trading system and the role of multilateralism. The CUSFTA, NAFTA, and EAI have coincided in Europe with the EC's 1992 program, the creation of a European Economic Space, and efforts to incorporate Eastern Europe (see Chapter 2), and in Asia with the discussion of a new regional grouping. This is ironic, as many developing countries have only recently begun to play an active role in the GATT, offering concessions and helping to design the new rules. Failure to secure major results in the Uruguay Round risks undermining their domestic liberalization efforts.

CONCLUSIONS

Bargaining over day-to-day trade policy with the United States is increasingly being handled in a quasi-judicial way. The scope for administrative or political discretion is being eroded. Flexibility in the application of trade law cuts both ways for developing countries. Domestic political interests may be given priority over foreign. Nonetheless, the U.S. administration is still able to use foreign policy considerations to buy time (e.g., over China). Yet the development of trade law, both domestically and through the GATT, remains politically charged, with the administration sensitive to pressures in Congress.

The trend in this direction in Canada is somewhat less pronounced. The quasi-judicial process has been rationalized and given greater transparency with the formation of the Canadian International Trade Tribunal, allowing for some political and administrative discretion.

Some countries have sought to avoid such problems by bilateral free trade agreements. For example, the CUSFTA provides for Canada to be consulted before it is included in any proposed change in U.S. trade legislation. Another key element is the chapter 18 and 19 dispute settlement mechanisms. But while these do not provide complete insurance for Canadian exporters, there is considerable opposition in the United States to extending similar treatment (especially Chapter 19) to other countries, notably to Mexico.

For the United States, the agreement with Canada served as a useful model for its multilateral agenda, as a warning to those who would not accept its GATT demands, and as an invitation to others to follow suit. It is also partly designed as an insurance policy, securing a preferential zone for U.S. exporters in the event that the world trading system becomes more fragmented.

Some of the CUSFTA elements have contributed to the Uruguay Round discussions, a priority also for Canada. It is less clear, however, that the CUSFTA has hastened concessions from other parties like the EC or Japan. Any final deal will be struck on the basis of bilateral bargaining, for instance, changes in EC and Japanese agricultural policy for changes in the U.S. Section 301. It is unlikely that the EC, with its European preoccupations, will be disarmed by the prospects of a North American trade agreement.

The shift to regionalism has inevitably undermined the position of countries who have sought to work through the GATT, particularly in dealing with the United States. Many have responded positively to the EAI. This will not be an easy course to follow. It is not guaranteed to generate more secure or greater access, while there may be a higher price to pay than in the GATT. In particular it will be trade distorting.

Besides the issue of trade distortion, other countries may lose in various ways. First, they too will be expected to pay more for improved access to the U.S. market. Second, there is a strong risk of the GATT system's being weakened. Third, fragile South-South trade efforts may suffer, even if the EAI is pursued plurilaterally. A successful Uruguay Round, including a strengthened GATT and dispute settlement mechanism, would diminish some of these concerns by reducing the scope of trade diversion and reasserting the primacy of the GATT.

NOTES

I am grateful for the research assistance of Andrew Clark and Han Soo Kim. I would also like to thank the other project participants and G. K. Helleiner for helpful comments on an earlier draft and the International Development Research Centre for its funding.

1. For example, Kuttner, 1989, 17: "The Administration has never been clear to itself or to its allies, about which of these are temporary adjustment expedients; which ones are merely tactical manoeuvres intended to be bargained away for reciprocal liberalizations; which ones are adjuncts of domestic industrial policies; which ones are craven capitulations to domestic pressure groups; and which are necessary long-term regimes in industries which don't lend themselves to Ricardian trade."

2. The Economic Council of Canada (1988), for instance, found sectoral policies had retarded rather than promoted adjustment to change. It recommended that general labor adjustment policies, e.g., the expansion of the Industrial Adjustment Service, substitute for capital subsidies.

3. An initial study by Cox and Harris (1991) suggests that the gains will be restricted to lower consumer prices. Oligopolies, however, may diminish both the price changes and the productivity gains in cases of foreign ownership.

4. This reflects many smaller countries' frustration with the GATT's dispute settlement process (the ultimate sanction of retaliation still depending on market size) and a preference for resolution through diplomacy.

5. For an articulation of the Canadian view that the time had come to look beyond the GATT to advance Canada's trade interests, see Curtis, 1985, 183: "Canada's trading relationship with the US will remain central to long-term Canadian economic performance....Bilateral agreements to reduce or eliminate barriers to cross-border trade...would contribute importantly to long-term investment, production and income growth in Canada." Curtis also notes the long history of Canada's bilateral deals with the United States, dating from the late 1800s. A number of earlier deals with the United States had been on a sectoral basis (agricultural machinery in the 1920s, arms production in the 1940s, and the 1965 autopact).

6. CARIBCAN, which began in 1986, offers all Commonwealth Caribbean countries duty-free access to the Canadian market for the bulk of their exports. Major exceptions include textiles and clothing, some leather products, lubricating oils, and methanol.

7. Once Canada (or the United States) has decided to pursue a dispute bilaterally under Chapter 18 or 19, it cannot be appealed to the GATT.

8. There are some parallels here with the lessons developing countries have had to learn with the GSP, though the expectations with the GSP should never have been as high, given that they were a unilateral concession.

PART III
NATIONAL RESPONSES

4

Out of the Crisis: Mexico

CLAUDIA SCHATAN

When negotiations began over the NAFTA, the Mexican economy was quite different from that of the early 1980s. With 70 percent of the country's exports in oil, the oil price slump of 1982 put Mexico in a difficult situation. Faced with high international interest rates, massive capital flight,[1] a debt of $82 billion, almost no foreign exchange reserves, and an inward-looking economy, Mexico was forced to take a drastic turn in its economic policy. Since the mid-1980s, trade liberalization has been one of the key elements of the new orientation.

Mexico also had to undertake active international trade negotiations in order to secure access to markets abroad. The new trade policy was used not only to stabilize the economy but also to improve the bargaining power of Mexican trade negotiators. With little prior experience in the latter arena (Bueno, 1991), Mexican officials had to learn quickly. Bilateral negotiations were the most urgent and were intended to limit or avoid retaliation and protectionism and to gain greater access to the U.S. market. Multilateral negotiations were intended to give Mexico credibility as a serious trading partner and thus increase leverage in bilateral bargaining.

The purpose of this chapter is to assess Mexico's bargaining power and bargaining strategies as it attempted to improve its position in the U.S. and world markets[2] in the 1980s. It begins by analyzing the liberalization of trade policy, then examines trade bargaining, both multilateral and bilateral.

ADJUSTMENT, CONDITIONALITY, AND TRADE LIBERALIZATION (1982–1990)

Macroeconomic Policies and Trade Liberalization

After a decade of economic growth led by industrial expansion—supported by import-substitution and export-promotion policies—the external shocks Mexico suffered in the 1980s, mainly as a result of the oil price collapses of 1982 and 1986, changed the parameters for economic strategy. A package of stabilization measures was applied in 1982 and included budget cuts, reduction of real wages, and three strong devaluations, which lowered the value of the peso in real terms. As a result, the fiscal deficit was brought down sharply, the current account showed a surplus in 1983, and the inflation rate dropped from almost 100 percent in 1982 to less than 60 percent in 1984. Success in stabilization efforts was short-lived, however. The measures were not consistently maintained (for example, the exchange rate was allowed to appreciate in 1983–1985), while new oil price declines in 1985 and 1986 disrupted the foreign accounts, encouraging speculation against the dollar and capital flight.

As for trade policy, the initial reaction was to tighten protection to overcome trade disequilibria. The process of very gradual opening that had begun in the late 1970s came to a halt, and in 1983 Mexico registered one of its highest levels of protection ever.

The repeated oil price shocks made it clear, however, that in the long run oil could not play the role it had previously had in financing development. If Mexico was to diversify its exports, it would have to restructure its economy. A more competitive position in the world economy could be achieved only if domestic producers were able to compete with imports. This became urgent in 1985, when manufactured exports declined by 12 percent. At that point, the Mexican government faced the problem squarely by launching an accelerated program of trade liberalization, a key component of its macroeconomic strategy for the post–oil boom period. A decree signed in July 1985 established the massive elimination of import permits. The result was that only 11 percent of the tariff's items, or 36 percent of the value of production (see Table 4.1), was subject to import permits by mid-1987. (Almost 100 percent of them had been under direct control from 1983 to mid-1985.) Most of the products that still required import permits were agricultural products, oil–related durables, pharmaceuticals, automobiles, and other consumer goods.

The tariff level and structure also changed quickly. The government announced a unilateral, four-stage program of tariff reduction to start in May 1986 and end in October 1988. According to this plan, the maximum tariff of 100 percent was lowered to 50 percent in 1986. The intention was to reduce these maximum tariffs to 30 percent and the weighted average to 10 percent by 1988.

The drop in oil revenues in 1986 was followed by a new set of stabilization policies, this time complicated by mounting inflation. The latter accelerated after the stock market crisis of October 1987. Although 1987 saw some growth, the accumulation of $12.5 billion in reserves, and equilibrium in several indicators, such as public finances, monetary supply, and the exchange rate, lack of confidence persisted, and unexpected

Table 4.1   Mexican Domestic Production Covered by Import Licensing (percentages for June of each year)

	1985a	1986	1987	1988	1989	1990
Agriculture	95.8	62.6	57.6	44.3	44.3	40.1
Crude oil & natural gas	100.0	100.0	100.0	100.0	100.0	100.0
Other mining	51.8	4.3	4.3	0.0	0.0	0.0
Foodstuffs	98.1	55.8	31.7	25.9	25.3	20.2
Beverages & tobacco	99.5	99.4	62.6	20.6	19.8	19.8
Textiles	90.7	9.6	9.6	2.4	3.1	1.0
Apparel & footwear	99.1	81.4	78.1	0.0	0.0	0.0
Wood products	99.9	46.8	11.6	0.0	0.0	0.0
Paper & printing	74.5	6.7	6.7	0.3	0.3	0.0
Petroleum refining	94.3	87.4	87.2	87.2	87.2	86.4
Chemicals	86.8	24.8	18.0	2.5	2.4	1.6
Nonmetallic mineral products	95.6	15.3	3.6	2.1	2.4	0.0
Basic metal industries	86.8	0.4	0.0	0.0	0.0	0.0
Metal Products	74.0	8.6	1.6	1.0	1.0	1.0
Machinery & equipment	85.6	15.6	6.1	2.4	4.8	2.8
Electric materials	97.2	36.9	24.0	0.0	0.0	0.0
Transport equipment	99.0	76.8	64.0	57.4	41.4	39.4
Miscellaneous manufacturing	91.8	22.8	17.0	0.0	0.0	0.0
Total production of goods	92.2	46.9	35.8	23.2	22.1	19.0

Source: Reprinted from *World Development*, vol. 20, no. 5, Adriaan Ten Kate, "Trade Liberalization and Economic Stabalization: Lessons of Experience," p. 664, ©1991, with permission from Pergamon Press Ltd, Hedington Hill Hall, Oxford 0X3 0BW, UK.
Note: a. The liberalization decree was passed in July 1985.

pressure on the dollar forced a strong devaluation of the peso. The devaluation of the domestic currency in 1987 in the free market was 143 percent and that of the controlled exchange rate 138 percent. Prices rose by 159 percent that year, accelerated by these drastic devaluations (Banco de México, 1988).

An Economic Solidarity Pact (PECE) to combat inflation was signed in December 1987 by the government, business sector, and the trade unions; it included not only orthodox stabilization measures but also anti-inertial inflationary tools. The extraordinarily strong devaluations were partly offset by a reduction of the maximum tariff to 20 percent and the elimination of the across-the-board 5 percent tariff on imports. This resulted in an average tariff of only 11.0 percent in June 1988 (Table 4.2)[3] and the coverage of about 23 percent of production (20 percent of import value) by permits (Table 4.1). These measures exceeded all previous liberalization targets and, as will be seen later, foreign conditionalities.

In this way, the opening of the Mexican economy took place in only three years (1985–1987). During that period, import permits were dismantled and tariffs lowered to levels comparable with those of developed countries. After 1987, a few other liberalizing measures were undertaken. These included two decrees gradually liberalizing automobile imports and a decree eliminating import permits for microcomputers (1990) (though another allowed strong subsidies for local production of microcomputers under development plans; see Pérez, 1990). Since it took office at the end of 1988, the government of Carlos Salinas has tried to make effective protection rates more uniform across sectors by reducing the dispersion of nominal rates (Zabludovsky, 1990). At the beginning of 1989, tariff rates were raised for goods that had no tariffs or only paid 5–10 percent. Tariff dispersion was reduced considerably, while the average tariff rose marginally (Table 4.2).

This deepening liberalization was supposed to be anti-inflationary, lowering costs of production through cheaper inputs (which were especially expensive because of the high exchange rate) and by exposing domestic producers to foreign competition. Tariff reductions were fiscally feasible partly because of the foreign currency surplus accumulated in the previous period. Whether the liberalization policy was successful in curbing inflation is not at all clear, partly because of the high exchange rate, which increased the cost of imports. According to Ize (1990), direct price controls played a more important role in stopping inflationary inertia than did import liberalization, though the latter may have reduced inflationary expectations. In the longer run, as prices are decontrolled, foreign price arbitrage may play a greater role if it helps to keep prices of oligopolistic producers lower than they would be in a protected market. As for the impact of trade liberalization on exports (which grew at a remarkable rate in the second half of the 1980s), this is difficult to separate from the impact of exchange rate policies and domestic recession (Zabludovsky, 1990).

**Table 4.2   Production-weighted Tariff Averages in Mexico
(percentages ad valorem)**

	1985	1986	1987	1988	1989	1990
Agriculture	8.6	12.1	12.9	6.4	9.7	9.2
Crude oil & natural gas	0.0	0.0	0.0	0.0	10.0	8.6
Other mining	19.1	17.7	16.4	8.0	11.0	10.9
Foodstuffs	22.6	29.2	26.4	11.6	12.2	11.9
Beverages & tobacco	77.0	41.4	37.4	19.7	19.7	19.7
Textiles	32.5	37.2	33.3	14.7	14.8	14.8
Apparel & footwear	46.8	41.4	37.1	18.7	18.5	18.5
Wood products	37.0	37.0	33.5	16.8	16.9	16.9
Paper & printing	19.6	19.3	18.3	4.6	6.8	6.8
Petroleum refining	2.2	2.3	2.0	1.1	10.2	4.4
Chemicals	28.7	26.5	26.0	12.9	13.5	13.4
Nonmetallic mineral products	31.7	33.1	29.8	14.2	14.9	14.9
Basic metal industries	15.1	19.7	18.9	8.0	10.6	10.6
Metal products	35.7	30.1	27.7	15.0	14.6	14.6
Machinery & equipment	21.5	29.0	28.2	15.6	15.7	15.7
Electric materials	35.5	38.4	34.9	17.4	17.4	17.4
Transport equipment	39.2	29.0	28.6	14.8	16.0	16.0
Miscellaneous manufacturing	50.8	37.9	33.8	17.6	18.0	18.0
Total production of goods	23.5	24.0	22.7	11.0	12.8	12.5

Source: Reprinted from *World Development,* vol. 20, no. 5, Adriaan Ten Kate, "Trade Liberalization and Economic Stabalization: Lessons of Experience," p. 664, ©1991, with permission from Pergamon Press Ltd, Hedington Hill Hall, Oxford 0X3 0BW, UK.

Conditionality and Trade Liberalization

In the mid-1980s, trade liberalization acquired great relevance for Mexico in negotiations for loans from international financial institutions and in those aimed at improving access to international markets. I discuss the first set of negotiations in this section and the latter subsequently.

Unlike financial agreements signed before the 1980s, commercial bank loans, stabilization loans, and structural adjustment loans granted since then have all included trade policy conditions. How important was this conditionality in leading Mexico to open up its economy as quickly as it did?

The 1986–1987 period was one of strong World Bank and IMF conditionality. Although the trade policy loans (TPLs) granted by the World Bank in that period were not that large (two loans of $500 million each), because of cross-conditionality (Rodríguez and Griffith-Jones, 1992), all other loans from the World Bank and commercial banks (more than $7 billion to be given in six stages, from March 1987 to January 1988), would be disbursed only if trade liberalization were carried out as agreed with the World Bank (Olea, 1990a).

The new money included in the agreement for Mexican debt restructuring was composed of four kinds of financing: (1) $5 billion in parallel financing from the private banks and the World Bank; (2) $1 billion of cofinancing for the communications and transport sector from the commercial banks and the World Bank; (3) $500 million in contingency cofinancing for public investment by commercial banks; and (4) $1.2 million for oil contingency financing (Gurría, 1988; Olea, 1990a).

The first facility was given in six stages, and each disbursement was conditioned to the fulfillment of the World Bank TPLs and IMF contingency loan agreement (standby agreement) provisions. Facilities (2) and (3) would be granted only if the conditions imposed by the first facility had been met. Hence, the latter were also tied to the TPLs. Only the fourth facility was independent from these conditionalities.

The agreement with the World Bank in terms of trade policy to be accomplished by October 1988, was as follows (Olea, 1990a):

Maximum tariff rate	30.0%
Minimum tariff rate	0.0%
Average tariff rate	17.3%
Tariff dispersion	8.4%
Weighted average tariff	10.0%
Number of rates	5

In addition, the agreement included the reduction of NTBs (mainly import permits and official prices) to 30–40 percent of total imports by the end of 1988.

When the TPL and the agreement with the World Bank took place, the import liberalization program was already under way, and its aims were similar to those of World Bank conditions. Though there is no evidence that Mexico's unilateral liberalization announcement in July 1985 was linked to negotiations with the World Bank and IMF, in that year Mexico was in particularly urgent need of new international financing. On the IMF and World Bank side, both institutions were increasingly interested in dealing with the debt problem through a comprehensive macroeconomic package, of which trade liberalization was an important aspect (Gurría, 1988). Under these circumstances, the international financial institutions probably did—directly or indirectly—play a role in trade policy decisions. Its main effect may have been to increase consistency, credibility, and irreversibility of the liberalization policies.

Nevertheless, the acceleration of the trade policy measures in December 1987, in response to sharp inflation, together with the fact that such measures were more severe than those considered in any previous program (Mexican alone or in agreement with the World Bank), strongly suggests that the *final degree* of openness the Mexican economy reached has little to do with foreign pressures and international financial institutions conditionality.

THE BARGAINING PROCESS

Mexico's trade negotiating position changed from a weak and defensive one during its protectionist period to a much stronger and more active stance after trade liberalization had started. In fact, until 1985, Mexico had to spend much of its bargaining effort overcoming the difficulties arising from its refusal to join the GATT in 1980. Later, having changed its trade policy, thus surmounting some of the greatest obstacles to its exports, it could negotiate better conditions of entry to the neighboring market. Together with its new trade policy, Mexico's increased participation in multilateral trade negotiations since 1986 has widened its sphere of influence and strengthened its bargaining position at the bilateral level.

Multilateral Bargaining in the GATT

Mexico's entry into the GATT. Mexico completed negotiations to join the GATT in 1979, but because of insufficient support in congress and within the cabinet, in March 1980 President José López Portillo announced that the country's adhesion to the agreement would be postponed. According to the Finance Ministry, the reasons for not joining the GATT were the incompatibility of Mexico's global development plan and industrial development national plan with the GATT rules, especially in the areas of subsidies and compensatory rights (Olea, 1989b). Government officials believed Mexico needed a slower opening process than GATT required. Second, according to Mexico, the special treatment for less-developed countries agreed to in the Tokyo Round had not been adequately incorporated into the GATT codes of conduct. Hence, industrial countries were opening up their domestic markets for some developing countries' exports only under voluntary export restraint agreements or other restrictions. Third, Mexican legislation had not yet been adequately adjusted to the GATT legal framework, lacking clauses on subsidies and dumping, among others; this would leave Mexico at a disadvantage vis-à-vis other GATT members. Uncertainty about the legal links between the GATT rules and the U.S. trade agreement law of 1979 was another reason Mexico postponed GATT accession (Olea, 1989b).

The end of the oil bonanza greatly weakened the influence of the interest groups that had opposed the GATT accession in 1980; it also made Mexico's integration into the world economy through nonoil channels more urgent. Together these paved the way for a new attempt by Mexico to enter GATT.

A second round of negotiations was carried out in 1985–1986, following specific instructions from President Miguel de la Madrid. After several meetings (especially with the United States), Mexico was able to negotiate an extended standard protocol of entry to GATT. The advantage for Mexico was that it could include several conditions in the preamble of the protocol, not a commonly accepted practice. There were basically four conditions: Mexico's status as a developing country and the special treatment this affords in the GATT; Mexico's sovereignty over its natural resources; the social and economic importance of agriculture and the country's corresponding right to adopt policies to develop the sector and protect employment; and the right to implement policies required by its industrial development national plan and its sectoral versions.

The more detailed negotiations on products and tariffs were less advantageous to Mexico than they had been in the 1979 round. In fact, the United States refused to take the 1979 protocol of adhesion as a framework for the 1985 discussions since, according to U.S. officials, it required too few concessions from Mexico (Vega Cánovas, 1989b). The 1979 protocol entailed very few commitments in agriculture or industry and covered few products of interest to the United States. Mexican maximum tariffs were also high (100 percent in some cases), and the period granted for removing imports permits was too long (ten to twelve years) (Vega Cánovas, 1989b; Bennett, 1989).

To become a member of GATT in 1986 Mexico agreed to eliminate import permits or reduce duties for 373 imported products, or 15.9 percent of total imports (a higher value and number of items than those involved in the previous negotiation). The maximum time allowed to implement the concessions was eight years, less than in the first protocol. (Almost no concessions were made, however, in health, automobiles, textiles, or iron and steel.) In addition, Mexico agreed to sign several codes of conduct in the months following its adhesion to GATT.

Although some (e.g., Olea, 1990b) would argue that the 1986 protocol is better than the 1979 one because it "establishes broader and more precisely defined safeguards," on the whole, the negotiations seem to have provided fewer advantages for Mexico than those agreed to in 1979 (Vega Cánovas, 1989b). This was a sign of how much U.S.–Mexican trade relations had deteriorated after Mexico had reinforced its protectionist trade policy in 1980. In economic terms, however, the concessions of 1986 were not significant, since the 1987 trade policy deepened liberalization beyond the targets fixed by GATT.

Mexico's role in the Uruguay Round. Mexico joined the GATT hastily in order to participate in the Uruguay Round negotiations, which began in 1986. Mexico's position changed quickly during these negotiations: it went from seeking preferences, like any other developing country, to taking a more independent stance that emphasized the country's particular circumstances. During the first two years of the round, Mexico stressed the need for relative reciprocity and special and favorable treatment for developing countries. This approach was replaced by demands for the recognition of unilateral trade liberalization by countries like Mexico and adequate reciprocal concessions by other GATT members.[4]

Mexico also changed its position on agriculture. During the first two years of the round, Mexico was somewhat defensive, as shown by its initiative in forming a group of net food-importing countries that demanded compensation for the elimination of subsidies by net exporting countries. After 1988, in contrast, Mexico adopted a more liberalizing policy than most countries (even the Cairns Group; see Chapter 10), proposing the total elimination of export subsidies for agricultural products.

By December 1990, the Mexican position in the Uruguay Round had become compatible with the goal of joining the North American trade bloc. Mexico also showed a receptive attitude toward the new issues put forward mainly by the United States in the round: the protection of intellectual property rights, greater flexibility of foreign investment-related measures, and greater openness to trade in services. Still, Mexico made certain demands related to the new issues that were widely supported by other developing countries; for example, Mexico played a strong role by calling for the liberalization of labor-intensive services.

The experience and exposure Mexico gained by in the Uruguay Round probably helped increase the country's bargaining power in the parallel bilateral negotiations with the United States.

Bilateral Bargaining for Market Access

Mexico signed bilateral trade agreements mainly with the United States in 1982–1990. There were at least three areas of negotiation: subsidies and compensatory rights; direct foreign investment and intellectual property rights (patents and trademarks); and the GSP.

The bilateral agreement on subsidies and compensatory rights of 1985.
The origin of this bilateral agreement was Mexico's refusal in 1979 to
sign the subsidies code created during the Tokyo Round of GATT negotiations (Vega Cánovas, 1989b); this refusal left Mexico vulnerable to
CVDs. The agreements reached in the Tokyo Round were included in new
legislation on trade in the United States in 1979, which explicitly discriminated against the countries that were not signatories to the code.
Only those countries that had signed or had bilateral agreements with the
United States equivalent to the code would be eligible for the injury test,
while the rest could be subject to CVDs each time a U.S. producer
showed evidence of a subsidy with some effect on its exports.

Mexico was particularly disadvantaged because the U.S. law did not
give special and differentiated treatment to developing countries. While
the GATT subsidies code allowed subsidies to stimulate development in
developing countries—as long as they were not damaging for the country
granting them and not substantially harmful to the importing country
—the U.S. law did not. Moreover, the law did not make a clear distinction between subsidies to exports and other subsidies, leaving the
exporting country subject to CVDs imposed upon the evidence of any
domestic subsidy.

By the early 1980s, these CVDs were affecting Mexican exports.
Between 1980 and 1984, U.S. actions against Mexican exports affected
$500 million, or 6 percent of Mexican nonoil exports to the United States
(Hernández, 1987). Even more important than the direct effect was the
uncertainty created for Mexican exporters by arbitrary CVDs. The problem was felt most acutely after 1982, when the economic crisis prompted
an outward-oriented strategy. Uncertainty for exporters had to be tackled
quickly and effectively.

In 1983 Mexico began talks with the United States to obtain the
injury test. The bargaining process was harsh for the Mexicans: the concessions demanded in return for the injury test were greater than those it
would have had to make as a signatory to the subsidies code in GATT.
Mexico also had to make concessions in other areas of interest to the
United States before a deal could be struck.

The agreement was signed in May 1985. Mexico's concessions were
the elimination of all export subsidies and a commitment not to impose
new ones. In exchange, the United States granted Mexico the injury test
prior to the imposition of a compensatory tax. Mexico was also allowed
to obtain a suspension of subsidy demands against its exports—according
to the protection given by the 1979 trade agreement law—as well as other
rights concerning subsidies and compensatory taxes considered in that
law. The terms of this bilateral agreement were tougher than those normally available to developing countries under Article 14 of the GATT
subsidies code, in that subsidies were treated more harshly. Another

difference with GATT terms was that the United States did not necessarily have to adopt reciprocal subsidy cuts for exports to Mexico.

Finally, the U.S. 1984 trade law (Section 201) weakens considerably the advantages that Mexico could have derived from the 1985 Subsidies and Compensatory Duties Agreement. According to that law, U.S. producers can "accumulate" the injury effect caused by the import of a particular good. In other words, there can be evidence of injury against a Mexican export to the United States if those exports, added to the exports of the same good from another country to the United States, cause injury to a particular producer. Alternatively, different causes of injury can be added (e.g., the reduction of the share of a U.S. product in its own market, export subsidies by a foreign producer, other forms of foreign government support to exports) (del Castillo, 1987).

In spite of the above shortcomings, the agreement served the purpose of stopping new demands against Mexican exporters. Since the agreement was signed, only two new cases against Mexico have been registered and only one of them succeeded, compared to twenty-four cases registered between 1980 and 1985. Furthermore, of the sixteen cases that were still valid, seven were retroactively revoked (Blanco, 1990). This resulted from the higher cost and greater difficulty to U.S. producers in providing evidence of injury (Nogués, 1986).

Intellectual property rights and foreign direct investment. In addition to obtaining the injury test, another priority of the Mexican government was to establish conditions for a greater inflow of foreign direct investment (FDI). At a time when foreign credit had dried up and the trade balance was poor, FDI seemed to be one of the few promising sources of finance in the early 1980s.

The first attempts to reach agreement with the United States completely failed in 1986, but the negotiating atmosphere improved and significant agreements were reached in 1987. Mexico's intention to review its 1976 law of patents and trademarks, which gave place to a bilateral negotiation on this topic with the United States in 1986, originated not only in the need to attract foreign resources but also in changes to U.S. trade policy. The U.S. trade law of 1984 emphasized the protection of U.S. intellectual property rights. It stipulated that if the rights, patents, or trademarks of U.S. authors were not respected by a trade partner, the United States could retaliate as if the foreign country had set up NTBs. The law also linked trade and FDI; countries that imposed restrictions on FDI could also suffer trade retaliation by the United States. The 1988 omnibus trade act reinforced the discretionary nature of U.S. foreign trade policy (see Chapter 3).

Negotiations between Mexico and the United States on patents and trademarks went badly. According to U.S. officials, the main problem with the new Mexican law was that the protection of patents for many products, including pharmaceuticals and chemicals, would be postponed for ten years (until January 1997) (Bennett, 1989). In the view of Mexican officials, U.S. proposals threatened the possibility of developing a domestic pharmaceutical industry.

U.S. officials not only objected to the new Mexican law but also took retaliatory measures. In January 1987 the U.S. government announced that it would suppress the GSP benefits for thirty-two Mexican products (with an export value of $200 million at that time). In addition, a Mexican petition to include 130 products in the GSP was rejected (Olea, 1990a; Vega, Cánovas, 1989b).[5] Mexico was also put on the "priority watch" list because of the poor patent protection it granted; it was removed from the list in 1990 only when Mexican officials announced changes in the laws regarding intellectual property (Lustig, 1991).

In contrast to the frustrating negotiations on patents and trademarks, an agreement on investment and trade was reached. In 1986 both countries started to negotiate the Principles and Procedure Framework for Consultations on Trade and Investment Relationships. This was seen as a complement to the GATT rather than a substitute for it. Mexico had an interest in this kind of agreement since the 1985 Subsidies and Compensatory Duties Agreement was signed, given that it almost simultaneously launched the PROFIEX (promotion of exports program). The latter attempted to provide a strategy to increase Mexico's access to the international market. Even after joining GATT, Mexico seemed obliged to make this effort because its participation in the U.S. market could be better secured through a bilateral agreement than through a multilateral one.

A declaration of principles was signed in August 1987 and included not only the principles but also a consultation mechanism.[6] The document gathered most of the requests from both sides, though no sectoral or detailed agreements were worked out.[7] The document:

- Stated that both countries agree to open their economies and dismantle NTBs;
- Recognized Mexico as a developing country;
- Acknowledged the role of GATT as the suitable legal framework for handling trade issues and, eventually, the regulation of trade, services, and investment;
- Maintained that a positive trade balance is essential for Mexico to meet its debt obligations;
- Asserted FDI's complementary role in economic growth, transfer of technology, development, etc.;
- Included commitments that intellectual property rights would be regulated by GATT, the WIPO, and Author's Rights Universal Convention; and

- Acknowledged Mexico's trade liberalization process ("Entendimiento," 1987).

This negotiation on trade and investment was one of the few that made an explicit link between the debt problem and trade concessions. This led Mexico to expect greater access to the U.S. market to facilitate repayment of its debt.

In November 1989 a complementary agreement, the Accord on Talks to Facilitate Trade and Investment, was signed. Its purpose was to "change the spirit and philosophy of the 1987 Agreement" and to "identify trade and investment opportunities" (Blanco, 1990). Several sectors were given priority, including petrochemicals and agriculture.

Additional efforts to attract FDI were also undertaken, including four important decrees. The first, signed in May 1989, allows investments with up to 100 percent of shares held by foreigners.[8] The repatriation of profits was also made easier by these new rules.[9] The decrees of December 1989 and June 1990 permit foreigners to own up to 49 percent of the shares in nonbanking financial institutions and 34 percent of the shares in private banks. Finally, a decree on patents, trademarks, and technology transfer was signed in January 1990 to grant greater protection to patents and industrial secrecy and greater freedom for technology transfer and royalty payments.

Notwithstanding the above changes, the Mexican FDI law will probably remain on the agenda for future trade negotiations between Mexico and the United States, since the United States still wants greater openness to FDI.

The GSP and Mexico. Following revision of the United States' GSP scheme in 1984, Mexico, like many other LDCs, found it more difficult to maintain and expand existing preferences. Since the GSP was no longer an unconditional unilateral concession (Molina, 1985), Mexico had to make concessions of its own. Countries that did not provide acceptable treatment to U.S. investment and intellectual property, as well as internationally accepted treatment to its workers, could face an accelerated "graduation" process. They would be susceptible for graduation when a specific product composed 25 percent of U.S. imports of that item instead of the 50 percent level normally applied (Molina, 1985).

The 1987 revision of GSP for Mexico—including considering graduation, an annual product review, GSP redesignation and other mechanisms—resulted in a $637.5 million loss in product eligibility through GSP for Mexico, mainly because of the 25 percent measure for graduation (Vega Cánovas, 1989b).

In recent years, though, the United States has shown a more generous attitude toward Mexican entitlement to GSP benefits. In 1989 Mexico asked for the reincorporation of 306 products into the GSP; 275 of these were approved. Other revisions were also made, allowing further use of the GSP.[10]

The NAFTA

Notwithstanding its active participation in multilateral trade negotiations, the Mexican government in 1990 again chose the bilateral arena to negotiate the trade conditions needed for its export-oriented economic model. The multilateral route to market access was expected to be slow and cumbersome, and Mexican officials had to act quickly to support their export strategy and attract badly needed foreign investment. Such investment had not increased sufficiently even after the debt renegotiation had been successfully accomplished and the foreign investment law had been made more flexible. These considerations prompted the search for a bilateral FTA with the United States, which later turned into a North American FTA. The rich experience of the multilateral and bilateral negotiations Mexico carried out during the 1980s, together with its more open economy, put the country on firmer ground than it had been a decade earlier in its efforts to negotiate a better trading relationship with the United States.

The differing characteristics of the countries involved in the NAFTA negotiations have created many difficulties. Countries with size and income dissimilarities like those of Mexico, the United States, and Canada have widely divergent interests in the NAFTA.

The United States and Canada will not be able to gain significant markets for the export of goods from opening up the relatively small Mexican market and will therefore try to complement such market expansion with other advantages. Hence the importance U.S. officials give to trade in services, "national treatment" to foreign investment in Mexico, intellectual property rights protection, and access to strategic resources, namely, oil.

Also reflecting these differences, Mexico wishes to be acknowledged as a developing country and will therefore want from the United States concessions similar to those granted to Israel in its FTA with the United States. Those include the right to eliminate tariffs and NTBs at a slower pace than the United States and Canada and to impose temporary tariffs to protect infant industries and/or overcome temporary balance-of-payments crises. By mid-1992, it appeared that the results on this point would be mixed. Although the United States and Canada will not grant Mexico developing-country status, they may make exceptions in specific areas.

Beyond these asymmetries, the three countries are expected to benefit from greater specialization, economies of scale, and hence greater efficiency (Lustig, 1991). Nevertheless, the NAFTA road to market access is not free of shortcomings, as shown by the Canadian experience (see

Chapter 3). Furthermore, adopting NAFTA will rule out other forms of trade promotion that have been successful in the East Asian countries, such as targeting potentially competitive industries and supporting them with activist policies (see Chapter 9).

Mexico's reasons for an FTA with the United States. Although the United States improved its attitude toward Mexican exports in the late 1980s, about 600 Mexican products faced 10–20 percent U.S. tariffs, and a few were subject to much higher tariffs (Blanco, 1990; Lustig, 1991). Additionally, NTBs were still an obstacle for Mexican exports, particularly in iron and steel, textiles, apparel, and agricultural products.[11]

Second, the export–oriented economic model was vulnerable to unpredictable protectionist measures by the United States. Experience had shown that once an imported product made up a significant percentage of total U.S. imports of that good, protectionist measures were almost sure to follow. In principle, an FTA would curb this.

Third, the Mexican government felt its liberalization strategy to be threatened by trade diversion resulting from the 1988 CUSFTA. As barriers between the United States and Canada were dismantled, Mexico would progressively have been discriminated against (Helleiner, 1991).

Investment diversion would probably be as important as trade diversion. Potential investments in the automobile, petrochemical, chemical, and other industries would have been concentrated in the country with best access to the U.S. market, that is, Canada.

Finally, Mexican officials believed that an FTA would convince national and international investors that the new economic strategy would be permanent, and thus encourage investment.

The United States' reasons for an FTA with Mexico. The CUSFTA is part of a wider U.S. strategy of developing closer ties with countries on the American continent, partly in response to the integration of Europe in 1992. The EAI and the NAFTA are both signs of this strategy.

Even if an FTA does not significantly increase exports of U.S. goods to Mexico in the short run, in the long run, a more prosperous Mexican economy may provide a significant market for U.S. products, at least in some sectors. Perhaps more important, the FTA would also provide clear and more favorable rules for U.S. foreign investment in Mexico, permitting U.S. enterprises to improve their competitiveness by incorporating Mexican comparative advantages in their production process. More generally, the FTA would permit U.S. transnational corporations to restructure their operations in the three nations' territory according to the advantages of each.

Finally, the United States has at least three strategic targets in the FTA with Mexico: guaranteeing the supply of Mexican oil to the United

States; reducing illegal Mexican migration to the United States through increased growth of the Mexican economy; and the political stability that might accompany economic growth.

The agenda for negotiations.   While it is premature to draw conclusions about Mexican bargaining power in the NAFTA negotiations before the talks come a close, a few tentative comments can be offered on some of the major issues. The weight that some topics will finally have in the negotiations will depend in part on how successful the Uruguay Round is in solving present trade problems. If little progress is made in that arena, the issues to be dealt with in the NAFTA negotiations will be more numerous.

The central purpose of an FTA is to eliminate tariffs among the countries signing the agreement. This is not the most difficult aspect of the negotiations, since tariff levels in the three countries are not high (a maximum of 20 percent for most products). More difficult will be the reduction of nontariff barriers, some of which may survive even in the long run. Mexico will at least try to widen its quota of exports to the United States, especially in textiles, apparel, iron and steel, and agricultural products. The United States will probably demand the dismantling of Mexican NTBs in automobiles, electronics (especially computers), pharmaceuticals, and agricultural products.

Since tariff and nontariff exemptions are granted exclusively to FTA members, the exported product's "nationality" becomes crucial. Rules of origin are therefore one of the most important topics of negotiation. In the existing bilateral agreements (U.S.-Israel and CUSFTA), preferences are given only to those products that have 50 percent of their value added in the FTA country of origin.

Nevertheless, in the case of Mexico, the United States and Canada fear that many countries may try to take advantage of its cheap labor and proximity to the United States by exporting, with minimum transformation, products coming from third countries. Hence the negotiations on rules of origin have been very heated. The greatest difficulty has arisen in the automobile industry, where General Motors, Chrysler, and Ford have asked for a 75 percent rule of origin, which would tend to exclude non-U.S. firms from NAFTA preferences.

An additional challenge for the NAFTA negotiations is the harmonization of a wide range of variables, including differences in salaries, taxes, and subsidies among Mexico, the United States, and Canada. This is a sensitive topic, since harmonization may have negative social effects on health care, education, basic products, and services. Furthermore, the gains in competitiveness from tariff and nontariff dismantling could be more than offset by the higher costs resulting from subsidy elimination.

Another topic of discussion is FDI and intellectual property rights. The United States views FDI as a way to preserve U.S. producers' leadership in world production, while Mexico needs FDI to set up competitive firms and finance its export strategy. Mexico also needs investment inflows to preserve its macroeconomic equilibrium and avoid balance-of-payments difficulties. In spite of earlier liberalizations, there have been constant complaints by U.S. foreign investors of the rigid Mexican FDI law. It may be expected, then, that the U.S. and Canadian side will demand that Mexico give "national treatment" to foreign capital.

As a complement to improved conditions for FDI, foreign investors demand protection for patents and other property rights. This will probably not pose great problems, since the 1991 Mexican industrial property rights law is quite similar to those of the United States and Canada. Among other things, it protects patents for twenty years and makes it easier to register new patents.

Another difficult area is banking and financial services. Mexico is particularly defensive here, since its financial market is very small compared to that of its potential partners (only about 1 percent of the U.S. financial market). The limit that Mexico intends to put on foreign ownership in the Mexican financial market (30 percent), even within NAFTA, and its resistance to giving U.S. and Canadian financial institutions "national treatment" have been matters of contention in the negotiations.

Finally, the CUSFTA inclusion of an important clause on oil resources and the expectation that Mexico will accept a similar agreement have created two of the biggest stumbling blocks for the first draft of NAFTA. The Mexican constitution reserves property and direct exploitation of oil for the Mexican government. The primary petrochemical industry is also reserved for Petroleos Mexicanos (PEMEX). The United States, besides wanting rights to full participation in all stages of production, distribution, and sales, is asking for priority in the supply of hydrocarbons, so that at least 70 percent of the present Mexican supply to the United States is sustained in case of international conflicts, for example.

SUMMARY AND CONCLUSIONS

Mexico entered the 1980s by strengthening its protectionist policies. It then entered an arid period of bilateral trade negotiations with the United States, which lasted until Mexican trade policy shifted toward openness and multilateralism. By the mid-1980s, Mexico had started a unilateral trade liberalization and joined the GATT. By the end of the decade, Mexico's economy was as open as those of many developed countries; it was playing an active role in the Uruguay Round negotiations of the GATT and was preparing to sign an important FTA agreement with the United States and Canada.

The unilateral trade liberalization carried out between 1985 and 1988 was a policy response to the difficulties Mexican exporters were facing in the post-oil boom era. It was also a result of structural adjustment conditionality of the World Bank, which linked its individual loans and those of commercial banks to fulfillment of the TPL conditions. Nevertheless, the degree to which liberalization was carried out—much greater than originally planned—was a result of macroeconomic adjustment policies applied in December 1987 to curb very high rates of speculative inflation. Trade conditionality, in this sense, did not require the abandonment of the government's economic policy but, rather, blended naturally with the existing one. Although it left Mexico with little leverage to bargain for reciprocal liberalization with trade partners later, the policy of trade liberalization improved Mexico's credibility and thus its bargaining position, particularly with the United States.

The Mexican experience in trade bargaining in 1980–1990 seems to demonstrate that bilateral negotiations may be more efficient than the multilateral ones for quick trade expansion and the removal of tariff barriers and NTBs by the trading partner. This was particularly the case with the United States in the 1980s, since its trade laws gave increasing power to the executive to retaliate and demand reciprocity from trading partners. Still, joining the GATT gave Mexico some basic rights in international trade and a forum in which to expose arbitrary measures.

Several questions arise regarding Mexico's experience with trade bargaining in the 1980s. What was the relationship between trade policy and trade negotiations? To what extent were the trade negotiations successful in achieving their goals? Was such active negotiation necessary within the model of economic openness pursued by the government?

Trade negotiations and trade policy seem to have been complementary throughout most of the decade, although this mutual support seemed to be more effective once the first steps of liberalization had been taken. Before 1984, trade negotiations were intense but slow and concentrated on surmounting the difficulties derived from Mexico's decision not to join the GATT in 1980. Since then, although there were some negotiating failures (especially with regard to intellectual property rights) and retaliatory actions by the United States, trade negotiations were quite successful in securing wider markets for Mexico in the United States. By the end of the period, the benefits of the GSP had been increased; export quotas for textiles and iron and steel were larger; some regulations for agricultural products had been eliminated; few legal actions against Mexican exports to the United States were under way; and discussions on an FTA had started. All of these are the results of effective trade bargaining.

To what extent the trade negotiations in themselves were responsible for the successful Mexican export performance in the second half of the 1980s is difficult to know, but it probably did not account for most of it. Trade liberalization, exchange rate policy, and anti-inflationary fiscal and monetary policies were more directly responsible. Nevertheless, given the considerable capacity to produce some export goods and the concentration of exports in the U.S. market, it would have been impossible to achieve a significant increase in some exports (such as iron and steel or textiles) without negotiation with the United States. The agreements reached with the United States and the accession to GATT also helped to reestablish confidence among foreign and domestic investors and international financial institutions and hence stimulated capital flows to Mexico.

As for the costs of the trade negotiation strategy, a few issues should be pointed out. The postponement of GATT entry shortly before a deep economic crisis and a radical change of economic policy strategy toward openness meant that liberalization had to be carried out unilaterally, preventing Mexican officials from demanding reciprocity from trade partners. As for other possible costs, although Mexico had to make concessions both to enter GATT and to reach bilateral agreements with the United States, these concessions have not been important, given that the Mexican strategy was in the end very liberal in any case.

While the outcome of the NAFTA negotiations is as yet unclear, the mere prospect of the agreement seems to have attracted considerable investment to Mexico. At the same time, Mexico has not neglected its links with the rest of America (and to some extent Europe and East Asia). Although results may be slow to materialize, recent negotiations over FTAs with other Latin American countries (Chile) or other forms of integration (Central America, Colombia, Venezuela) should facilitate the diversification of markets and reduce dependence on a successful NAFTA negotiation.

NOTES

1. "Errors and omissions" in the balance of payments exceeded $12 billion in 1981 and 1982.

2. Although Mexico had trade-bargaining experiences with other countries, especially in Latin America, these will not be covered in this chapter because Mexico's trade with that region is only 3 percent of its total foreign trade. During 1991 several new agreements were signed with other Latin American countries to expand trade, but the results are still to be seen.

3. This is a production-weighted average. The average tariff is even lower if weighted by imports (5.7 percent in 1988).

4. This shift was not uniquely Mexican. After holding a relatively defensive stand in the GATT, Argentina (see Chapter 6), among others, started actively seeking acknowledgment for its trade liberalization at that time.

5. Argentina and Brazil endured similar U.S. pressures on the patent issue, although the United States did not retaliate in the case of Argentina (see Chapters 6 and 7).

6. As to the consultation mechanism, it privileges the promptness of the procedure. If a difference arises between the two sides as they try to solve a problem, each can look for a solution according to its own legislation or they can turn to the GATT. If the problem arises in the investment sphere, then the effort to solve the controversy within the bilateral working group would be deepened. Finally, the mechanism called for an annual bilateral meeting at a cabinet level to review and discuss the relations among the two countries (see "Entendimiento," 1987).

7. Nevertheless, the agreement comprised an agenda for immediate action that included the beginning of consultations on textiles, agricultural products, iron and steel products, investment, technology transfer and property rights, electronics, and services-sector information exchange as an input for the Uruguay Round negotiations.

8. This is not valid for all industries. Several still have FDI ownership restrictions.

9. Still, the foreign investment law imposes restraints to FDI, including the requirement to bring all funds from abroad to make the investment, the stipulation of a balance in the firm's foreign exchange during the first three years, and the $100 million ceiling for automatically approved investment—all of which are probably seen as serious obstacles to foreign investors.

10. Argentina and Brazil, after having undertaken unilateral trade liberalization, also benefited from greater openness of the U.S. market toward their exports in the late 1980s (see Chapters 6 and 7).

11. The highly concentrated trade of Mexico with the United States makes NAFTA a plausible solution for expanding its exports markets. The agreement would not be feasible for a country like Brazil, whose export markets are much more diversified (see Chapter 7).

5

The Multiple Tracks of a
Small Open Economy: Costa Rica

ENNIO RODRÍGUEZ

Costa Rica's relatively favorable person/resource base was a condition for its rapid postwar growth rates. The growth strategy was based on a diversification of exports: agricultural commodities to third markets and industrial goods to the Central American Common Market (CACM). Import-substituting industrialization had started unintentionally in the early 1950s but rapidly engendered protectionist interests that merged with what was then accepted wisdom in Latin America: an-inward looking industrialization strategy was adopted. High tariffs and rapid industrialization formed the backdrop against which the Economic Commission for Latin America and the Caribbean (ECLAC) proposed the formation of the CACM. The countries involved reached agreement on a common external tariff and free movement of industrial goods.[1] Costa Rica joined the CACM in 1963, two years after the market's creation.[2]

CACM had a two-pronged trade strategy. First, industrial exports to the CACM were promoted not only by high tariffs but also by a generous system of incentives, including tax holidays; tariff–free imports of raw materials, inputs, and capital goods; and abundant and cheap credit. The second leg of the strategy was the attempt to diversify agricultural exports. To the pivotal coffee and bananas, meat, sugar, and cocoa were added. Incentives to the agricultural sector also included the allocation of cheap credit and heavy investment in rural infrastructure.

Trade bargaining during this period was centered on the Coffee Pact and in the CACM. Results achieved in the coffee negotiations were perceived as benefiting primarily large producers. Moreover, in the late 1980s Costa Rican negotiators were instrumental in the breakdown of the pact, as they adopted a tough stance demanding larger participation. Negotiators also perceived that a market solution could end up being more favorable than the existing arrangement based on product differentiation, as Costa Rican coffee is high quality and suffered from the general categories of the Coffee Pact.

In the CACM, after the common external tariff was agreed upon, endless trade negotiations ensued. No dispute mechanism was designed, and nontariff barriers and payments difficulties filled the agenda of the common market secretariat and the meetings of ministers for the economy and central bank presidents. Sometimes disputes were the result of particular commercial interests, but mostly they were a consequence of macroeconomic difficulties, as fiscal and trade deficits were recurrent problems. The more global issue, the distribution of benefits among participating partners, was never properly addressed. The relatively more developed economies of the region benefited most, leading Honduras to withdraw in the early 1970s. There were only two minor attempts to allocate industries following other than market criteria, and there were no compensatory schemes based on regional budgets.

Two reflections need to be made at this stage. The recurrent argument that import-substituting industrialization took place at the expense of the primary export sector cannot be easily sustained without a complex calculation of net subsidies. Another important consideration is that based on indicators such as the percentage of trade in GDP, the countries of Central America were never closed economies. Import-substituting industrialization was conducted in relatively open economies and only made final-stage production processes attractive.[3]

The importance of trade performance for achieving growth thus cannot be overemphasized. The CACM, however, acted as a buffer against the downturns in prices and markets of very vulnerable third-market exports.

The growth strategy based on primary export diversification and import-substituting industrialization was successful. Costa Rica was transformed in four decades. A low-income, rural society gave way to a middle-income, increasingly urbanized population. As a modern welfare system evolved, health and social conditions began to match those of southern Europe (see Table 5.1). A democratic political system was thus strengthened and the record on human rights has been impeccable.

CRISIS AND CHANGE

The second oil shock of the 1970s hit the CACM economies particularly hard, as there was no increase in regional trade to compensate for the downturn in the terms of trade with other countries. The two engines of growth faltered simultaneously. Political and military instability and the exhaustion of the easy import-substitution phase meant a crisis for the CACM that coincided with the crisis of trade with third parties. Trade within the CACM decreased from $1.5 billion in 1979 to $300 million in 1983.

Table 5.1   Social Indicators in Costa Rica

	1960	1979	1987
Life expectancy at birth (years)	62	70	74
Infant mortality rate (thousands)	80	28	13 [a]
Population per physician	2,700	1,410	960 [b]
School registration as percentage of			
age group:			
Primary school	96	106	102 [c]
Secondary school	21	47	42 [c]
Higher education	5	20	24 [c]
Adult Literacy rate	86	90	93
Income distribution, percentage			
received by:			
20 percent lowest	5.0 [d]	3.9 [e]	
50 percent lowest	20.4 [d]	18.4 [e]	

Sources: World Bank, World Development Reports, 1980–1985, and Trejos and Elizalde 1988.
Notes: a. 1990.
       b. 1984.
       c. 1986.
       d. 1971.
       e. 1977.

In Costa Rica the manifestation of the deep structural crisis was post-poned until August 1981. Virtually unlimited access to commercial bank credit enabled the government to hold off the engulfing fiscal and trade deficits until the payments crisis hit. The economic crisis was the worst in postwar history. Disposable per capita income decreased by 10 percent during 1982, real wages declined 30 percent, and unemployment doubled. A landslide victory for the incoming administration in May 1982 expressed a clear mandate to end the crisis. A stabilization program combining both orthodox and heterodox measures was successfully implemented and the external debt renegotiated (Rodríguez, 1988 and 1992; Castillo, 1987).

Policymakers never seriously considered a return to the past in terms of trade strategies, recognizing clear limits to traditional primary exports and to import-substituting industrialization. On the contrary, they saw export promotion to third markets as the new engine of growth. Export incentives for nontraditional activities had been in place since 1976 but without much impact. These incentives were strengthened in new legislation approved by the legislative assembly in 1984. The background was a relatively stable macroeconomic situation, improving relations with the international financial institutions, and unmistakable political signals that export promotion was here to stay. A key indicator, the exchange rate, was to reflect the relative changes in prices between Costa Rica and the major trading partners; overvaluation of the currency was to be avoided (see Table 5.2). An Export Ministry was created (later to become the Foreign Trade Ministry) and a simplification of import and export procedures initiated.

Table 5.2   Key Macroeconomic Indicators in Costa Rica, 1985–1989

	1985	1987	1988	1989
GDP[a]	9,785	10,818	11,190	11,827
GDP per capita[b]	3,703	3,876	3,904	4,021
Flow of external funds[c]				
Gross	956	838	1,059	na
Net	258	312	421	na
Exports[c]	976	1,158	1,270	1,444
Imports[c]	1,098	1,385	1,409	1,757
Public sector deficit as				
percentage of GDP	1.7	0.3	0.3	2.1
Unemployment	6.8	5.5	5.5	3.8
Average monthly wage[b]	1,612	1,706	1,669	1,741
Interest rate	20.0	23.0	23.5	23.5
Consumer price index	15.1	16.8	20.8	16.5
Exchange rate[d]	50.4	62.8	75.8	81.5
Adjusted real exchange				
rate index[e]	117.1	120.5	128.1	126.3

Sources: Academia de Centroamerica and ECLAC databases.
Notes: a. Constant million colones.
     b. Constant colones.
     c. Million U.S. dollars.
     d. Colones per U.S. dollar.
     e. Adjusted by the relative price index of Costa Rica and the United States; 1978 is
       the base year.

Some of the key elements of the 1984 law for financial-sector equilibrium had been negotiated by the executive with the U.S. Agency for International Development (AID) as conditions for the Economic Support Fund (ESF) of 1983. Approval of the law was not easy in spite of the ample majority the ruling Partido Liberación Nacional held in the legislative assembly. The controversial issues were not, however, related to the export incentives but rather the privatization of public enterprises and the strengthening of the private banks.[4]

The law defined three types of export regimes, each with different incentives: (1) the temporary admission program, or *maquila,* designed for offshore processing, exempting industries from tariffs on inputs; (2) the free trade zones privately owned and administered, which became tax havens in which the central bank had no control over hard-currency transactions; and (3) the export contract signed between the government and exporting firms designed to compensate for the existing "antiexport bias" and to promote exports of nontraditional goods to third markets. The contract grants tariff exemption for the imports of raw materials and capital goods, an income tax holiday, and a direct subsidy as a percentage of the value of third-market sales in the form of a tax credit certificate (Herrera, 1992).

During 1984 the first structural adjustment loan (SAL) was being negotiated. The key trade-related issue included in the negotiations was the tariff system. The World Bank called for an immediate reduction of tariffs, which could not but provoke Costa Rica's withdrawal from the CACM's common external tariff. The government was determined to reduce both tariff dispersion and protection and was negotiating simultaneously with three sides: the World Bank, the private sector, and the CACM trading partners. Negotiations were difficult on all fronts. Other Central American countries had not arrived at the conclusion that protection had to be reduced. Common markets were not yet seen as an acceptable second best to (unilateral) freeing of trade; there was a bias against common markets in the international financial institutions. Geopolitical conflicts in the region and the attempts to isolate Nicaragua further complicated the defense of the CACM, from which Nicaragua could derive benefits. The region was inclined to a discount of bilateralism with the consequent weakening of multilateral fora.

The president himself was, however, fully committed to remain within the CACM, and the Chamber of Industry started to play a progressive role supporting the need to reduce protection, although arguing for gradualism and defending the export contracts insofar as other "distortions" prevailed in the economy. The CACM survived, and the SAL tariff reduction targets were conditioned to the results in the negotiations for a new common external tariff. The reduction in effective protection can be seen in Table 5.3. Trade in the CACM has slowly recuperated from its 1982 low. Costa Rica's position in favor of negotiating within the CACM and at the same time insisting on tariff rationalization and reduction served to pull CACM partners in the direction of revising the strategy of import substitution.

The creation of attractive conditions for nontraditional exports starting with the stabilization program of 1982 and the export incentives of 1984 coincided with the unilateral concessions the United States granted

Table 5.3   Effective Protection Rates by Branch

	1984		1987		1992	
	Number	**%**	**Number**	**%**	**Number**	**%**
Less than 10%	5	10	5	10	6	12
10–50%	17	34	18	36	22	44
51–100%	13	26	14	28	18	36
101–150%	3	6	9	18	3	6
151–200%	3	6	1	2	1	2
More than 200%	9	18	3	6		
Total Branches	50		50		50	

Source: Instituto de Investigaciones en Ciencias Económicas, Universidad de Costa Rica databases.

under the CBI. No trade bargaining was required, as Costa Rica had created the internal conditions for taking advantage of such an initiative and was thus the country in the region that benefited most. At the same time, favorable external and internal conditions resulted in an expansion of exports and investment. Table 5.4 shows the positive results in terms of exports to the United States, employment creation, and attracting foreign investment.

The success of nontraditional exports is impressive. Sustained high growth rates more than doubled the 1985 figure in six years (see Table 5.5). The export structure changed; nontraditional exports represented 38.3 percent of total exports in 1985 and increased to 54.8 percent in 1990.

The export strategy centered on the promotion of exports of nontraditional goods to North American markets, especially to the United States. Table 5.6 shows that most of the increase was in nontraditional exports destined for the United States (including Puerto Rico), rising from one-third to almost half of the total. Traditional exports to the EC expanded partly because 1985 was an unusually low year (the figure for 1986 was $294 million) value added under the *maquila* is virtually all destined for the U.S. market. In addition Costa Rica has always been a very open economy, even during the import-substitution phase. In 1989 trade was 90.6 percent of GDP. The structural change has to a large extent come from increasing the share of nontraditional exports rather than opening the economy.

Initially, there was no trade bargaining to speak of, as concessions in the CBI were unilaterally granted and seemed to reinforce the view that only internal conditions had to be created in order to gain access to third

Table 5.4 Investment, Employment, and Sales of Interviewed Enterprises in Central American Countries Benefiting from CBI

	Investment		Employment		Sales	
	US$000	%	Number	%	US$000	%
Countries						
Costa Rica	89,510.8	38.8	11,827	32.6	67,066.7	41.4
El Salvador	13,619.8	5.9	3,697	10.2	10,439.7	6.4
Guatemala	63,180.6	27.4	11,388	31.4	40,384.6	24.9
Honduras	64,668.6	28.0	9,388	25.9	44,119.3	27.2
Total	**230,979.8**	**100.0**	**36,300**	**100.0**	**162,010.3**	**100.0**
Products[a]						
CBI eligibles						
(except agric.)[b]	70,549.6	30.5	6,776	18.7	50,546.6	31.2
Agriculture	112,086.4	48.5	16,910	46.6	72,977.0	45.0
Noneligible						
(except textiles)	684.4	0.3	304	0.8	3,356.4	2.1
Textiles/clothing	44,509.4	19.3	11,823	32.6	34,830.3	21.5
Tourism	1,950.0	0.8	268	0.7	200.0	0.1
Other services	1,200.0	0.5	219	0.6	100.0	0.1
Total	**230,979.8**	**100.0**	**36,300**	**100.0**	**162,010.3**	**100.0**

(continues)

Table 5.4 *(continued)*

	Rate of Growth					
	1983–1984	1984–1985	1985–1986	1986–1987	1987–1988	1983–1988
Imports from the United States						
Costa Rica	21.2	4.4	32.1	3.8	14.1	11.7
El Salvador	6.3	3.7	-6.0	-26.6	3.6	-5.3
Guatemala	19.1	-10.5	53.8	-20.7	-10.3	5.4
Honduras	8.0	-6.0	16.4	12.1	-9.0	5.8
Total	**13.8**	**-2.1**	**24.7**	**-7.3**	**0.6**	**5.2**

Source: U.S. Department of Commerce, International Trade Administration, "Caribbean Basin Investment Survey," November 1988.
Notes: Data compiled from enterprises interviewed.
  a. Accrued data for surveyed enterprises for the period 1984–1987.
  b. Includes traditional and nontraditional.

Table 5.5   Total External Sales in Costa Rica, 1985–1990
(in millions of dollars)

	Exports		Tourism	Total
	Traditional	Nontraditional		
1985	594.1	368.4	118.3	1,080.8
1986	721.7	404.7	132.7	1,259.1
1987	678.4	492.3	136.3	1,307.0
1988	671.5	583.5	170.0	1,425.0
1989	707.3	749.6	206.6	1,662.5
1990	666.5	809.2	193.3[b]	1,669.1

Sources: Centro para la Promoción de Exportaciones e Inversiones, based on Dirección General de Estadística y Censos, Banco Central, and Corporación de Zonas Francas databases.
Notes: a. Includes value-added for offshore processing under the *maquila* and in free trade zones.
b. Preliminary.

markets. Table 5.5 suggests, however, that the issue of access is critical, as most new exports were directed to the country that had improved access. Yet as exports to the United States increased, CVDs, voluntary restraint agreements, and export quotas began to materialize. As a result,

Table 5.6   Total Costa Rican Exports by Destination
(in millions of dollars and in percentages)

	1985				1989			
	Traditional		Nontraditional[a]		Traditional		Nontraditional[a]	
	US$	%	US$	%	US$	%	US$	%
Central America	0.0	0.0	134.4	40.3	1.2	0.2	128.4	19.6
United States	238.6	40.2	100.3	30.0	256.0	36.2	277.8	42.4
EC	148.4	25.0	13.9	4.2	300.6	42.5	66.9	10.2
Canada	5.0	0.8	5.9	1.8	6.4	0.9	47.6	7.3
Panama	0.0	0.0	38.9	11.7	0.0	0.0	40.9	6.2
Puerto Rico	13.5	2.3	9.5	2.8	18.2	2.6	26.4	4.0
Rest	188.6	31.7	30.5	9.2	124.9	17.6	66.5	10.3
Total	594.1	100.0	333.4	100.0	707.3	100.0	654.5	100.0

Sources: Centro para la Promoción de Exportaciones e Inversiones, based on Dirección General de Estadística y Censos, Banco Central and Corporación de Zonas Francas.
Note: a. Value added by maquila not included.

huge amounts were spent on lawyers' fees. On the positive side, exporters and the government developed organizations with functions such as the monitoring of exports, quota allocation, and handling of legal cases. The CBI provided for no protection or dispute settlement mechanism. The alternatives for ensuring continued access to U.S. markets appeared to be joining the GATT or signing an agreement with the United States granting the injury test. It became clear that the latter was highly unlikely. Joining GATT was also consistent with the overall trade strategy of greater participation in world markets and a way to lock in the reforms.

JOINING GATT

Before we look at Costa Rica's accession to GATT, we need to make a brief point about the macroeconomic conditions. The crisis at the beginning of the decade was followed by relatively high growth rates, which meant a return to near full employment and rising real wages (see Table 5.2). This occurred at a time in which other CBI beneficiaries were starting to offer competitive conditions to attract investment. The Coalición de Iniciativas de Desarrollo (CINDE), a private-sector investment and export promotion agency, reported increasing costs of investment per job from $6.58 million in 1986 to $7.97 million in 1988 and $13.34 million in 1989. This rise reflects the growing number of capital-intensive plants being attracted to Costa Rica as the low-wage sector became uncompetitive.

Full employment had been an objective of the trade strategy. The low-wage export activities, particularly the *maquila,* contributed largely to employment creation. But once nearly full employment was reached, these activities began to be threatened. A problem of industrial restructuring in the nontraditional, newly created export activities thus emerged. Some argued for real wage reductions to remain competitive, suggesting continuing specialization in low-wage activities and therefore raising the issue of technological upgrading.

Joining GATT was relatively costless. Costa Rica's major trading partner seemed satisfied with the 1984 fulfillment of the ESF conditions and later implementation of the SAL. After Costa Rica negotiated with the United States from February to October 1989, the rest of the negotiations were closed without further ado in the last week of October 1989. No major new concessions were required (see Table 5.7 for the reduction of average tariffs and dispersion). The maximum tariff in the second SAL was 40 percent, whereas in GATT the commitment was to reach 60 percent a year after adhering to the protocol and to reduce the maximum to 55 percent within the next three years. For fiscal reasons, automobiles, together with a few other goods, were excepted, allowed a 100 percent maximum tariff; shoes remained with an 80 percent maximum tariff.

Existing surcharges—1 percent of customs value, 2 percent on all imports, and 6 percent on some raw materials—were to be phased out within four years, and the importation permits for some agricultural goods were to be made GATT-consistent within four years. On November 24, 1989, Costa Rica signed the protocol of accession.

Table 5.7 Average Tariffs in Costa Rica

	1986	1989	1992
Final Goods			
Average tariff	27.4	21.0	19.7
Variance	596.8	320.5	260.2
Standard deviation	24.4	18.2	16.5
All goods			
Average tariff	22.3	16.8	15.9
Variance	492.5	281.4	253.3
Standard deviation	22.2	16.8	15.9

Source: Based on Herrera, 1992.

Another advantage of adhering to GATT mentioned by the Chamber of Exporters of Costa Rica (CADEXCO) was obtaining the injury test for goods entering the United States with no tariffs. The cut-flower industry had been badly damaged in 1986 by the absence of this defense mechanism (CADEXCO, 1990). As mentioned earlier, this was one of the reasons for the decision to join GATT. Furthermore, the elimination of the cumulative damage clause in CBI II (which means that CBI exports will not be added to other countries' exports in the determination of injury to U.S. producers) makes the 80 percent of Costa Rican products entering the United States (those that pay no tariffs) less likely to continue suffering from CVDs. In order to obtain the injury test for the remaining 20 percent, it was necessary to adhere to the code on subsidies and CVDs, which was being questioned in the Uruguay Round and could be reformed. It was decided to postpone the decision until the end of the round (Herrera, 1990). Not so with other codes: Costa Rica declared its intention to sign the codes on import licenses and customs valuation within three years and the antidumping code immediately after concluding negotiations with the CACM partners.

At the beginning of negotiations, the United States made clear that the export subsidies involved in the tax credit certificates could be subject to compensatory measures. Costa Rican negotiators argued that the subsidy was compatible with the disposition enabling developing countries to establish subsidies to foster productive activities; they also indicated that the subsidy was subject to revision in compliance with SAL II. The two sides finally agreed that Costa Rica would inform the United States of any changes made to tax credit certificates.

Previous success in export promotion had encouraged the view that Costa Rica was a special case and could easily handle access to export markets because it was a small country. The experience of joining GATT and the participation in the Uruguay Round have, however, strengthened the view that skillful trade negotiators are a sine qua non for adequate participation in markets in which the language is one of reciprocity, dispute settlement, and bloc bargaining.[5] In particular, there is growing awareness of the need to develop joint positions with the other CACM partners.

Costa Rica's participation in the Uruguay Round has been far from proactive. The benefits of joint efforts with other CACM countries have also clearly emerged, as the costs of relatively large negotiating teams are prohibitive for a small country and make little sense in terms of actual power. A strategy of coalition formation is probably the best option.

In a second SAL, additional tariff cutbacks were set. A 1992 maximum of 40 percent was to be implemented, with few exceptions extending to 1995. The new tariff reductions were implemented as if consistent with an escape clause of the common external tariff treaty, an interpretation that in different circumstances other CACM members would not be prepared to accept, since the provision only allows for tariffs to be temporarily raised for short-term, fiscal or balance-of-payments purposes. The environment had, however, changed. El Salvador also embarked on tariff reductions faster than Costa Rica. This has obviously undermined the common external tariff. But the political revival of the CACM after the Central American Peace Plan and the loss at the polls of the Sandinistas in Nicaragua have given rise to a new calendar. The harmonization of the common external tariff has been agreed on for 1993, with a commitment to further advance tariff reduction; the maximum is to be 20 percent and the minimum 5 percent. Honduras has rejoined the CACM by a process of "multilateralizing" the existing bilateral treaties signed with CACM members, and Panama is seriously considering joining.

An important result not only of the multiple bargaining process of joining GATT, reducing tariffs, facing U.S. protectionist measures, negotiating with the EC, solving transport problems for nontraditional exports but also of the political process in Central America has been the increased participation of the private sector. The organizations have been strengthened and bargaining capabilities developed.[6]

EMERGING FREE TRADE ZONES IN THE REGION

The indefinite extension of CBI in 1991 included important improvements such as the exemption from the cumulative damage clause. The positive impact, however, is expected to be limited, and the benefits of CBI are likely to decrease as a result of Mexico's joining the NAFTA. Although Costa Rica has continued to attract investment, Mexico is becoming an irresistible pole. Mexican goods also compete with Costa Rican exports to the United States, and Mexico could end up having better access than the CBI concessions on two accounts: first, concessions obtained by Mexico would be contractual and not unilateral as in the CBI, and, second, they could be better. Mexican sugar exports, for example, might squeeze out current Central American sugar exports under the quota system. The favorable external environment for exports and investment Costa Rica has enjoyed so far is being eroded by the prospect of Mexico's FTAs. Most nontraditional goods Costa Rica exports to the United States are also produced by Mexico. There is further erosion as a result of trade concessions granted to the Andean Pact countries in exchange for anti-drug production efforts. On these grounds, continuing efforts are needed to ensure access to export markets and make investment attractive beyond the continuing liberalization of the economy.

One such possibility emerged from George Bush's Enterprise for the Americas Initiative (EAI). Its three elements—trade, investment, and debt—amount to a wide proposal addressed to countries or groups of countries pursuing market policies. Initially, the EAI seems to be concentrated on the free trade negotiations with Mexico (see Chapter 3). Nonetheless, many countries, including Costa Rica, have moved fast to sign "framework agreements" that contain little besides an intention to negotiate an FTA at a later date. In spite of the U.S. administration's clear indications that it is prepared to negotiate only with groups of countries, Costa Rican authorities seem to be attempting to negotiate ahead of other CACM partners. The reality of regional treaties and practical considerations on the part of the United States may, however, at some stage hinder this attempt.

Costa Rica's intention to negotiate independently may be explained by its strategy of differentiation from the rest of the region to attract investment. In terms of bargaining strengths, it may not be a wise move. But there may be an incentive for individual countries' preferring individual negotiations to the extent they are firstcomers. Trade and investment diversion may create growth to the detriment of third parties, giving the firstcomer a competitive edge in terms of market share, which may prevail in view of the initial difficulties of latecomers (see Chapter 3). The critical issue, however, seems to be that the longer the time span between Mexico's joining the NAFTA and Costa Rica's being able to sign an FTA with the United States, the higher the costs in terms of potential investments lost and competition of exports. Under the assumption that the Mexican agreement will predate any other FTA, the costs to the Costa Rican strategy of export promotion can be very high. There are complex political issues involved in the Mexican negotiation that may postpone approval by Congress, and further delay may arise from the intention to evaluate the results of Mexico's joining NAFTA prior to additional FTAs. Moreover, Central America could suffer from lack of political priority, as it may be argued that the region has already benefited from two trade initiatives (CBI I and II).

For Costa Rica and CBI beneficiaries in general, the attraction of the EAI resides in the critical importance of increasing and guaranteeing market access. This includes: 1) moving from the unilateral trade concessions of CBI to a contractual format and 2) increasing market access at least to conditions similar to those to be obtained by Mexico but, preferably, even better access in textiles and apparel, leather, and agricultural and tropical products.

The USTR has suggested that Central America will benefit as a result of growth within NAFTA. This assessment, however, does not fully take into account the consequences for trade and investment competition. First, it was suggested that given that Mexico is likely to benefit most from NAFTA, Central America should increase its trade links. Exports to Mexico were only $8 million in 1989, thus even a fantastic growth rate is not likely to have a large impact. Second, because the United States is the single largest market for Central American goods (40.2 percent of total exports), competitive access is critical. Moreover, most nontraditional exports from Costa Rica are destined for the U.S. market. Expansion of exports to the United States spurred by NAFTA may be offset by the loss of actual and potential market share to Mexico. The key issue, as already mentioned, is competitive access to the U.S. market.

The Federation of Private Sector Organization of Central America and Panama (FEDEPRICAP) has proposed four options for the CBI beneficiaries to gain improved market access to the United States within the same time frame of negotiation and implementation of NAFTA (FEDEPRICAP, 1991):

1. To negotiate a regional FTA under the fast-track authority, which would supplement CBI and provide NAFTA-type concessions in exchange for market-opening concessions from CBI. A fast-track approval of the legislation may be necessary for concessions on sensitive products. CBI concessions would be less than those necessary for a full-fledged FTA but sufficiently attractive to the U.S. business community to gain its support for the arrangement. The arrangement would be

temporary to keep the pressure for economic reform and leading to a full-fledged FTA or to dock with NAFTA.

2. To pursue improvements on CBI through legislation. The pending CBI III bill, which includes repeal of provisions excluding ineligible items, could be expanded to equate the concessions to the benefits included in NAFTA, particularly making concessions contractual.

3. To negotiate CBI improvements (making the initiative contractual and improving access for specific CBI imports) in the Uruguay Round or on the fringes of the round for inclusion in the implementing legislation for the round.[7]

4. To provide special status for CBI within NAFTA. Interim solutions could include providing NAFTA associate status with full benefits but only partial obligations, treating CBI products as NAFTA products for origin purposes.

These alternatives illustrate that so long as there is the political will, a way to avoid further deterioration of the CBI investment climate can be found. The response of the USTR to FEDEPRICAP proposals was, however, cautious, suggesting the enactment of a satisfactory intellectual property regime and bilateral investment treaties while Central America proceeded with economic reforms. In spite of the unilateral concessions granted under CBI, there is no evidence of an adverse impact on U.S. industry. In fact, 1990 was the fourth consecutive year in which the United States registered a trade surplus (1.8 billion) with CBI beneficiaries and record U.S. exports ($9.3 billion).

The EAI raises at least three other strategic issues: the vulnerability to shifts in U.S. economy, the need for greater technological development in the Costa Rican productive sectors, and the ecological consequences of an FTA.

During the 1980s Costa Rica's attempts at export promotion meant an increased share of exports to the United States. One obvious reason for this was geographical proximity. The United States is a very large economy with high wages and a temperate climate; as a consequence, technologically simple, low-wage goods and tropical and winter "window" agricultural products have a comparative advantage, provided they have market access. Other destinations in the industrialized countries for such products may face problems of market access, transportation costs, and time of delivery. The issue of proximity is thus a vital one and the current trends toward reducing lead time and requiring greater flexibility have increased the weight of this factor. Markets in other developing countries tend to have competing export structures and are prone to wide fluctuations in exchange rates. Thus in an "easy" export-promotion phase, new exports are likely to flow to the nearest industrial market. The effect of the export strategy is greater reliance on the industrial economy's ability to grow. A possible FTA may increase vulnerability to the fluctuations in the U.S. economy.

The second issue is whether moving up the technological ladder is a spontaneous process to be achieved by unaided market forces. The attraction of foreign investment is already being targeted to more capital-intensive sectors, raising the problem of the unarticulated productive structures developed for final-stage import substitution or simple, low-wage exports. At this point the trade strategy has become unavoidably linked with the industrial policies. Issues such as creating the conditions for research and development, innovation diffusion, linking training and education to the emerging comparative advantages, making risk capital available, and so on need to be addressed in connection with the export strategy, in particular in response to the nature of external markets. New tactics may include macropolicies as well as sector-specific approaches. In the apparel sector, for example, it could mean moving from *maquila* to offering the full package, and this would require development of marketing, sourcing, and financial capabilities currently lacking. Possibilities could be defined on a sectoral level. At present advances are being made in some of these areas, but there is no integrated view of where the economy could be heading, linking industrial and trade policies.

The relationship between an FTA and the potential for technological leapfrogging is a complex one. On the one hand, reliance on foreign capital for the modernization of export activities and the competitive pressures in the U.S. market would encourage the adoption of best-practice techniques. On the other, it is not clear how the conditions of the FTA may favor or hinder technological development. In particular, detailed evaluations of the impact of a standardized intellectual property rights regime and investment need to be assessed.

Third, increased exports in the past have generally tended to harm the environment. This effect, however, may now be more complex. The increasing lobbying strength of environmentalist groups in the United States may end up improving environmental conditions in countries signing an FTA, both as a direct result of stipulations negotiated by these groups as well as a consequence of alliances with the already powerful Costa Rican environmentalist groups, which may produce joint action. Expansion of production for exports may then not necessarily destroy the environment. The pressure for forms of sustainable development may increase as a result of an FTA.

Central America is also bargaining with its larger Latin American neighbors. In January 1991 President Salinas and the Central American presidents signed an agreement for economic complementation,[8] a far-reaching initiative on four areas of cooperation: politics, economics, technology and science, and education and culture. In trade matters it calls for the creation of a free trade zone between the CACM and Mexico in 1995. The underlying concept proposed is that of a "asymmetric reciprocity," which is supposed to imply a recognition of the different levels of development between trading partners and would mean different speeds of tariff reduction and allowance for subsidies and other developmental policies to subsist for longer periods in the cases of the less-developed members. A provision is made for the later incorporation of Venezuela and Colombia.

At the Central American summit meeting in San Salvador in July 1991, Venezuela announced its intention to grant greater access to CACM products. The potential for a free trade area from Mexico to Venezuela is a promising initiative in the short run. The suggested mechanisms for investment promotion could also provide for badly needed savings in Central America. The potential beneficial impact is, however, severely constrained by the low volume of exports from Central America to Mexico and Venezuela.

The complementation agreement provides a framework for negotiations with Central America as a group and leaves the bilateral option as a default. Again Costa Rica initiated bilateral talks. Free trade between Costa Rica and Mexico is slated for 1993. Yet Costa Rica's attempts at differentiation do not seem to create the conditions for greater concessions. The authorities may be more concerned with signals to investors and with the potential firstcomer gains than with the actual bargaining of conditions of access. Costa Rica's hurry may even push the slower partners to action as regional agreements and treaties lead to certain joint negotiations. A regional approach may be forced for practical administrative reasons on the part of Mexico and Venezuela. In terms of bargaining strengths, a regional approach would favor Central America. One of the obstacles to such an approach is the weakness of Central American institutions and the absence of experience in joint public and private regional negotiating teams. Yet joint bargaining can and will have to be learned.

In June 1990 the intention to move toward the creation of the Economic Community of the Central American Isthmus was announced, partly in response to a petition from the private sector. The ambitious plan called for wide-ranging trade reforms, including: (1) the removal of trade obstacles; (2) creation of a free trade zone; (3) coordination of economic policies; (4) formulation of a regional science and technology program; (5) coordination of regional sustainable development strategy; and (6) formulation of a regional poverty alleviation strategy. The targets for the implementation of the economic community were perhaps overambitious and suffered from the weakness of the regional institutions. The political directives are, however, clear.

Another arena of trade negotiations emerged in an unexpected forum. Since 1984 the ministers of foreign affairs of the EC and Central America

have met yearly in a series of talks called San José, after the first conference site. The framework for the European cooperation is the
Luxembourg Accord. The San José VII meeting in Managua in May 1991
was a departure from the preceding ones—and illustrates the potential
effectiveness of joint negotiations. Previously, trade matters were not discussed. This time the Central American negotiators, concerned that the
concessions given to the Andean Pact countries were going to outcompete
Central American products, demanded discussion of the issue.[9] The topic
was raised at the technical level and was later given top priority at the
ministerial meeting. A similar treatment of tariff-free access to the EC
was requested.

CONCLUSIONS

During the past decade, trade bargaining has increasingly been recognized
as an integral part of trade strategies. As exports have diversified and a
greater burden has been placed on the external sector, market access has
become a central policy priority.

There are important changes in global trade relations and in trade-
liberalizing efforts. Costa Rica is on the fringe of one such integrationist
attempt, NAFTA. In the recent past, geopolitical reasons facilitated market access to the U.S. economy. Today wider considerations enter into the
picture. The negotiation of access to the U.S. market is the critical trade
issue. Moreover, as Latin America awakes from the debt-lethargy of the
1980s, outward-looking growth strategies in changing global trade patterns point to the need to consolidate trading partners in both the South
and the North.

Central America became a locus for East-West tensions during the
1980s. CACM declined, as did investment and growth. In contrast, Costa
Rica's efforts at differentiation from the region met with considerable success in terms of growth and investment. In the 1990s, however, the CACM
has revived, with enlarged goals and a role as a natural coalition for negotiating trade, investment, debt, and even certain political issues. Negotiating
within the CACM and from the CACM is one of the key lessons of the
decade. Costa Rica's valid attempt at differentiation from the region may be
useful but it will have to be used tactically rather than strategically.

As full employment is reached and the easy export-promotion phase
is left behind, trade strategies and bargaining have become intertwined
with broader industrial and financial policies. A more explicit consideration of these interrelationships is a strategic requirement of increasing
importance in the 1990s.

Experience has demonstrated that small as it is, Costa Rica may not
be small enough, as many nontraditional markets are relatively limited

and the technologies are standard and easily available in the region. The more competitive environment means that beyond market access, product flexibility and marketing skills will also play a critical role. It is in this latter sense, however, that smallness can be a positive factor, given that flexibility and niche marketing can be more significant for a small than for a large economy. Costa Rica has an advantage in having developed export experience earlier than competing countries. It may thus be able to keep ahead, but here the broader strategic issues mentioned earlier become a necessary condition for success.

By and large, there had been no consistent bargaining strategy and for good reasons. Bargaining became necessary as exports began to succeed, the approach has been flexible and may have to remain so. A combination of bilateral negotiations and use of multilateral fora may continue to be appropriate: the latter, participation in coalitions, will generally be preferable, probably without launching major initiatives. Free riding probably offers the greatest benefits to small participants. As more and more countries are likelier to join trading coalitions, Costa Rica would benefit most by promoting and actively participating in a relatively permanent coalition with the other CACM partners, even if, at times, it may want to move at a different pace.

NOTES

1. High tariffs were not proposed by ECLAC but preceded it and were at the time accepted "wisdom."

2. Costa Rican negotiators played an important role in the definition and launching of the CACM, but in 1962 a change of government put traditional exporters into critical posts and delayed Costa Rica's joining the CACM.

3. Taken together, the CACM is not larger than the Peruvian economy.

4. Banks had been nationalized in 1949. Later interpretations of the nationalization decree allowed the operation of private banks but with restrictions (banning current accounts, for example).

5. See Chapter 9, which analyzes the links between access and bargaining as well.

6. CINDE, CADEXCO, and the Industry Chamber have become especially active. In the case of transport negotiations with transport cartels and ports, users' committees have been created in each country of Central America by FEDEPRICAP. Joint regional negotiations have had considerable success in cheapening transport costs. See CADEXCO, 1990, for an evaluation of the private sector's participation in GATT.

7. Brazil made a proposal on similar grounds for securing the GSP in the Tokyo Round (see Chapter 7).

8. For the reasons involved in Mexico's decision to take such an initiative, see Chapter 4.

9. See Chapter 2 for a detailed exposé of the EC's bargaining strategies.

6

Bargaining at
a Crossroads: Argentina

DIANA TUSSIE

Prior to the Uruguay Round, the bias of protection against developing countries could have been attributed to inward orientation and self-exclusion; the trading system was more open among active participants in trade negotiations than between participants and onlookers. Potentially negotiated concessions were extended by virtue of the MFN principle; nonetheless, the principal-supplier rule in GATT as well as a biased selection of the products included in negotiations did not allow the trickle-down of the benefits that accrued to active participants.

The Uruguay Round was a milestone in this respect. In sharp contrast to previous rounds, developing countries were exceptionally active. Altering the way trade bargaining had been conducted since the postwar, many countries veered from their traditional inward orientation and to an unprecedented degree were alert to the challenges and opportunities offered by the round.

Argentina was one such country with a high profile throughout the negotiations. Early on, insofar as it has been one of the countries most penalized by the historical exclusion of agriculture from the system of reciprocal bargaining, it assessed that it had much to gain from an active part in the round. Moreover, it was ready to take the initiative in trade bargaining after having completed significant liberalization. The expectation was that willingness to open its economy and to negotiate on liberalization of trade barriers could influence the formation of trade policy in industrial countries. Instead of waiting passively, Argentina used unilateral liberalization both as a goodwill gesture and a moral argument to push for increased access to markets.

This chapter tries to describe and assess the choice of strategy and procedures that Argentina used to bargain. It starts by tracing the changing determinants of trade bargaining. The first section provides a background description of adjustment and trade structure; the next outlines the impact of conditionality on the direction of trade policies.

Changing relations with the United States are subsequently examined, then bargaining in the GATT. The chapter ends with a look at past results and expectations for the future.

ADJUSTMENT:
THE SHIFT FROM INWARD TO OUTWARD ORIENTATION

Two forces traditionally inspired Argentine economic diplomacy: agricultural protection abroad and import substitution at home. The process of adjustment has resulted in a gradual erosion of the bases of import-substitution culture and has thus watered down some of the issues surrounding this duality of interests.

As is well known, Argentina is endowed with a highly efficient and competitive agricultural sector. This sector has provided the country with about 80 percent of its export earnings. Primary and agrobased manufactures represent 35 percent of gross national product (GNP) and account for 32 percent of employment. Import-substitution industrialization was first undertaken as a defensive reaction to the international economic crisis of the 1930s, but it became deliberate policy as of the 1940s.

The espousal of import substitution entailed discrimination against agricultural exports in which Argentina holds absolute advantages. Export taxes on food and grains have traditionally been used as means to counter unwanted income-redistribution effects, given that the state has been unable to tax landowners to any significant extent. Since traditional exports are overwhelmingly wage goods, over and above explicit export taxes, dual exchange rates were also used to collect "quasi rents." This policy was rendered possible by the international competitiveness of traditional exports.

On the production side, export taxes were typically reinforced by the purchase of inputs and machinery at prices higher than international ones, the result being negative effective rates for the agricultural sector (Berlinski, 1989). Nevertheless, the farm sector continued to play a critical role as supplier of foreign exchange. Sturzenegger (1988) has calculated that about 40 percent of agricultural GDP was transferred to other sectors between 1960 and 1980.

The production of resource-based intermediates was favored with tax exemptions and other fiscal advantages in the early 1970s. These heavily subsidized industries—petrochemicals, aluminum, pulp and paper, and steel—were spared from Argentina's first experiment with trade liberalization in the mid-1970s, the brunt of which was concentrated on final goods. With the ensuing structure of protection, final goods were severely penalized while the effective rate of protection (ERP) for intermediates was raised. Although the production of automobiles and other consumer durables, machine tools, ships, and capital goods in general fell by 50 percent, steel enjoyed an ERP of about 90 percent. In relative terms this figure was among the highest in a sample of manufacturing industries (Berlinski, 1978).

When the debt crisis broke out, the production of intermediates was characterized by overcapacity, high external indebtedness, negligible penetration of international markets, and heavy reliance on fiscal support. By 1986, industrial investment subsidies amounted to nearly 4 percent of GDP.

Adjustment on external accounts has been impressive. Since the onset of the debt crisis, export earnings have exceeded import expenditures in all years (see Table 6.1). The trade deficit, which was equivalent to 3 percent of GDP in 1981, was turned into a trade surplus equivalent to 10 percent of GDP in 1990. Export earnings have not been able to close the current account deficit. Until 1988 this turnaround took place amid falling international prices. The effort of adjustment was double; more physical goods had to be sacrificed from consumption and investment and a higher proportion of GDP had to be spared to achieve a positive trade balance. It has been calculated that the terms-of-trade loss in 1980–1986 amounted to 4.5 percent of GDP. Simultaneously, gross investment declined from 25 percent to 7 percent in the decade. The fall in the investment ratio is among the worst for indebted countries. Until 1992 macroeconomic instability continually undermined investment and conspired against competitiveness. Reflecting the drop in investment, the share of capital goods in total imports declined from 20–24 percent before the debt crisis to less than 10 percent since. In 1981–1991 GNP fell by 7.7 percent.

Table 6.1   Balance of Trade in Argentina
(current values, in thousands of dollars)

	Exports	Imports	Balance
1980	8020	10539	-2519
1985	8396	3814	4582
1986	6852	4724	2128
1987	6360	5819	541
1988	9133	5322	3811
1989	9577	4204	5373
1990	12079	3843	8236
1991	11721	7767	3954

Source: Argentina, Secretaria de Industria y Comercio Exterior, 1991.

In 1987, subsidies for non-agrobased exports were implemented to counter the impact of falling international prices for agricultural goods. Argentina's response was quick, as can be seen in Table 6.2.

Table 6.2   Composition of Argentine Exports (in percentages)

	1985	1986	1987	1988	1989	1990
Primary products	43.79	36.85	27.45	26.51	21.75	28.22
Agrobased manufactures	30.92	39.21	44.43	43.17	42.00	37.86
Industrial products	18.37	21.72	26.96	28.73	33.13	27.10
Fuel	3.74	2.13	1.37	1.52	3.09	6.78

Source: Argentina, Secretaria de Industria y Comercio Exterior, 1990.

Since then, and even though subsidies have subsequently been severely curtailed, the structure of exports has been shifting, with such products as seamless tubes, ethane, pulp, and paper becoming more important. The traditional payments deficit of the industrial sector, which used to run at about $2 billion, has been turned into a small surplus. Steel exports in particular have grown very speedily, and in 1989 they contributed about a one-tenth of export earnings. The state enterprise SOMISA (in the process of being privatized) became the leading exporter, having left traditional food-exporting firms behind. Despite the withdrawal of fiscal incentives and severe overvaluation of the rate of exchange, this trend continued into 1991.

Since 1988 the rate of growth of Argentine manufactured exports has exceeded by far the rate of growth of world exports, especially in terms of volume (see Table 6.3). This is a marked change from historical trends (Bouzas and Keifman, 1987). In fact, manufactured exports have served as a sort of buffer for the wild fluctuations in the volume and value of agricultural exports.[1]

Coupled with the increased export propensity and the changing composition of exports has been a shift in destination. The Soviet Union, Argentina's main market in the early 1980s, was replaced by the United States and Brazil, which now compete for first place and together account for nearly one-fourth of exports. Performance in the U.S. market has been influenced by the dynamic growth of steel exports. Other goods exported to the U.S. are hides and leather goods, textiles, clothing, and wool. Trade with Brazil is composed mainly of wheat and fruits, but the overhaul of trade policies has induced the reorganization of the car sector in both countries, and Argentina is now exporting parts to Brazil. As a result the

Table 6.3 Comparative Rates of Export Growth (annual variation)

	1976/85		1987		1988		1989		1990	
	Argentina	World	Argentina	World	Argentina	World	Argentina	World	Argentina	World
Total										
Value	8.8	7.6	-7.0	16.9	43.6	13.7	3.8	7.5	29	13
Volume	7.0	3.0	3.4	5.5	22.8	8.5	-1.2	7.0	-0.8	5
Agriculture										
Value	10.1	5.3	-22.6	14.5	54.7	13.8	-11.0	5.0	30	6.5
Volume	11.5	3.1	-15.8	6.0	20.6	5.0	-12.2	4.0	-5.7	3.5
Manufactures										
Value	7.9	8.7	8.5	19.4	54.0	16.8	24.3	7.0	27	13.5
Volume	3.9	5.1	26.3	6.5	24.5	10.5	18.2	8.0	9	5.5

Sources: Bouzas and Keifman, 1987; GATT, *International Trade*, various issues; ECLA, data base.

traditional deficit in bilateral trade flows has been turned into a surplus. Yet wildly fluctuating relative rates of exchange conspire against predictable conditions of competition between the two countries. Nonetheless, the plan to create a regional common market by 1995 is regarded as a means of consolidating adjustment and countering the regionalization of trade policies (see Chapters 2 and 3).

For the first time, the industrial sector has backed the new orientation, and traditional import substituters have begun to increase their reliance on export markets. The general overhaul of trade policies has, for one thing, watered down the differences between traditional agricultural exporters and the import-competing sector over the balance of incentives. For another, it has diversified the composition and interests of the export lobby. A political consensus has emerged over the opening to trade. The government in office since 1989 has transformed the consensus into an active reform policy.

THE IMPACT OF CONDITIONALITY
ON THE DIRECTION OF TRADE POLICY

Before the onset of the debt crisis, the exchange rate was grossly overvalued, and the nominal average tariff was set at an average of 30 percent. Reflecting the import-substitution drive, three criteria had been used as a basis to order the tariff schedule: type of good (i.e., consumer, intermediate, or capital), availability of domestic supply (produced or not produced locally), and value added. Rates were higher for consumer goods than for capital goods and intermediates. Import-competing goods enjoyed higher rates, and these increased with the degree of processing, which resulted in a structure of effective protection that was higher than the one shown by nominal rates, although tariff dispersion was not high (Berlinski, 1978).

This structure of protection kept historical expenditures on consumer goods at less than 6 percent of the import bill. When import liberalization of final goods was implemented in 1979–1981, expenditures on consumer goods added up to 14 percent. More than two-thirds of imports consisted of raw materials and intermediates, the volume of which was directly related to the level of domestic activity.

Pressed by the foreign exchange crisis at the end of 1982, across-the-board import licensing was introduced, and imports were drastically cut by half. Tariff levels were not modified, but strict QRs operated by dividing imports into three categories: prohibited imports, consisting mainly of consumer goods and domestically produced industrial inputs; "prior consultation" goods, for which consent from producers' associations was first required and including domestically produced capital goods and selected inputs; and permitted imports.

All imports had to be cleared by the Industry and Trade Secretariat, for which a document called a sworn declaration of import need was required. The first attempt to stabilize the economy under the Austral Plan in 1985 did not involve trade liberalization. On the contrary, the standby agreements with the IMF in that period included tariff surcharges and export taxes for budgetary purposes.

Tariff surcharges amounted to 15 percentage points, and they pushed up the average nominal level of tariffs from 30 percent to about 43 percent (production weighted). In 1987—barely a few months after a standby agreement was signed relying on an across-the-board tariff increase for short-term fiscal purposes—trade liberalization became part and parcel of negotiations with the World Bank, as one of the steps for joining the Baker Plan.

Argentina's overall bargaining with the World Bank under Baker Plan guidelines has been analyzed elsewhere (Tussie and Botzman, 1992). In 1986 President Raúl Alfonsín's government had hoped that external pressures and the spearhead provided by conditionality would allow it to further its own policy goals in relation to trade and structural reform. In respect to trade policy, a consensual rather than a shock approach was seen as preferable. The government, unwilling to confront vested interests head on, would need to reach an agreement with the oligopolistic domestic producers of intermediates who benefited from the structure of incentives.

A two-step compromise was reached. A first TPL implemented in 1987 reduced the antiexport bias of the import-licensing system with the implementation of a broad temporary admission regime that provided exports with a free trade status. It increased the effective exchange rate for exporters through reimbursement of indirect taxes and the elimination of export taxes on manufactures and agrobased products. Export taxes remained in place, however, on soybeans, and the government also retained its ban on the export of raw hides to favor local processing.

This TPL operated in tandem with an IMF standby loan. Three lessons of previous liberalization experiments were built into the new reform: (1) sequencing with a strong emphasis on the free trade status for exporters early in the reform process, coupled with a phaseout of various specific export-promotion measures; (2) a negotiated, sector-by-sector approach; (3) an attempt, which was not always successful, to maintain a competitive exchange rate for trade transactions

Subjecting the hard core of import protection to external competition was left for a subsequent operation, by which time industrial production was shifting to export markets. A second TPL, negotiated during 1988, was also designed as a two-step procedure. The approach to reform was a gradual one, focusing on areas that would generate support to build momentum for liberalization. The idea was to begin by intermediate goods with highly uncompetitive structures; this would raise the ERP of user industries and thus increase the range of acceptability of the reform. It was also hoped that the initial focus on intermediates would generate additional support, given the high price linkages to the rest of the economy. According to a World Bank industrial study of Argentina, "as such, they [intermediates] become a critical link in the mechanism which propagates inflationary pressures. Import competition would help sever this link" (World Bank, 1987, 86).

The most important policy change adopted under the program was the removal of QRs, the withdrawal of iron and steel imports from the control of the General Directorate of Military Industries, and the abolition of the process of prior consultation with producers' associations for all other imports. For first-tranche release, QRs—which then applied to two-thirds of the value of production—had to be reduced to cover a maximum of 18 percent; this ceiling had to be reduced to 15 percent for second-tranche release. Equally important was the lifting of the import-licensing system for all imports without QRs. Imports without QRs—the overall majority—had to be fully automatic for second-tranche release.

The main items retaining QRs were textiles, cars, and metal products and machinery. In some cases, such as textiles and electronics, protection was reinforced with the introduction of new specific tariffs. In other cases, such as cars, tariffs were reduced from 115 percent to 50 percent, the maximum allowed rate under the loan contract. But since QRs were retained, the reduction in the tariff level may well have produced an illusory opening effect and reduced fiscal revenue.

When it came to bargaining over tariff items, the World Bank was not too worried if rates were initially hiked, so long as QRs were removed. The opening effort was centered on replacing QRs with equivalent indifference tariffs at a level that did not add new water to the system. The program was aimed primarily at curbing the discretionary power over imports and providing greater overall transparency to the system.

Tariff protection on steel and petrochemicals was significantly reduced. Yet aside from these sectors, the thrust of the tariff program was a return to the level prevailing before the Austral Plan, that is, an average ad valorem rate of 30 percent. Ironically, this is about the average at which they stood before IMF-monitored adjustment began in 1985. This component of conditionality was thus more or less easily fulfillable; such a broad measure of protection allowed ample room to tinker with the average.

Tariff dispersion in nominal terms was not altered; the majority of tariffs remained in the 10–40 percent band, with a few exceptions (the car sector among them) set at 50 percent. No estimates of shifts in the rate of effective protection are available, but it is highly probable that aggregate ERP remained constant, except for steel and petrochemical end-users, which benefited from an increase in trade protection.

In sum, the most important policy reforms were the removal of QRs and the introduction of automatic import procedures on the great majority of imports. Except for steel and petrochemicals, tariffs were not supposed to fall dramatically: on average they went back to pre-Austral levels.

The import liberalization program was introduced at the end of 1988 and proceeded according to the preestablished time frame in the loan contract. However, the macroconditionality attached to this tranche of the trade loan was not met. Indeed, a particular feature of this TPL was that it was not supported by an IMF standby because of the dissolution of the Baker Plan during the last phase of the Reagan administration. The ensuing disagreements split the twin institutions over the soundness of the Argentine economic program, so the World Bank stepped ahead of the IMF, judging that leadership was required in order to catalyze other external creditors. As the World Bank stated, "The economic situation in Argentina is at an important turning point and timely international support is warranted. Extended delay in agreeing on an external financing programme might jeopardise the success of the stabilisation programme and risk bringing about an outcome unfavourable to all creditors" (World Bank, 1988, 20).

Deprived of the safety net of an IMF standby and straightforwardly set to provide balance-of-payment support, the Bank tied the loan to a macroframework. Trade targets were accompanied by a letter of development policy that specified macro-objectives. The letter included a clause whereby the second disbursement of the loan would be made conditional to favorable overall macroeconomic performance. Besides action on trade policy, "satisfactory progress on putting in place an external financing program will be an important criterion against which to assess macroeconomic performance" (World Bank, 1988, 20).

While the government proceeded to fulfill the trade conditions, it was unable to come to an agreement with the IMF and to comply with the macroprogram. The loan was suspended in early 1989, just before a severe hyperinflationary bout. Hyperinflation and the drying up of external finance were a final blow to the government of President Alfonsín and led to a call for early elections in May.

The new government promptly renewed contacts with the IMF and complied with the conditionality of the TPL in order to obtain disbursement of the second tranche. Conditionality in relation to trade policy was fulfilled—indeed overfulfilled. Moreover, import liberalization continued throughout 1990 and 1991, no longer linked to conditionality but as part of the government's own initiative to pursue deregulation in all spheres of economic activity. Practically all QRs were abolished at the end of 1990; those still in force apply to cars and car parts. Specific tariffs protecting textiles and electronics were also removed. The new tariff structure implemented in April 1991 comprises three levels: 5 percent for raw materials and food products, 13 percent for intermediates, and 22 percent for final goods. The average production-weighted tariff thus fell from the 30 percent agreed upon with the Bank in October 1988 to 9 percent in April 1991.

Conditionality has, then, played a complex and changing role. In the initial steps, when the import-substitution culture was still strongly rooted, it gave a weak government the external technocratic support it required to take up reform of the system of incentives. In such circumstances it may not always be easy to distinguish between what countries want to assume by way of commitments for domestic political reasons and what they are obliged to accept by way of strict conditionality. Subsequently, in the latter phases of the reform process, import liberalization has gone far beyond what was required to comply with loan conditions. Full unilateral opening to trade has continued as part of a wider-ranging design to deregulate the economy.

The real weight of conditionality was applied to NTBs, QRs, and import licensing. As regards tariffs, rates have not been immoderately low, a production-weighted average of 30 percent. Since tariff conditionality was specified in such aggregate terms as production-weighted averages, the selection of tariff positions subject to reduction remained open to policy preferences or vulnerable to the reaction of lobbies. When bargaining with the Bank, for example, Argentina maintained protection for textiles and cars.

The fact nevertheless remains that levels of commitment have now become a good deal greater than in the pre-Baker Plan, pre-Uruguay Round mid-1980s. For this reason, but also because of the internal political consensus that has emerged over the timeliness of liberalization, a rollback of reforms and a return to the past seems unfeasible. Even if they are not yet bound in GATT, these reforms are permanent. The evolving process in this respect seems quite akin to that in Mexico and Costa Rica (see Chapters 4 and 5). Like Mexico and Costa Rica, Argentina has also made an effort to develop good relations with the United States.

RELATIONS WITH THE UNITED STATES: THE DYNAMICS OF CROSSCUTTING INTERESTS

The evolution of bilateral relations with the principal demandeur in the Uruguay Round has been an important factor in shaping multilateral diplomacy. Argentine exports to the United States amount to $1.5 billion, equivalent to 15 percent of total exports. They consist of light manufactures such as hides and leather goods, steel products, canned and packaged meat, fruit juices, and so on. Bilateral trade relations have been tinted by two major issues: subsidies (and CVD action) and intellectual property rights (and the threat to apply Special Section 301 of the U.S. trade act; see the Introduction). Both topics illustrate the growing involvement of the industrial sector in international negotiations and its growing need for a nonconfrontational relationship with the United States.

In the heyday of import substitution, Argentina had refused to sign the 1979 Tokyo Round code on subsidies and CVDs under which countries had to undertake a commitment to phase out export subsidies in exchange for the injury test. For one thing, the industrial sector relied heavily on fiscal incentives and subsidized credit; for another, agricultural exporters rejected the code on matters of principle, given that it excluded primary products.

Since then, CVDs have been applied to wool and woolen garments, leather apparel, textiles, nonrubber footwear, and cold-rolled steel sheets (Bouzas, 1992). Two sectors, steel and hides, have been particularly vulnerable to the lack of the injury test. Exports of hides to the United States amount to about $200 million, equivalent to about 40 percent of domestic production. To encourage domestic processing a ban on exports of untanned cattle was implemented in 1985. The measure resulted in CVDs ranging from 8 percent to 25 percent, depending on the degree of processing that each exporting firm carries out.

Steel products as well have consistently suffered from CVD action, not only because of the panoply of fiscal incentives they have enjoyed but also because of the industry's rejection of a VER under the U.S. 1984 steel program. The quota offered then was fixed in volume terms and entailed a two-thirds cut of actual exports of 300,000 tons. Moreover, such a severe cut had little growth potential since it was accompanied by a ceiling of 200,000 tons. The industry rejected the discipline of the VER forthrightly. Unrestrained by a VER, Argentine steel exports to the United States were able to grow quite rapidly, amounting to about $150 million. Yet without a VER and without the injury test, they have also been vulnerable to recurrent CVD action.

The collapse of the domestic market with the fall in investment ratios, the increasing reliance on the U.S. market, and the curtailment of subsidies that came with adjustment changed the sector's initial refusal to agree on subsidies. Following the Mexican matrix, Argentina has taken the bilateral road to the injury test and has signed an agreement on similar terms.[2] The government pledged to impose a standstill and a gradual phaseout of existing subsidies.

Growing dependence on the U.S. market has also increased the vulnerability of business to bilateral coercion on intellectual property rights and action under Special Section 301 (see Introduction). In 1988 Argentina was formally threatened with the application of Special 301 for excluding pharmaceutical products from its patent system. In their petition against Argentina, the Pharmaceutical Manufacturers of America (PMA) estimated losses of $84 million per year caused by slack patent protection. Argentine law recognizes patents on processes, though not on products.

Since Section 301 is unilateral and GATT-illegal, the conditions for its application are highly discretionary and open-ended. Trade remedy laws, in contrast, must conform to the GATT codes on dumping and subsidies, so there is an attempt to define which subsidies are prohibited or to provide guidelines for the calculation of the value of a given subsidy or a dumping margin. Section 301 merely requires that the president find a foreign practice "unreasonable, unjustified, or discriminatory." Cases are opened when an interested party in the United States submits a petition to the USTR. In practice most petitioners approach the USTR informally prior to submitting a petition; the USTR then makes informal contacts and negotiations with the country involved before actually imposing a sanction.

The USTR was due to take a decision in the case against Argentina in September 1989. The date coincided with the annual IMF–World Bank meeting during which Argentina hoped to obtain renewed support from the United States for a $1.4 billion standby loan. As part of the bargaining over the standby loan, Argentina promised to reform legislation on patents. Three days before the deadline, the Foreign Ministry sent a note to the USTR pledging to send a draft law to Congress within two years.[3]

Even if access to external finance had not been threatened, Argentina's room to maneuver was limited. When confronted with a threat, a country's "main economic consideration is whether the net social benefit of low patent protection is higher or lower than the social costs of retaliation" (Nogués, 1990). The quantity of trade that might be affected is suggested by the injury the PMA claimed. In other words, on a narrowly focused commercial evaluation, the cost of retaining the status quo might have cost Argentina at least the equivalent of the amount the U.S. manufacturers claimed.

Under Section 301 the president has broad discretionary power in selecting the sanctions—exclusion from the GSP, tariff surcharges, and so on. The law also specifies that the sanction may be applied to products or services other than those that are the subject of the investigation. Thus there need be no logical economic linkages between the selected products and those under investigation. Cross-sectoral retaliation is certain in the case of pharmaceuticals. Argentina, for instance, exports barely $6 million to the United States, while imports from the United States amount to $25 million, most of which are intrafirm flows. The United States had sanctioned Mexico by excluding it from GSP benefits, but more frequently retaliation has meant imposing 100 percent ad valorem tariffs on selected imports, as in the case of Brazil. The United States first threatened Argentina with hiking ad valorem tariffs on dynamic export lines, but it also considered excluding Argentina from the GSP.

The precedent set by the Brazilian informatics dispute showed that the selection of imports to be penalized had excluded exports from U.S. affiliates (Hurrell and Felder, 1988). The list was designed with the object of converting local exporters, be they footwear producers or orange growers, into active advocates of the U.S. position. One should bear in mind that a sanction is a means rather than the objective of both the petitioning industry and the U.S. negotiators. The threat is a means of obtaining concessions without actually having to resort to sanctions. The purpose of any punitive action is deterrence ex ante facto and not revenge ex post facto.[4]

To avoid an actual resort to sanctions, the USTR made exporters of a variety of products aware of the potential loss of access to the U.S. market if the government failed to be accommodating. This drove a wedge in the domestic front, inducing local exporters to lobby for the required concessions. Although a target list was not formally drawn up or made public, in the period following Argentina's commitment to send a law to Congress, the USTR heightened the awareness and vulnerability of local exporters to the alternative threats. On the one hand, an increase in ad valorem tariffs to 100 percent would have hit the most dynamic exports, prominent among them steel. The leading firm, Siderca, part of the Techint holding, was especially vulnerable. With the narrowing of domestic demand in recent years, over 80 percent of Siderca's production is sold abroad, the U.S. representing a leading market for seamless tubes. With a tariff increase of 100 percent, the company would be priced out of the market.

On the other hand, exclusion from the GSP would have hit $250 million worth of exports, or one-fourth of Argentine exports to the United States, among which hides are prominent. This alternative was a smaller "punishment" to overall Argentine exports, but for the United States it holds the attraction that it does not lead to violation of GATT obligations. The United States could therefore avoid confronting a panel in GATT, as it had to do as a result of its sanctions on Brazil. (see Chapter 7).

In any alternative, local pharmaceutical firms were thus confronted with waning support for their resistance to U.S. pressure. They canvassed public opinion at home and abroad but also started to adjust by seeking licensing agreements from multinational patent holders. At the end of the two-year period agreed with the USTR, Argentina acquired the right to the injury test with a bilateral agreement on subsidies and CVDs and sent a draft law to Congress in order to remove the pending threat of Special 301 on its main exports to the United States.

BARGAINING IN GATT

The relevance of agricultural trade for Argentina cannot be exaggerated. Several studies have shown that Argentina is the country most affected by protectionist policies (World Bank, 1986). Despite the growing diversification of Argentine exports, grains, oilseeds, and by-products are still the main sources of foreign exchange.

Prior to the Uruguay Round, the GATT had been marginal to Argentine economic diplomacy. In the GATT Argentina had been largely driven by its dual interest in supporting import substitution and attacking the pervasive effects of agricultural protectionism. But because GATT offered negligible prospects for agriculture, Argentina (like most other developing countries in the GATT) devoted its bargaining resources to protecting its domestic market protected from foreign competition, using Article 18b. Argentina negotiated few tariff positions in GATT and bound even fewer. Those bindings were done at 50 percent as a result of negotiations for accession during the Kennedy Round.

For Argentina as for other developing countries (see Chapter 1), the Uruguay Round marked a remarkable break with precedent. Argentina leapt from its historical low profile to an activist strategy. The upsurge of coalition activity offered new alternatives to small countries with limited bargaining power in multilateral trade negotiations. Moreover, as Argentina undertook adjustment and unilateral liberalization simultaneous to the Uruguay Round, it was able to put its own opening on the bargaining table both as a goodwill gesture and a moral argument.

In the period leading up to the launching of the Uruguay Round, the definition of Argentine interests remained ambivalent. Despite a scenario in which agriculture was gradually but clearly becoming negotiating matter, Argentina first concentrated its resources in joining the Group of Ten (see Chapter 11), using stalling tactics and trying to delay the launching of the round. But as the Cairns Group crystalized during 1986, Argentine inclinations in favor of a round that offered some hope for agriculture gathered weight. At Punta del Este, Argentina, together with the United States and Australia, was in the frontline in obtaining a commitment on the inclusion of agriculture.

Agricultural exporters played a significant role in this shift; they lobbied to change the official perception that agriculture would be sacrificed to the so-called new issues and promoted the adoption of an attitude more proximate to the overall interests of the United States (de las Carreras, 1985). The private sector was subsequently given an active role in international trade negotiations, especially landowners' associations which were advantageously positioned to articulate their interests in respect to foreign markets. Representatives of all landowners' associations, were not only kept punctually informed and consulted, they also took part in several official missions abroad to lobby for an agreement. With a clear-cut private-sector view of the issue and grassroots support, the government was able to make headway more easily in agriculture than in any other group in which bureaucrats alone were left to take the lead. High stakes were placed on the Cairns Group, and as a member of the coalition, Argentina was always hopeful that U.S. backing might ultimately persuade the EC to overrule its farming lobbies.

Other factors also contributed to changing perceptions. One was a generalized fresh evaluation of the Uruguay Round. The period leading up to the launching of the round had been one of deep-seated dissension over the new issues, reflecting trenchant North-South divisions. Developing countries feared the new round would neglect traditional issues and would simply impose the new outcome from negotiations on the new issues in a "take-it-or-leave-it" option, as had been the case with the Tokyo Round codes. As the round began to evolve, new configurations of interests seemed possible. Above all the round seemed to offer a better chance than ever before of achieving results in agriculture because of the manifest intention of the United States to negotiate a multilateral solution to the problem of agricultural protectionism and the congealing of the Cairns partnership. Both multilateral diplomatic endeavors helped defuse some of the Argentine passion behind the North-South cleavage. They opened the possibility of untried forms of international cooperation.

At a bilateral level U.S. diplomatic pressure was also unrelenting. The run-up period before the launching of the round was contradictory for Argentina. It coincided with negotiations over the Baker Plan, and Argentina's debt strategy was centered on joining it. In November 1985 David Mulford visited Argentina to sew up some of the details in relation to the Baker Plan, and he made it publicly known that Argentina could not expect to be "favored" with Baker funds if it did not "cooperate" on issues in the GATT that interested the United States (Aicardi and Tussie, 1986).

The mix of bilateral pressures coupled with the factors that contributed to the dilution of the import-substitution model described in the previous sections increased Argentina's readiness to take on multilateral obligations. More importantly, Argentina became keen to secure recognition in the field of agriculture for its own unilateral opening. Given the process of unilateral opening and as yet budding industrial export interests, the range of issues of interest naturally narrowed; at the same time they were more pressing and meaningful. As the Uruguay Round evolved, the same process that had given Argentina a high profile gradually turned it into a one-issue country. If Indian bargaining strategy could be characterized as service-centered (see Chapter 8), Argentine strategy has been primarily agriculture-centered, the inward-looking development model withering away. As Felipe Solá, former secretary for agriculture, described it, "Argentina's growth model is predicated upon a successful resolution to the agricultural crisis in GATT." The transparency of such a stance carried with it the disadvantage of a certain loss of flexibility. The element of uncertainty over possible Argentine positioning was thus removed from the bargaining process.

Even in comparison to those of other major Cairns Group countries, Argentina's trade interests are significantly less diversified, its dice overwhelmingly loaded in favor of liberalizing agriculture above all other sector interests (see Chapter 10). Both as a member of the coalition and individually, Argentina expended most of its negotiating capacity on consolidating the ground for agricultural negotiations. In March 1988 it presented a paper to the services group that served as a procedural contribution. It did away with certain stumbling blocks, narrowed the North-South gap on the issue, and created the climate for the subsequent, more substantial negotiations. The paper laid the groundwork that eventually led to the Montreal decision on services (see Chapter 1). Michael Samuels, then deputy USTR with responsibility for GATT affairs, described the Argentine paper as a "positive initiative which moves the negotiating process forward. The importance of the Argentine proposals is that they are the first real effort to spell out the view of a developing nation" (*Financial Times* , March 25, 1988).

This initiative marked a change from the defensive attitude prevailing in the run-up to the launching of the round. Such activism culminated in the Montreal midterm review in December 1988, when the disagreement between the United States and the EC on the short-term versus the long-term approach to farm reform galvanized Argentina into vetoing progress in other areas. When cross-bargaining tactics proved insufficient to push forward the agricultural issue, Argentina moved in the opposite direction to block agreements obtained by the other eleven negotiating groups. With the support of the Latin American members of the Cairns Group, negotiations were put on hold in Montreal pending the results of further negotiations in Geneva in April of the following year. The impasse was resolved with a Cairns proposal to freeze existing levels of support, an early cutback in 1990, and a commitment to formulate a longer-term package by the end of 1990. The move highlighted the importance that Argentina had attached to better access to agricultural markets.

While agriculture held a pivotal role in overall bargaining, in the other groups Argentina participated along the lines of the North-South debate, especially in safeguards, textiles, and services. In contrast to the situation regarding agriculture and intellectual property rights, there has been less involvement of the private sector and less empirical work. Pharmaceutical firms closely monitored the evolution of negotiations in intellectual property rights in an effort to use the GATT as a countervailing instrument against Special 301. The industry provided negotiators with substantial support and key inputs to argue their case. In services (except for shipping and insurance, in which substantial regulations still persist) it is important for Argentina to use the binding of its rather open and deregulated service sector to obtain credit or as a pawn in other negotiations.

Argentina offered to bind the entire tariff schedule at a maximum level of 35 percent, the maximum applied rate being thirteen percentage points lower. The United States considered the offer insufficient on the grounds that the applied rate was below the binding offer. The pressure has been to force the binding of applied rates rather than accept the reduction of high unbound tariffs and the tying of the entire tariff schedule as a contribution, even though few developed countries have bound their entire schedules. The widespread hope of obtaining credit for liberalization measures implemented in the course of adjustment was not realized, partly because of the stalemate in negotiations.

CONCLUSIONS

Before the Uruguay Round, Argentina, like most developing countries, had concentrated its trade diplomacy on the defense of import substitution, applying its skills mainly to securing import protection. In the initial phases of the round, old attitudes lingered. But gradually Argentine interests focused on issues of market access, both in the bilateral and the multilateral arena.

Although conditionality—by virtue of its highly aggregate design —left some room to bargain in GATT, indebtedness has restricted Argentina's options and alternatives in a broader sense. Not only were concessions extracted under duress at critical phases of debt negotiations, but the structure of industry shifted from its traditional inward to outward orientation, policy options were altered accordingly. Moreover, unilateral opening meant that Argentine expectations of an adequately functioning trading system with opportunities for reciprocal deals were heightened.

Multilateral bargaining strategy was defined by the overriding importance of agriculture and good relations with the main demandeur of the round; tactics were circumscribed by the process of adjustment and the overspill of debt pressures and priorities. Thus the country was constrained by the limits imposed by the combination of a high-profile role and a restricted range of options.

The readiness to take the initiative and the firm expectation of payment in kind have produced a mirror image of the traditionally passive bargaining stance. Adjustment and unilateral liberalization have heightened the interest of the private sector in an adequately functioning multilateral system. The advantages offered by GATT surveillance have acquired a new and growing relevance. The example of the Cairns Group has also led to a growing awareness of the benefits of joint action. Thus a desire to replicate the model with increasingly tighter coordination with Brazil under the proposed regional common market, MERCOSUR, can be expected in the near future.

NOTES

Research assistance by Maria Wagner is gratefully acknowledged.

1. Despite this growth trend, Argentina's share in world trade has continued its historical decline. During the 1980s it fell from 0.42 percent to 0.17 percent of world trade.

2. For a discussion of the alternatives of going bilateral or multilateral on this issue, see Chapter 4.

3. For similar types of diplomatic concessions under duress in Brazil, see Chapter 7.

4. For similar implications of such threats in the case of debt, see Tussie (1988).

7

Trade Policies and Bargaining in a Heavily Indebted Economy: Brazil

MARCELO DE PAIVA ABREU

My main objective in this chapter is to consider the formulation and implementation of trade policies in Brazil during the 1980s, a period marked by overall balance-of-payments vulnerability due to heavy foreign indebtedness accumulated before 1982 and by very poor economic performance compared to the long-term trend. I try to show how distinct and changing vested interests affected negotiating stances as well as the links between trade developments on the bilateral level and stances in multilateral trade negotiations. I also examine the increased leverage of multilateral financial agencies as a factor in shifts in trade policy and assess the recent overhauling of decisionmaking arrangements in the trade policy area and liberalizing moves in terms of policy sequencing, coherence, and sustainability in the longer term.

The chapter is divided into four sections. The first considers trends in trade performance and evidence of the obstacles that have constrained access of exports to developed markets since the early 1980s. The next section deals with negotiations in the GATT, especially in connection with the Uruguay Round. The third section examines relations with multilateral financial agencies, especially the World Bank and the IMF, and implications for trade policy. The final section considers recent liberalization in Brazilian trade policy in the context of past policy trends and offers conclusions.

TRADE PERFORMANCE AND MARKET ACCESS
IN DEVELOPED COUNTRIES IN THE 1980s

The 1980s are commonly referred to as the lost decade in Brazil, as GDP per capita actually fell, in sharp contrast with long-term trends. GDP in 1980–1989 increased at the yearly rate of 2.2 percent, whereas it had increased at 7.1 percent yearly in 1973–1980 and 11.2 percent in

1967–1973. In 1990 it decreased by 4.6 percent. International economic policy was based on a blend that included export promotion, import substitution, and foreign indebtedness. Mediocre growth performance resulted from a particularly destructive combination of high inflation and foreign exchange constraints as Brazil's role as an importer of real resources was reversed after 1982. This is not the place to delve into the main causes of the deterioration of growth performance, but a balanced view of the process would certainly require a mix of arguments related to the structural inability to finance public expenditure and the generalization of indexation rules that made inflation at least partly an inertial phenomenon. (See Table 7.1 for data on GDP, inflation, foreign debt, and the flow of real resources.)[1]

Table 7.1   Key Macroeconomic Indicators in Brazil, 1980–1990

	GDP Yearly Rate of Change (%)	GDP Deflator Yearly Rate of Change (%)	Foreign Debt ($ billion)	Balance of Trade and Nonfactor Services (% GDP)
1980	9.3	90.3	64.2	-2.5
1981	-4.4	107.0	74.0	-0.4
1982	0.6	105.0	85.3	-0.7
1983	-3.4	140.0	93.6	2.4
1984	5.3	213.0	102.0	5.7
1985	8.0	232.0	105.1	5.2
1986	7.5	146.0	111.0	2.5
1987	3.6	204.0	121.2	3.3
1988	-0.1	648.0	113.5	5.2
1989	3.2	1,323.0	115.1	3.2
1990	-4.6	2,848.9	121.0	1.6

Source: Central Bank of Brazil.

Attempts to face the debt crisis in the early 1980s led to the adoption of recessive policies together with a realignment of the real exchange rate in relation to the dollar. This adjustment of around 40 percent in 1983–1986 was, however, followed by appreciation of the domestic currency against the dollar: in 1989 the average real exchange rate was back to its 1981–1982 level. It fluctuated significantly as a result of successive failures of stabilization efforts in 1990–1991.

Export performance was outstanding between 1979 and 1984 but has been less so since the mid-1980s. There was a marked product diversification away from raw materials or semiprocessed goods in favor of manufactures (see Table 7.2). Manufactured export prices fell until the mid-1980s as a result of the vent for surplus stance of domestic producers.[2] At the end of the 1980s, Brazilian exports remained small both as a proportion of world total exports (around 1.1 percent) and of GDP (around 10 percent). Product diversification was matched by market diversification until the early 1980s, as the shares of Latin America, Africa, and the Middle East in total exports increased significantly partly because of the growing importance of barter trade with the Middle East, as Brazil was severely hit by the rise in oil prices. After the debt crisis and with the fall in oil prices, these trends were reversed, and markets in developed countries partly regained their former importance. The United States in particular recovered from the recession in the early 1980s, and the dollar was overvalued in relation to other key currencies. These trends were even more marked for manufactured exports.[3]

Table 7.2   Brazilian Exports and Imports, 1979–1990
(in millions of dollars)

	Total Exports FOB	Manufactured Exports (Braz. def.) FOB	Total Imports FOB	Mineral Fuel Imports FOB
1979	15,244	6,645	18,083	6,773
1981	23,293	11,883	22,091	11,340
1982	20,175	10,253	19,395	10,623
1985	25,639	14,063	13,153	6,176
1986	22,348	12,404	14,044	3,541
1987	26,224	14,839	15,052	4,709
1988	33,787	19,188	14,605	4,136
1989	34,383	18,634	18,263	4,430
1990	31,391	16,988	20,593	5,288

Source: Central Bank of Brazil.

The sharp reversal of the trade balance in the early 1980s is explained not only by the rise in exports but also by a significant contraction of imports, initially as a result of a strengthening of controls under the provisions of GATT Article 18b and other protective policies, then mainly by the reduced rate of growth of GDP. Import volume by 1989 was still almost 20 percent below its 1979 level in spite of a GDP growth over the decade of more than 30 percent. The low level of imports is in large part explained by the sharply reduced reliance on imported oil achieved through a combination of substitution in consumption and increased domestic production. This dual strategy led to a decrease of the share of oil in total imports from more than 50 percent to about 25 percent between 1981 and 1990. Nonoil imports were also significantly reduced. The geographical origin of imports reflected the importance of oil imports. Indeed, the nonoil import shares of the United States and the EC in Brazil have been similar and stable since 1979.

Exports faced severe restrictions of access to the markets of developed countries. Evidence of this limited access is notoriously difficult to interpret: data on the proportion of trade affected by NTBs suggest that barriers to Brazilian exports to developed countries in 1986 were relatively more important than those faced by Latin America as a whole or from all developing countries, especially in the U.S. market (which was, however, significantly less protected than the EC). These obstacles affected especially exports of processed tropical products, certain temperate agricultural exports, some iron and steel products, textiles and clothing, and shoes.[4] There is evidence that at least in the United States and Japan these restrictions have been reduced since 1986, as data presented in Table 7.3 suggest.

Table 7.3 **NTB Coverage of Ratio of Brazilian Exports to the Main Developed Economies, 1986–1989**

	United States		Japan		EC	
	1986	1989	1986	1988	1986	1988
Food products	25.5	16.9	96.4	99.0	13.6	12.2
Agricultural raw materials	1.8	0	14.7	14.9	5.1	6.3
Minerals, metals	37.1	46.3	0.1	0	11.7	16.7
iron, and steel	81.9	81.9	0	0	74.2	88.0
Fuels	92.0	97.9	0	0	0	0
Chemical products	37.6	3.3	100	92.8	2.2	1.5
Manufactures	19.5	7.3	62.7	56.3	22.9	32.6
Leather	0	0	20.6	13.6	24.4	99.6
Textiles	74.6	71.1	50.3	37.8	90.8	86.5
Clothing	96.7	97.0	0	0	92.6	96.6
Shoes	0	0	79.1	0	100	100

Source: Computations based on Smart data base. EC ratios concerning food products may have been affected by incomplete information.

Bilateral trade disputes—especially with the United States but also with the EC—have affected the growth of many exports. Barriers take the form of ADDs and CVDs, the imposition of VERs, and actions under the U.S. trade act to redress alleged injury to U.S. interests (see Chapter 3). Brazil faced more CVD initiations than any other developing country in 1980–1986. After Mexico, it also led the list of countries affected by provisional measures and definitive duties. Similarly, on antidumping (with the exception of initiations, in relation to which it has suffered marginally less than South Korea) Brazil was at the head of developing countries subject to the imposition of provisional measures and definitive duties as well as price undertakings.[5]

In the U.S. market, antidumping and countervailing actions have affected exports such as airplanes, iron and steel products, paper products, plywood, tools, cotton yarn, chemical products (ethyl alcohol, fatty acids, oxalic acid, and cyanuric chloride), petrochemical products, orange juice, castor oil, and footwear. EC actions have primarily influenced steel products, paper products, textiles, pig iron, footwear, and soybean products.[6] Bilateral negotiations aiming at the suspension of ADDs or CVDs usually result in the introduction of VERs. In the case of Brazil, they mainly affect steel and iron products both in the U.S. and EC markets.

There are indications that after 1986 Brazil was relatively less affected by ADDs and CVDs at least in part because of the use of other instruments. Thus Brazil has faced U.S. actions under Section 301 of the trade act of 1974, as amended, and Super 301. Of seventy-nine investigations under Section 301 between 1975 and the end of 1989, twenty-nine were against developing countries, of which five were against Brazil (with eight against the Republic of Korea, six against Taiwan, five against Argentina, and three against India) (GATT, 1990b, 262–265). Brazil was the only country to suffer retaliation. In October 1988 the United States imposed tariffs of 100 percent on Brazilian paper, pharmaceutical, and electronic products because of a complaint by the Pharmaceutical Manufacturers Association that the Brazilian intellectual property legislation did not provide adequate protection. This case prompted Brazil to ask for the establishment of a GATT panel (see the following section) and was resolved only in June 1990 as Brazil provided assurances that it would change its legislation so as to increase the protection of process patents. Another notorious 301 case was related to the informatics policy, in particular concerning software legislation. The case was initiated by the USTR in 1985 based on grievances concerning access to the Brazilian software market, protection of intellectual property in relation to both software and hardware, and administrative procedures in the informatics. The case was not concluded until October 1989, after changes were made to relevant Brazilian policies (SELA, 1987, 15–28).

In May 1989 Brazil was designated with Japan and India as one of the priority countries for possible retaliation under Super 301 in relation to the import-licensing system. The striking feature of this decision is that its focus on the trade surplus made explicit the contradiction of U.S. foreign economic policy insofar as foreign debt cannot be serviced—even at a much reduced level in relation to initial contractual terms—without the generation of trade surpluses with developed countries. The controversial first application of Super 301 was suspended in May 1990 in the wake of Brazil's decision to significantly liberalize its import-licensing procedures. Brazil's good behavior may have helped it avoid statutory retaliation, although other countries have escaped Super 301 retaliation without making substantial concessions (Dam, 1970, 368–370; Hudec, 1977, 222; GATT, 1966, 18). The United States further expressed its goodwill toward a more liberal Brazil by reversing a long-standing policy concerning graduation under GSP, as preferences were restored in 1990 for products whose trade covered about $0.5 billion.

BRAZIL IN THE GATT

Brazil was a poor but active founding nation of GATT.[7] Before the early 1960s, its involvement mainly related to the renegotiation of tariff schedules and the Brazilian-Uruguayan initiative concerning nullification or impairment of obligations (Article 23), which proposed the principle of financial payments by developed to developing countries for violations of the GATT.[8] The best efforts in commercial diplomacy until the Tokyo Round, however, were devoted to the negotiations in UNCTAD, in particular in connection with GSP.

Brazilian trade policy up to the 1960s was to a large extent that of a commodity exporter with a fragile balance of payments and an industrial policy based on import substitution. Import substitution has had a long and, until the early 1980s, extremely successful history in Brazil.[9] "Modernization" entailed by a change in political regime in the mid-1960s included the strengthening of links with the international economy, but this was a rather asymmetrical affair. A more liberal attitude toward direct foreign investment, less-distorted foreign exchange policies, and export-promotion policies were not matched by a significant reduction in barriers to imports.[10] On the contrary, balance-of-payments difficulties in the 1970s provided an argument for the imposition of severe quantitative import controls.

In the 1970s the issue of reform of the GATT brought about closer Brazilian involvement in the Tokyo Round. Negotiations within the so-called Framework Group originated with a Brazilian proposal that included the provision of a standing legal basis for GSP so as to make the preferences legally binding and their withdrawal subject to compensation, greater flexibility in the use of Article 18 for balance-of-payments and development purposes, improvements in dispute settlement, and the right of developing countries to nonreciprocity. Developed countries were mainly interested in dispute settlement matters and in limiting the use of export controls by developing countries. The United States stressed its unwillingness to relegate the MFN clause to a residual role and insisted that developing countries forgo special treatment as they achieved their development goals (Maciel, 1978; Windham, 1986, 144–146). The Framework Group negotiations resulted in four agreements. An enabling clause consolidated nonreciprocity based on differential and more favorable treatment for developing countries, and as a quid pro quo a general statement was made as regards graduation and fuller obligations with higher levels of development. Resort to Article 18 for both balance-of-payments and development purposes was made easier or more expedite, but there were no fundamental changes. On notification, consultation, dispute settlement, and surveillance, the United States pressed for a more automatic process based on majority vote, but EC support for a consensus approach avoided a backfiring of the Brazilian initiative. No agreement was reached on export controls (Windham, 1986, 274ff). The concessions made by developing and developed countries were thought to have been more or less equivalent. The initial Brazilian objective to try to compensate the inherent disequilibrium of retaliatory power due to differences in size was certainly contained by the counterproposals of developed countries.

In the period before the launching of the Uruguay Round, Brazil took a markedly defensive stance in the discussions preceding the 1982 GATT ministerial declaration, as did several of the more-advanced developing countries. They resisted the introduction of new issues related to trade-related intellectual property (TRIPs), investment measures (TRIMs), and especially trade in services in the draft agenda for the next MTNs. The main objection to the inclusion of services was that these would dim traditional GATT issues, the backlog of unfinished business of great importance to developing countries. Moreover, there were doubts, shared by some developed countries, on whether services should be treated in a multilateral framework and within the GATT in view of the large number of sector-specific issues involved and of the work of other specialized international organizations.

In several instances in the history of multilateral negotiations, Brazil was vulnerable to bilateral pressures, especially from the United States, to modify its stance. The most important code negotiated in the Tokyo Round from a Brazilian point of view was the one on subsidies. This was basically a negotiation between the EC and United States, but it had implications for Brazil given that U.S. countervailing actions on code signatories had to be based on material injury findings and given that the U.S. market is relatively more important for manufactured exports than for Brazilian total exports. The quid pro quo was a commitment by

Brazil to freeze levels of subsidy and to abolish by June 1983 the subsidies entailed in the credit premia system, which allowed tax credits over and above export tax exemptions. The concession resulted from the assessment by the Ministry of Finance that the position in relation to the United States was untenable. Relations between the Brazilian ministries of Finance and Foreign Affairs had reached a low ebb (de Lima, 1986, 330–336).

In 1982 trade and debt negotiations were linked in a very peculiar form. The 1982 GATT ministerial declaration included an explicit statement about several of the new themes that was at least partly related to the wavering stand of some of the more active developing countries. Brazil, for example, agreed to the inclusion while at the same time stressing that this did not affect its position in favor of a backlog-based agenda. In the second semester of 1982, Brazil was in an extremely fragile external financial condition following the Mexican debt crisis. A bridge loan by the U.S. Treasury was an important source of foreign exchange while the IMF considered the Brazilian position. And in November 1982 the U.S. agreed to a two-year extension of the dealing imposed on the export credit premia scheme. It is difficult to see all these questions as unrelated.[11]

The long negotiation process in the GATT that preceded the launching of the Uruguay Round in September 1986 was marked by continuous friction over the agenda. On one side of the issue was a small group of developing countries—the so-called G10 formed by Argentina, Brazil, Cuba, Egypt, India, Nicaragua, Nigeria, Peru, Tanzania, and Yugoslavia; on the other side were the developed countries.[12] The debate continued to center on the new issues, especially on services. Two agenda proposals were presented at Punta del Este: one, by Colombia and Switzerland, was initially supported by the developed countries and many developing countries and included all the new themes; the other, by the G10, included only the backlog (see Chapter 11). The Colombian-Swiss draft, however, could not resist the EC's opposition to its wording on agriculture. The EC was also important in supporting the principle of unwritten consensus, unwritten rule, thus undermining the U.S. attempt to bring matters to a vote and so break the resistance of the G10 more effectively.[13]

The Uruguay Round declaration formally reflected a compromise, as new themes other than services were included in the undertaking to enter into the general negotiations according to the General Agreement and separate negotiations were launched for trade in services. It was decided to create a Group on Negotiations on Services—outside GATT but with GATT support and applying GATT procedures and practices—postponing a decision on the implementation of its conclusions.[14]

The Brazilian agenda of active interests in the Uruguay Round consisted of tariff matters, temperate agricultural products, textiles and clothing, as well as "rule-making" issues, such as antidumping, subsidies, CVDs, as well as safeguards. In relation to the new themes, Brazil was of course defensive, especially so in the case of TRIPs and TRIMs.[15] Tariff matters include graduation under GSP schemes, tariff escalation, and tariff preferences. Tariff graduation under GSP may hit some specific products but is not an overall important issue, as trade gains entailed by GSP are thought to be around 1 percent of total exports. Tariff escalation affects a high proportion of Brazilian exports of primary and semimanu-factured products, especially in the case of coffee and cocoa product chains. Brazilian interests are also unfavorably affected by the continua-tion and expansion of such preferential trade arrangements as those entailed by the Lomé Convention and the CBI. But to press for the elimi-nation of these would involve major political costs and would undermine relations with a large number of developing countries.

Brazil was an early member of the Cairns Group formed to overcome protectionism in agricultural products.[16] Its initial motivation in joining was political, as it was not a priori clear whether Brazil would gain from the dismantlement of temperate agriculture protectionism. Estimates of the impact of the removal of all barriers on this trade suggest that gains in relation to sugar and beef would more than compensate for losses related to higher wheat prices and decreased soy exports as inefficient purchasers of feedstuff (such as the EC) are superseded by more efficient meat pro-ducers using more land-intensive technologies.[17] Previous qualitative assessments of the impact of a dismantlement of the MFA on Brazilian textile exports suggested that Brazil would lose from it. These estimates have been reversed by more recent research work, which includes Brazil among the big gainers from liberalization (Trela and Whalley, 1988). The importance of ADDs, CVDs, and VERs has already been noted in the pre-vious section, but it is extremely difficult to assess the concrete losses entailed by such actions, given the importance of export deterrence.[18]

As for the new issues, given supply response difficulties in develop-ing countries, it is unlikely that they would be significant demandeurs in services. It is, of course, true that liberalization of services would improve the competitiveness of developing-country exports, as it would enhance economic efficiency, but this an altogether different argument that has to do with economics and not with negotiations in the GATT, which are based on the exchange of "equivalent concessions." It is also hard to see developing countries as demandeurs in TRIPs and TRIMs.

As the Uruguay Round evolved, it became increasingly difficult for the small group of developing countries to maintain their opposition to considering the new themes before the backlog. Political support in the capitals flagged as some countries faced severe macroeconomic problems and became more vulnerable to pressures to give in. There was a growing sense of isolation. The heterogeneity of interests became clear not only in relation to trade-debt links but also in trade matters: the importance of agricultural issues for Argentina, for instance, became an increasingly dominant factor in shaping that country's stand in relation to other issues (see Chapter 6). So the difficulties that had plagued the working of a G77-style coalition of developing countries started to become explicit within the G10 (see Chapter 11).

Even before the change of course toward trade liberalization, when the administration of Fernando Collor de Mello took office in early 1990, Brazil's stance in the GATT became less visible; objections were toned down, positions reversed. Membership in the Cairns Group, which had initially been viewed with mixed feelings, became more significant as agricultural liberalization was singled out as the most important issue in which Brazil could be a demandeur. So Brazil played a crucial role at Montreal's 1988 GATT midterm review, turning Argentina's strong reaction to the lack of results in agriculture into a position of all the Latin American members of Cairns. This obstruction, counting on U.S. support, made it possible to put results on hold until more acceptable drafts could be negotiated in Geneva in April 1989. Brazil's newly found agricultural enthusiasm led to a still clearer stand in the ill-fated Brussels meeting at the end 1990, as once again Brazil played a major part in refusing to proceed with the negotiations while results were not obtained in agriculture. These new stances have to be understood in the context of the fatigue with obstructive policies concerning the new issues, the change of course in economic policy, and the importance the new administration ascribed to improvement of relations with the United States in order to win support in the foreign debt negotiation.

In the course of the 1980s, Brazil was very active in the GATT consultations and panels, both as a complainant and as a defendant. In the former role, Brazil took part in the 1980 Brazilian-Spanish panel on the tariff treatment of unroasted coffee, the consultations held in 1982 on the EC sugar export refund system (Brazil was one of ten countries involved), the 1986 Brazilian-U.S. consultations on U.S. tariff on ethyl alcohol, the protracted dispute with the United States on CVDs on non-rubber footwear, and the 1988 consultations on the unfavorable impact of the U.S. Export Enhancement Program on Brazilian exports of soy bean oil. In the latter role, Brazil faced a 1983 complaint by the United States on a violation of the subsidies code in relation to poultry exports, aborted consultations with the United States on restrictions on microelectronic products in 1987, and a 1989 U.S. complaint on the Brazilian quantitative import control regulations.[19]

By far the most significant issue of bilateral interest discussed in GATT in the 1980s was the retaliatory action taken by the United States in 1988 by imposing tariffs of 100 percent on selected Brazilian paper, pharmaceutical, and electronic products as the result of a complaint on the protection provided by intellectual property legislation on pharmaceutical products. Brazil asked for the establishment of a panel to consider the questions of principle involved. The United States was slow to respond, but the panel was eventually established in early 1990. There was no agreement on its terms of reference, the United States insisting that the substantive Brazilian legislation should be examined and Brazil centering its case on the conflict between the U.S. action and GATT rights and obligations. Terms of reference limited the panel to the examination of compatibility of the action with the GATT. The U.S. faced criticism for failing to try to settle the dispute using GATT machinery. The conflict was eventually solved bilaterally: retaliatory tariffs were withdrawn following Brazilian assurances on changes in the relevant intellectual property legislation. These changes were still being discussed in the Brazilian congress in mid-1992.

Attempts to establish more cordial relations with the U.S. did not prevent a flare-up of an old dispute on CVDs on nonrubber footwear exports. With support of other contracting parties, Brazil blocked the adoption of the panel's report in favor of the United States.

TRADE AND DEBT VULNERABILITY

Balance-of-payments provisions have traditionally played a major role in GATT from the point of view of many developing countries and certainly also in the case of Brazil. Article 18b provided a sound legal basis for effectively closing domestic markets to imports. Barriers that would be better justified by pointing to infant industry or national security were presented as necessary because of balance-of-payments difficulties, it was easier successfully to invoke Article 18b than other GATT articles.

Indebted countries had originally hoped that their need to generate trade surpluses would lead creditor countries to improve access for their exports in developed markets. But in spite of the pious words of the 1985 Leutwiler Report that "the health and even maintenance of the trading system are linked to a satisfactory resolution of the debt problem" (GATT, 1985, 49–50), there is no sign that the trade-debt link has had any concrete implications for MTNs. In fact, not only did commercial banks abstain from lobbying to improve market access of debtor countries, but they turned initial ideas about the trade-debt link upside down, backing the U.S. insistence in obtaining right of establishment for services industries in developing countries. Deterioration of the balance of payments, moreover, meant increased vulnerability in relation to conditionalities imposed by international financial agencies; the IMF and World Bank have pressed foreign-exchange-starved debtors to adopt unilateral trade liberalization as part of a deregulation/liberalization package.[20]

An important trade-debt complication is the contradiction between GATT's traditional basis of reciprocal negotiation and unilateral liberalization as a result of conditionalities imposed by multilateral financial agencies. To the extent that there is no equivalent pressure on other GATT contracting parties to reform their trade policies unilaterally, a perverse asymmetry is created that penalizes developing countries—in particular, indebted countries. (Supposing that at least in relation to certain issues, some developing countries or coalitions of developing countries are not "small" from a technical viewpoint.) Given that these tariff reductions are unlikely to be taken into account as concessions—since they are not bound—and given that financial vulnerability will in any case assure that they are permanent—even if not bound—it would make sense to bind them and try to extract counterconcessions as soon as possible.[21]

Trade policy conditionalities were included rather loosely in the letters of intent to the IMF that Brazilian authorities signed during the 1980s. Initially vague commitments in early 1983 to reduce quantitative restrictions "after the economy adjusts" were followed by commitments in 1983–1988 to substitute tariffs for import licenses, to reduce controls on imports of agricultural commodities, to reduce tariff levels, and to reduce certain types of quantitative restrictions.[22] Similarly, the Brazilian government was reluctant to agree with World Bank proposals to eliminate NTBs (in particular, licensing or prohibition of imports), reduce tariffs, eliminate export incentives, and devalue the exchange rate to the extent proposed (World Bank, 1989). Since the mid-1980s modest trade reform has curtailed the more lavish export-promotion schemes and has undertaken import liberalization through a cut in tariffs and the number of items subject to licensing and prohibition. This reform was partly a result of trade conditionalities that were included in agricultural-sector and "export development" World Bank loans and partly due to IMF conditionalities. But negotiations on a full-fledged trade reform loan remained deadlocked.

Differing views on liberalization policies tend to concentrate on timing and the sectoral distribution of the consequences of liberalizing rather than on its inherent validity. The sequencing of policies acquires critical importance in the context of stabilization programs designed to control high inflation. The crucial question is whether the simultaneous adoption of trade reform, foreign exchange devaluation, and tighter fiscal and monetary policies is to be preferred to a sequencing of reforms that would improve their chances of success.

Those in favor of a shock as opposed to a more gradual approach (for instance, Rodrik, 1990; World Bank, 1989) emphasize the credibility argument: with immediate commitment to reform, economic agents are more likely to believe that the reforms will be sustained. Political costs of implementing reform over a longer term are also thought to be higher, as economic agents tend to use breathing space to preserve their privileged positions.

The gradual approach suggests, more convincingly, a stabilization strategy in which fiscal adjustment policies should precede other policies such as foreign exchange devaluation and trade liberalization and underlines the need for new foreign finance as the exchange rate is targeted on inflation and not on external balance (Sachs, 1987). The experience of Latin American countries would suggest that those proposing a shock approach tend to underestimate the difficulties inherent in the formulation of a comprehensive reform package with adequate timing and, more importantly, that while there could in principle be some merit in a shock strategy, this is less likely to be the case when previous shocks have already affected expectations of economic agents.

There is no crude trade-off between increased imports prompted by liberalization and the level of payments entailed by debt settlements, since exports would also increase. It is clear, however, that trade liberalization in developing countries without a corresponding liberalization by developed countries requires bigger devaluations than would be required by a concerted move to reduce protection in developing and developed countries, as exports are to some extent constrained by barriers in developed countries. This link further strengthens the argument for multilateral rather than unilateral liberalization. Alternatively, the reduction in trade surpluses can be compensated by large transitory financial facilities to support liberalization.

TOWARD TRADE LIBERALIZATION

Brazilian economic diplomacy in multilateral trade fora has traditionally been a direct responsibility of the Ministry of Foreign Affairs. Policy formulation has basically been the task of the Ministry of Finance, which to a large extent acted as an interface with the private sector. Until the 1980s, Brazilian interests were classically concentrated on obtaining access for commodity exports and protecting the domestic market for manufactures from foreign competition. These interests were shared with the bulk of developing countries and explain the developing-country coalition of the 1960s in UNCTAD, especially in relation to the adoption of a GSP. Export diversification and fast growth since the early 1960s made Brazilian concrete interests in the global trading system more complex; questions such as market access for exports of manufactures and, to a lesser extent, some of the new themes, especially services and intellectual property, became part of the relevant agenda in the 1980s. Because import substitution nevertheless remained a pillar of trade policy, Brazil played as if the interests of developing countries had not significantly diversified in the 1970s and, particularly, in the 1980s. Negotiating stances in the GATT until the late 1980s tended on the one hand to stress the desirability of dealing with the backlog of themes, in relation to which developing countries had special interests, and on the other hand to be defensive or even obstructionist in relation to initiatives that would have resulted in opening up the domestic market to foreign competition.

Until the mid-1960s domestic lobbies with trade interests included commodity exporters, mainly interested in exchange rate policy, as well as domestic producers of manufactured goods (both domestic and foreign firms) interested in a high level of protection affecting competitive imports and access to cheap imported inputs and capital goods. As the export structure diversified, the domestic industrial sector became increasingly concerned with export promotion through access to fiscal and credit incentives. Concern with foreign exchange policies ceased to be restricted to commodity producers as the export lobby diversified. Commodity producers as well as producers of temperate agricultural products tried to maximize their extraction of subsidized credit from the government and, in the latter case, also lobbied for import substitution. The private sector fully appropriated rents related to export quotas both because of domestically imposed export restrictions and the imposition of restraints in foreign markets—notably, the case of textiles and clothing quotas under the MFA and steel exports regulated by VERs.[23]

With its combination of export promotion and import substitution, Brazilian foreign economic policy in the 1980s was built on the assumption that a relatively large politically relevant, and rapidly growing developing country could effectively exchange trade concessions with the major developed blocs. The Brazilian position cannot be analyzed in the same perspective as, say, the case of Chile, a small economy with a comparatively unsatisfactory growth record after having pursued an import-substitution strategy that its limited domestic market could not sustain.[24] Brazil's long history of successful import substitution was also a powerful factor in its reluctance to adopt liberalizing packages in the 1980s (as opposed, for instance, to the stand of Argentina and Mexico; see Chapters 4 and 6). But it is not particularly helpful merely to use hindsight to examine the shortcomings of past Brazilian policy. Instead, we turn to an analysis of Brazil's current situation.

Since March 1990, with the beginning of a new presidential term of office, Brazil has reversed its economic policy and undertaken a stabilization plan. An initially hesitant withdrawal of import prohibitions was followed by tariff reductions on a wide range of products, in particular textiles and agricultural inputs and capital goods. Decisionmakers whose primary target was stabilization focused on the possible role of expanded imports in dampening domestic price increases. They also expected trade policy changes to help persuade the U.S. government to support Brazil in debt negotiations. Strictly industrial or trade policy considerations receded to a secondary position among arguments favoring trade liberalization. World Bank conditionalities had no major direct influence on these decisions, which were among a massive—though not necessarily coherent or comprehensive—effort to deregulate the economy and reduce the role of the state as a producer of goods and services. A significant additional import liberalization program to reduce the modal and average tariffs to 20 percent and 14.2 percent, respectively, in 1994 (as compared to 40 percent and 32.2 percent in 1990) was introduced in early 1991.[25]

The Brazilian stabilization program does not fit either the shock or the gradual reform typology. The major difficulties faced on trade policy involved the overvaluation of the exchange rate and its impact on the trade balance. Hopes that imports would contribute to lower domestic prices were rapidly disappointed with the introduction of automatic import licensing, which—by initially restricting the access of economic agents to a list of approved firms—only transferred rents from import-substitution to import-trade activities. Access by final importers was subsequently allowed, but markups show downward rigidity. Import volumes have not increased significantly because of severe recession.

An extremely powerful new Ministry of the Economy in principle concentrated much of the decisionmaking in the trade area. A Department of Foreign Trade was made responsible for tariff reform—theoretically in coordination with industrial policy—and for implementation of trade policy. Actual decisionmaking, though, seems to be rather fragmentary, and lines of command are hazy. While on paper there was further weakening of the influence of the Ministry of Foreign Affairs, the secondary position of trade relations in the priorities of decisionmakers in the economic departments contributed to maintaining the authority of Foreign Affairs. More recently, diplomats have widened the scope of their influence by occupying key positions in the economic decisionmaking agencies.

Initially, as mentioned above, there was a visible improvement in the rather tense bilateral relations with the United States, as trade policies that had long been promoted either directly by U.S. authorities or indirectly through the efforts of the IMF and the World Bank were finally adopted. It is not surprising that Brazil should seek to improve its position in debt negotiations even at the expense of some traditional objectives of trade policy, insofar as debt service is substantial in relation to prospective trade liberalization "gains."[26] Despite the more cooperative attitude of U.S. authorities, as well as of the IMF, Brazil still feels that its good behavior has gone unrewarded. Trade policy accommodation may have countered U.S. retaliatory threats, but that is meager compensation.

The most recent and significant U.S. minilateral initiative, even if sustained, will probably not provide substantial relief for a country such as Brazil, at least in a midterm perspective. In June 1990 President Bush launched the EAI, which contained proposals on trade, foreign investment, and foreign debt. The trade proposals seem to offer Brazil more than those on investment and debt. The $500 million to be contributed to the Interamerican Development Bank over five years to foster investment is unlikely to make much impact if there is no change in macroeconomic conditions in Brazil. Nor is the reduction in debt service likely to provide much relief in the case of Brazil: the Overseas Development Council suggested only $286.9 million of debt service over 1991–1994. It is difficult to see Japan, and especially the EC, enthusiastically providing additional funds to a project that is clearly meant to counterbalance their initiatives in the respective areas of main economic influence (see Chapters 2 and 3).

In the commercial field, the EAI considers the creation in the long term of an FTA to liberalize the trade of the associated countries. As a transitory step the U.S. would negotiate framework agreements. An FTA would be an interesting opportunity for Mexico, the bulk of whose trade is with the United States (see Chapter 4) or for Chile, whose tariffs are already low. For Brazil, because of its higher tariff and the importance of non-U.S. trade, joining an FTA would have costs similar to a nondiscriminatory unilateral liberalization, since the United States is a potential supplier of the bulk of imports and export benefits are restricted to the U.S. market. A major obstacle to success is that the United States is unlikely to include in its offers a significant reduction of NTBs in those sensitive sectors in which Brazilian interest is concentrated. In principle there would be certain advantages for Brazil in negotiating a framework agreement with the United States jointly with other Latin American countries, for which the project of a common market in the Southern Cone must effectively materialize (Fritsch, 1990). There are, however, important obstacles, in particular the conflict of interests on the desired level of the common tariff between Brazil and the more open and smaller economies. Brazil's basic trade interests seem to lie in multilateral liberalization rather than in any trade bloc formation.

Trade liberalization has partly subverted the previous equilibrium in the size and distribution of trade-related rents. Other likely developments, such as a foreign debt settlement, additional sales of public assets, and further trade liberalization (including services), should also affect a new distributive equilibrium. The widespread expectation of gains has allowed reforms to advance, albeit somewhat slowly and with a far from comprehensive scope. But as liberalization proceeds, political stumbling blocks are likely to become harder to surmount, with losers facing increasing (real and perceived) difficulties to adjust to new conditions.

Debt negotiations remain crucial; together with a deep fiscal adjustment, they could provide a significant basis for lasting stabilization in a context marked by continuous progress in trade liberalization and other structural reforms. Yet as political constraints continue to menace, the obstacles in the path of such an adjustment loom large.

NOTES

The author thanks Leane Naidin, Alexandre Parola, and Guida Piani for the information they provided; Adriana Barbosa for research assistance, as well as participants in the project for their comments. The usual caveats apply.

1. A full treatment of Brazilian economic policy in the 1980s appears in Carneiro and Modiano, 1990, and Modiano, 1990.

2. Subsidies and exemptions (fiscal and credit) declined from 28.8 percent of the value of exports in 1979 to 3.9 percent in 1980 then rose back to almost 30 percent and fell rapidly to around 5 percent in the mid-1980s. See Baumann and Moreira, 1987.

3. The U.S. share rose to almost 30 percent of total exports in the mid-1980s but in 1989 was down to 23.3 percent in comparison to an EC share of 28.9 percent. The combined share of the Middle East and Africa and the Latin American Integration Association (LAIA), which reached more than 26 percent in 1982, fell to around 17 percent at the end of the 1980s. The United States was, however, absorbing 35 percent of manufactured exports as compared to 21.5 percent by the EC and 23.2 percent by the new markets. These new markets had bought more than 40 percent of Brazil's manufactured exports in the late 1970s.

4. Abreu and Fritsch, 1989, also presents a discussion of obstacles to Brazilian exports in relation to graduation from GSP, tariff escalation, agricultural products, textiles and clothing, as well as CVDs, ADDs, and VERs.

5. GATT, 1986, data provided by Brazilian government and GATT, 1990. The argument that countries that dump and subsidize more should suffer more actions fails, of course, to cope with the misuse of ADDs and CVDs to unfairly dissuade new suppliers (who are more competitive) from entering the markets of developed countries.

6. UNCTAD database, inventory on non-tariff measures, IPEA/CEPAL, 1985a and 1985b; as well as data supplied by CTT/Brazilian government.

7. For a detailed account of Brazilian experience in the GATT, see Abreu, 1991.

8. See Dam, 1970, 368–370. See also Hudec, 1987, 222; and GATT, 1966, 18.

9. This contrasts with the experience of other Latin American countries, notably Argentina but also Chile and Mexico. Brazilian GDP per capita in 1913 stood at 10 percent of the level of Argentina's, 30 percent of Chile's, and 40 percent of Mexico's. In 1989 Brazilian GDP per capita was considerably above the level of these other countries.

10. Import liberalization was an important element of the policy package introduced in the mid-1960s, but for reasons not entirely clear, the move toward tariff reduction in 1967 was reversed at the end of 1968. See Coes, 1991.

11. See also de Lima, 1986, 338ff. For similar debt-related vulnerabilities, see Chapter 6 in this volume.

12. See Chapter 11 on the coalitional behavior of developing countries since the 1960s.

13. Frictions between the United States and the EC included U.S. dissatisfaction with the EC's vague support of the G10 in exchange for a softening of commitments on agricultural liberalization. EC support of the consensus rule and of the two-track compromise is consistent with such understandings.

14. See Chapter 1 for an account of global bargaining.

15. For a detailed discussion of Brazil's concrete interests in the several negotiating groups, see Abreu and Fritsch, 1989. For an overall assessment of the interests of developing countries in the negotiations, see Abreu, 1989.

16. See Chapter 10 on the role played by the Cairns Group since 1985.

17. Abreu and Fritsch, 1989, provides rough estimates of the impact that a liberalization of protectionism in the developed countries would have on Brazilian trade of main temperate food commodities, More recent estimates by Anderson and Tyers, 1990, suggest that both Brazilian welfare and the balance of trade would gain from liberalization in the developed countries and from removal of all food price distortions in all countries.

18. Very rough estimates of impact of VERs on exports can be found in Abreu and Fritsch, 1989.

19. See GATT, *GATT Activities,* several issues.

20. Historically, the trade-debt link tended to be made explicit by the use of trade-bargaining power, defined on the basis of the size of the trade balance, to establish a preferential position for debt repayment of certain loans. Abreu, 1984 compares British use of such links in Argentina in the 1930s to the U.S. self-discipline in Brazil imposed by its strategic aim of reinforcing the multilateral trade system after 1934.

21. Whether developing countries will have the bargaining power to make sure that these tariff reductions are taken into account by developed countries is open to question.

22. For the successive Brazilian letters of intent and memoranda of understanding, see Central Bank of Brazil, *Brazil Economic Program: Internal and External Adjustment,* several issues.

23. For a similar process, see the case of Argentina as outlined in Chapter 6.

24. In 1990 Chile's GDP was equivalent to 7 percent of the Brazilian GDP. It is of course true that the Brazilian economy is more closed than the Chilean, but, the rising importance of investment as opposed to purely trade issues tends to weaken this classic qualification.

25. It is, however, important to stress that NTBs, such as minimum national content requirements to qualify for long-term credit, remained significant (see Fritsch and Franco, 1992). These NTBs are likely to be of special relevance to block imports of electronic products.

26. Potential gains generated by trade liberalization would be on the order of $4 billion additional Brazilian exports yearly (see Laird and Nogués 1989, 255). The present value of the Brazilian commercial foreign debt is much lower than the nominal value outstanding; interest payments, if accordingly adjusted, are likely to be at least of the same magnitude as liberalization export "gains."

8

The Walk Away
from Leadership: India

RAJIV KUMAR

India has been one of the most protected and regulated developing economies.[1] Since June 1991, when a new government took office, a series of wide-ranging and in some cases intensive reforms have been announced and implemented. These unprecedented reforms have sought to correct the many distortions that had come to characterize Indian economic policy.[2] India has also started to borrow heavily from the IMF, contracting not only under the lower, or first-credit, tranche, where conditionalities are limited, but also under the upper credit tranche and the oil facility. The country also undertook a SAL from the World Bank. In a parallel move, India has quite perceptibly changed its position in the Uruguay Round of MTNs. From what many contracting parties perceived as a confrontationist stance,[3] India has switched to a lower profile and a more constructive role. In keeping with this changed stance, the new government indicated its willingness to accept the Dunkel Draft as a basis for further negotiations toward reaching a conclusion of the round.

This chapter analyzes the determinants of policy reforms in India and their reflection on trade bargaining. These changes, whose early beginnings could be seen in the mid-1980s, were actually concentrated during 1991. In examining these determinants, this chapter attempts to answer the question whether these policy changes were entirely or even predominantly a result of external pressures, either multilateral or bilateral. I argue that these external pressures served the vital role of providing the necessary push and an identifiable exogenous reason for the government to undertake these reforms. Yet the reform package has been largely if not exclusively a result of indigenous initiatives both within and outside the government, as reflected in the incremental nature of these reforms. The immediate "real" cause was the emergence of the severe and unprecedented pressure on the balance of payments in April–May 1991, which brought India dangerously close to a default on its commitments for servicing its external debt.

In the last four decades (that is, until the end of the 1980s), India pursued development strategy perceptibly opposed to that followed by a number of successful Asian NICs. Although coupled with a leadership role in MTNs, the strategy could not enable the country to meet its self-specified development objectives. By the end of the 1980s, India suffered from severe macroeconomic imbalances. Vulnerability on the balance of payments precipitated a crisis of near bankruptcy and a severe resource crunch during April–June 1991. These crises reinforced the need to adopt the structural reforms endorsed by the multilateral financial institutions, who stepped in with nearly $3 billion in short-term and fast-disbursing credits to tide India over the crisis. Negotiating stances vis-à-vis the IMF and the World Bank as well as in the other multilateral fora, like the GATT, were changed to correspond more closely to the new set of domestic policy perceptions and imperatives.

This chapter is divided into four sections. The next provides a brief historical review of economic trends since independence in order to explain the nature and magnitude of macroimbalances that emerged during the 1980s and necessitated a change in policies despite a good growth record. The second section then reviews the evolution of trade and industrial policies, focusing on the reforms undertaken since mid-1991. The subsequent section relates the evolution of domestic trade and industrial policies to the position in external negotiations within the GATT and vis-à-vis the IMF and the World Bank. The last section offers conclusions and discusses future prospects. Negotiating positions may no longer be determined by considerations of leadership.

ECONOMIC PERFORMANCE

Economic performance during the first three decades after independence was mixed. The country did indeed manage to raise its savings rate from 10.2 percent in 1951 to 22.7 percent in 1980/81, but this could be translated into an annual rate of growth of only 3.8 percent between 1950/51 to 1979/80. This low growth rate was a result of the high capital output ratio, which was in turn due to high costs and inefficiencies in the industrial sector. A low rate of secular growth in GDP, combined with a population growth of 2.3 percent, yielded a per capita income growth rate of 1.5 percent per annum—not enough to tackle the problem of absolute poverty. Nearly half of India's population continued to exist below absolute poverty levels at the beginning of the 1980s.

India was able to establish one of the most diversified industrial structures anywhere in the developing world. Yet the majority of its industries were high cost and technologically backward. An average industrial growth rate of 5.2 percent over the three decades was insufficient to increase the share of the industrial sector in GDP.[4] The objective of food self-sufficiency was achieved by the mid-1980s.[5] Agriculture has, however, continued to remain dependent on monsoon behavior, and increases in productivity and yields have tended to plateau in recent years. This led to the reemergence of the agricultural constraint in 1990.

The export structure did change, and by the end of the 1970s, 75 percent of exports were sourced from the manufacturing sector. The share of foreign trade in the GDP, however, remained almost unchanged since independence. Worse still, India's share of exports in world exports declined throughout this period and dropped to a mere 0.48 percent in 1980 from about 2.5 percent in 1947. India, therefore, did not benefit from the sustained boom in global trade during the postwar decades.

By the end of the 1970s, it was clear that the development paradigm had failed to achieve either the growth or equity objectives. The economy became increasingly insulated from the rest of the world, and the objective of self-reliance came to be interpreted as self-sufficiency in physical terms.

The 1980s

During the 1980s, the Indian economy apparently broke through the low-growth syndrome in which it had been trapped for the previous three decades. India's GNP, as measured at factor cost, grew at a rate of 5.6 percent annually over the decade.[6] This higher rate of growth yielded an unprecedented rise of nearly 3 percent in per capita incomes per annum. To a large extent the improvement was a result of the sustained growth in industrial output, which increased at 7.71 percent during the 1980s and the beginning of 1990. Value-added in the manufacturing sector grew at 9.42 percent during this time, discounting all arguments that attributed the higher industrial growth to a surge in imports of components and semifinished products. The growth of the services sector was slightly lower than that of manufacturing, and the share of industry and services in national output remained unchanged throughout the decade.

The impressive performance of the industrial sector disguised some structural weaknesses. There was, first, a heavy bias in favor of chemicals and petrochemicals, with as much as 52.7 percent of investment flowing into this sector between 1982 and 1988. In contrast, metal-based industries and the machinery sector, where the country possesses both a natural and dynamic comparative advantage, received only 25.1 percent of the investment. The regional imbalance in the industrial structure was aggravated as the western part of the country pulled further away. Employment in the organized industrial sector stagnated, contributing to the sociopolitical instability experienced during the 1980s. Finally, higher growth could not reverse the decline of India's shares in global exports. Moreover, the share of exports in manufacturing output dropped further during the 1980s.

Yet the improved economic and industrial performance of the 1980s led to a weakened negotiating position, especially vis-à-vis the IMF and the World Bank, because of the emergence of some severe macroeconomic imbalances. The first such imbalance was represented by the inexorable increase in government budget deficits during the decade. Deficits in revenue accounts rose from 1.5 percent in 1980/81 to 2.7 percent of GDP in 1988/89 and further to 3.3 percent in 1990/91. The fiscal deficit, which reflected the overall financial position of the central government, increased from 6.2 percent of GDP in 1975/76 to 8.2 percent in 1990/91. These burgeoning deficits represented a breakdown in the financial discipline of the government and a dominance of populist policies.

The second macroimbalance came in the form of a sharp increase in foreign commercial debt. By the end of the 1970s, India's external commercial debt was $15 billion, amounting to a debt service ratio of less than 15 percent. The ratio went up to 18 percent in 1980/81 and 38 percent in 1987/88 and came down slightly to 34 percent in 1988/89. The volume of debt rose to $22 billion in 1980/81, then to $53 billion in 1988/89 and is currently estimated to be $78 billion. This represents a more than 500 percent increase in twelve years; including the debt from the erstwhile Soviet Union would push up the volume of total external debt to almost $100 billion. Suddenly, within the matter of less than a decade, India had been transformed from one of the credit-worthiest economies to a highly indebted country.

The Payments Crises of 1990/91

Macroimbalances led to a sudden loss of foreign exchange reserves in September 1990 on account of a sharp increase in imports of oil and refined products. From an average of $287 million per month in June–August 1990, these imports rose sharply to $671 million in the following six months because of the rise in prices upon Iraq's invasion of Kuwait and the need to contract large supplies through spot purchases to prevent shortages. Moreover, the years 1989 and 1990 had witnessed severe political instability in the country, with a hung parliament and a minority government in power. Political uncertainty and the sharp deterioration in the balance of trade in the second half of 1990 led to a net outflow from foreign currency deposits held by nonresident Indians.

This increase in imports and run on deposits was combined with the adverse effects of the Gulf War in the beginning of 1991. There was a mass return of Indian workers from Kuwait and a cessation of remittances not only from Kuwait and Iraq but also from other west Asian countries. The loss of exports to these markets is estimated to be about $280 million, and the total impact of the Gulf War is conservatively estimated at about $2 billion on India's external account.

The political events of 1990–1991—especially the government's inability to present its annual budget, which was expected to include a series of stringent measures to curb the loss of foreign exchange reserves —resulted in a complete loss of external confidence and a drying up of short-term credits by February 1991. Credits available at 0.25 percent above the London Inter-Bank Offered Rate (LIBOR) until November 1990 had to be contracted at 0.65 percent above LIBOR by March 1991. The cost went up to 1.25 percent above LIBOR in May that year. Thereafter, the cost was much higher, and credits were often unavailable as credit-rating agencies withdrew their ratings for India. The outflow of nonresident deposits, which also reflected the loss of confidence, went up to as much as $952 million during April–June 1991.[7]

Consequently, India had to pledge its gold reserves to meet debt-servicing and import requirements. The loss of reserves continued despite this and several other measures the government took to drastically curb imports of even essential commodities. As is usual in such circumstances, the balance-of-payment difficulties had been converted into a full-blown crisis of confidence by May 1991. For the first time in history, a default on payments had become a serious possibility by June 1991 (Government of India, 1992).

The unique conjunction of increasing balance-of-trade deficits, governmental financial profligacy and breakdown of financial discipline, sharp increase in external debts, an environment of extreme political instability and uncertainty, and adverse international events like the Gulf War precipitated a financial and payments crisis in May–June 1991. Yet the fundamental cause of the crisis lay in the uncompetitive economic structures that had evolved over the previous four decades. While taking steps to avert the immediate bankruptcy crisis, the government launched a program of structural trade and industrial policy reforms to address its fundamental cause. Although these reforms have been sequential and somewhat incremental, their overall coverage and scope mark a turning point in Indian history.

REFORM OF TRADE AND INDUSTRIAL POLICIES

India's development strategy since independence in 1947 has been cited as a classical example of an import-substituting regime that fostered a broad-based and diversified industrial structure. Domestic industries were almost completely insulated from global competition with the use of high tariff protection and a panoply of QRs. Indian planners adopted this policy regime soon after independence with full recognition of the dangers of overprotection.[8] This period of disengagement was to be utilized for the development of basic and capital goods industries. A competitive capital goods sector, policymakers thought, would ensure control over flows of trade and commerce. The structure of exports could be diversified on the basis of industrial growth. Foreign trade, however, was expected to play only a residual role in the growth strategy, as the domestic economy was sufficiently large to generate economies of scale in a majority of industrial sectors.

Capital formation depended on domestic savings. India was consistently able to finance as much as 96 percent of its investment requirements from domestically generated savings. Financial prudence, both on internal and external accounts, was accepted as one of the fundamental principles. In the latter half of the 1960s, following India's harrowing experiences with droughts and consequent food shortages that led to total dependence on food grain imports from the United States, India also made food security and self-sufficiency national development objectives. Agricultural investments were then assigned the highest priority.

During the 1980s India pursued a credit-driven demand expansion strategy to push up its rate of growth. This was successful inasmuch as the highest rate of growth for a sustained period since independence was achieved. This growth was, however, unsustainable because of the resource constraints. The continued high levels of protection to domestic industry and the distortions in the incentive structure premised upon effective tariff rates prevented the industry from becoming internationally competitive or increasing its share in global markets and generating a surplus on the balance of trade. This resource constraint was further intensified by the financial profligacy of the government, which allowed unsustainable revenue deficits to emerge annually. These revenue deficits were financed by both external and domestic debt, whose volumes rose inexorably during this decade. The basic policy framework continued during the 1980s with only some marginal changes. These included a decontrol of administered prices in some sectors and a reduction of the numbers of NTBs affecting imports. Measures were also put in place to improve the working of public-sector enterprises and provide them with greater autonomy.

There were many difficulties in dismantling the system of controls and regulation and in moving away from the policies of import substitution and physical balancing of input and outputs in the framework of central planning. The development paradigm, established after independence and in place until July 1991, represented a national consensus that had evolved during the national movement and the formative years of independence. Consequently, it continued to have widespread ideological appeal in the country.

Economic Reforms of 1991/92

The payment crisis of April–May 1991, which brought the country to the verge of bankruptcy, also provided the real and sufficient cause for initiating a process of structural reforms of the economy. The economic programs announced by almost all political parties at the time of the general elections in May 1991 admitted the need for such reforms. Public opinion, which had been gradually shifting away from the established paradigm, swung away decisively when the payment crisis broke out. This crisis, in terms of its magnitude and impact on public opinion, was comparable to the crises of food grain shortages of the late 1960s, providing the impetus for the turnaround.

The process of reform was initiated in July 1991. The reforms are to be undertaken sequentially and incrementally rather than implemented as a full-blown package of liberalization and stabilization. The size of the country and its social heterogeneity—and more so the uneven nature of regional economic development—necessitate such a measured approach.[9] There is also a political tradition of attempting large-scale change on the basis of broad-based consensus to the extent possible. Yet as the following brief description shows, the reforms, taken together, cover a wide scope and have been thoroughgoing, especially in the case of trade and industrial policies.

Macroeconomic Reforms

The government initiated a macroeconomic stabilization program within its first month in office. This included the devaluation of the currency by 21 percent in two stages and a further depreciation consequent upon the introduction of Export-Import Bank scrips and later the dual exchange rate in February 1992. The fiscal deficit was brought in check and the rising trend reversed in the first budget presented by the administration. A commitment to reduce both the overall fiscal deficit and the monetized revenue deficit was announced. Required budgetary measures, including reduction in subsidies and other government expenditures, were adopted in the two budgets presented so far. The fiscal deficit must be cut to 5 percent of the GDP within a year from the high level of 8.3 percent in 1990/91. The growth of money supply and the level of net credit by the central bank to the government are to be brought down within specified targets. The stabilization program has provided the overall context in which structural reform has been undertaken.

Trade Reforms

The trade policy regime as it existed prior to the reforms was complex (Kelkar, Kumar, and Nangia, 1990). The reforms aimed to (1) eliminate

NTBs affecting imports and exports, (2) simplify and broad-base the incentive structure for exports and thereby eliminate subsidies for exports, (3) eliminate existing monopoly rights conferred on public-sector enterprises for imports of bulk commodities, (4) lower the level and reduce the dispersion of tariffs on imports, and (5) move toward making the rupee convertible initially for trade transactions and shortly after to make it fully convertible, including the investment account.

The rupee has thus far been made partly convertible. Sixty percent of foreign exchange earnings, either from export of goods or services or invisibles such as remittances and tourism receipts, can be converted into domestic currency at the prevailing market rate. This represents in effect a dual exchange rate, with a tax equal to the difference in the market and official exchange rate being levied on 40 percent of foreign exchange inflows (except those received on official account). This is a transitory stage; full convertibility on the trade account is to be introduced as the economy is able to absorb an increase in the price of petroleum products and fiscal balances are restored so as to make enough budgetary resources available for official imports. Convertibility, even if partial, has ensured that the exchange rate for the rupee will not be overvalued in the future. In the first half of the 1980s overevaluation was the single most important disincentive for exports.

The dual exchange rate has improved incentives for exports, especially in products for which import content is not unduly high. The system has certainly simplified the structure of incentives and enabled the government to eliminate the plethora of industry-specific incentives and export subsidies that had come to exist over the years. Some of the export restrictions have already been done away with, and those that remain on the restricted list relate either to ecologically sensitive products or agro-products affected by overriding considerations of maintaining adequate domestic supplies.

QRs on imports have been virtually eliminated. The previous twenty-six import-licensing lists have been replaced by a short negative list that is largely confined to finished consumer goods. Monopoly import rights have been eliminated except in the case of eight products—which, however, do include the major imports such as oil, petroleum products, fertilizers, and so on. Actual user conditions have also been removed so that open trade activity in imports can now exist, perhaps for the first time.

Tariff rates have been lowered significantly for capital goods and raw materials. Ceiling rates were brought down in two stages to 150 and then to 110 percent in February 1992, reducing dispersion. Given that more than 40 percent of total customs revenues were earlier derived from imports with an import duty rate of above 110 percent, the reduction in ceilings has brought down the average tariff rates substantially. Yet significant ground still remains to be covered, in particular in simplifying custom procedures and lowering tariffs to levels comparable to those of other developing countries (see Chapters 4–6).

Trade policy reforms have also resolved some of the more specific and microconstraints that hampered exports. The advance licensing system has been modified to improve exporters' access to duty-free imports; exporters have been permitted to retain a part of their export earnings and maintain foreign currency accounts. Overall, the reforms have, in a matter of nine months, transformed the foreign trade regime and environment in the country.

The reforms have been undertaken during a time of widespread recessionary conditions in India's major markets, including the United States, Japan, and the former Soviet Union. Exports to the erstwhile Soviet Union went down by as much as 50 percent as markets suddenly collapsed. These exports were once covered by the bilateral payments arrangements, which have become inoperative. Export performance since the start of 1991 has consequently been unimpressive. While exports to convertible currency markets have grown by 6.5 percent, the overall volume has stagnated. Such lags are expected until the impact of the improved export profitability is felt.

Industrial Policy Reforms

In the industrial sector as well, one of the most complex and cumbersome systems of controls and regulations had evolved. During the 1980s, some measures were undertaken to relax regulations on capacity expansion and allow changes to the product mix within a broadly specified group. Yet elaborate controls on technology imports, capacity creation in new units, location of plants, and foreign collaborations remained unchanged. Moreover, a large number of sectors were reserved for exclusive operation of public-sector or small-scale enterprises. The larger companies, the so-called monopoly houses, faced an even more stringent set of controls and regulatory mechanisms. In effect, therefore, government clearances were required for almost any activity a firm undertook. An attempt to implement a new industrial policy was aborted in 1990 when disagreements emerged within the ruling coalition and could not be resolved before the government fell.

The objectives of the industrial policy reforms undertaken since July 1991 have been (1) to eliminate entry barriers both for all classes of domestic firms and for foreign investment; (2) to relax the government controls on technology imports, which—on grounds of self-reliance—had become retrogressive; (3) to reduce the number of sectors reserved for public-sector operations so as to provide greater areas for private capital; (4) to encourage inflows of direct foreign investment; (5) to remove constraints on large companies to expand capacities and diversify into other sectors; and (6) to lower exit barriers essentially by tackling the problem of labor redeployment and improving the conditions under which assets can be divested by firms that are unable to carry on business.

Most of these objectives were achieved swiftly. Most of the entry barriers, including those for large companies, have been eliminated. Licensing has been abolished for all except eighteen sectors.[10] Reservations for public-sector operations have been drastically reduced and are now limited to eight industries for security reasons. The monopolies and restrictive trade practices act has been amended to eliminate the need for large companies to seek permission for capacity expansion or diversification. Large companies are now allowed to hold up to 24 percent equity in small-scale enterprises.

Steps to facilitate direct foreign investment include the raising of the ceiling on equity participation from 40 to 51 percent and significant amendments to the foreign exchange regulation act so as to permit foreign companies to own real estate and establishments in the country. This law, which severely constrained foreign capital inflows, is being thoroughly overhauled. Automatic clearance mechanisms have been established for foreign investment proposals. The phased manufacturing program which required firms to undertake progressive indigenization of production has been discontinued. Technology imports have been liberalized, and government clearances are no longer required if the importer does not seek access to official reserves. For priority sectors, these imports are automatically cleared if the royalty rate is below 5 percent of domestic and 8 percent of export sales, and the lump sum payment is below 10 million rupees.

Industrial deregulation is intended to reduce the role of the government in directing industrial activity and even more so in actually undertaking production where the private sector can operate. The thrust for industrial policy reforms will now shift to improving public-sector performance; increasing the share of privately held equity capital in public-sector units and privatizing them completely where feasible; and putting into operation a broad-based social security network to facilitate corporate exit and labor redeployment.

The trade and industrial policy reforms have been accompanied by reforms in the financial sector that allow greater freedom to commercial banks but at the same time improve the operating norms. Both direct and indirect tax reform and a comprehensive review of government expenditure are well under way. The scope, coverage, and intensity of the reforms are unprecedented in the Indian context. Still the process is not complete, nor is it free from criticism. Some observers say these reforms have been far too gradual and incomplete. Others charge India with bowing down to IMF–World Bank pressure, compromising economic sovereignty; and adopting the ruinous path of market determined growth. In the next section we examine the extent to which these reforms have been undertaken as part of conditionality and the extent to which they have affected trade bargaining in the GATT.

INDIA'S EXPERIENCE OF TRADE BARGAINING

The Indian experience of multilateral trade bargaining and negotiating with the IMF and the World Bank is made up of three distinct phases. The first covered the period up to the beginning of the 1980s and prior to the launch of the Uruguay Round. The second stage began with the prelaunch negotiations for the Uruguay Round and extended to the end of the 1980s. The third phase of India's interaction with the IMF and the Bank and its role in the GATT began in the 1990s. Objectives and negotiating stances in each of these phases have been quite distinct since they were derived from qualitatively different conditions and policy concerns.

The first phase coincided with planned development since 1951. The country consciously chose to disengage its economy from that of the rest of the world. Paramount policy concerns were to establish a diversified industrial structure on the basis of import substitution and to achieve self-sufficiency in food supplies. During the period between 1951 until the end of the 1970s, India became an increasingly closed economy with reduced stakes in the global trading order. It strived for and achieved relative self-sufficiency in financial resources, derived, as some would argue, from a readiness to accept lower rates of growth in the economy. At the same time, in political terms, India had emerged undisputedly as one of leading countries in the developing world. Its size, the unique and historically exemplary nonviolent independence movement, and its acceptance of a genuine liberal democracy had provided it with a high level of political credibility and legitimacy both among developing and developed countries. Its status was consolidated by the leadership role it played in the nonaligned movement and the importance of this movement in the context of the Cold War.

During this phase India steadfastly upheld classical North-South positions differences in international economic negotiations. It became the major voice for developing-country interests and, along with Brazil and Yugoslavia, emerged as a key player in the developing-country coalitions like the G77. India contributed significantly to the working of the UNCTAD and the agreements the council reached on GSP; it also played a part in the GATT move to incorporate Part 4. The country's economic policies—and even more so its relative insulation from global markets—gave it autonomy to confront developed countries at times. Dependent neither on their markets nor on inflows to finance capital formation, India could, in economic terms, afford to take on the exalted negotiating role. Moreover, its political stature further reinforced its economic nonvulnerability, enabling it to play a leading South-oriented role in international trade negotiations.

The same set of economic and political factors also allowed it to bargain from a position of strength vis-à-vis the IMF and the World Bank. India's needs for concessional aid flows were apparently unquestionable. Its efforts to mobilize internal resources were also evident and actually commended by multilateral agencies, especially in the context of its low per capita incomes and poverty levels. The best example of India's resourcefulness was its ability to implement a series of tariff reductions and other measures to dilute the potentially contractionary effects of the devaluation in 1967, which had been undertaken as a result of pressure by the IMF. Again in the last years of the 1970s, India was successful in contracting a loan under the Extended Financial Facility of the IMF with light conditionalities. The measures already undertaken to marginally liberalize the trade regime and the price increase applied to petroleum products were considered sufficient to grant the loan. Further, India returned about 40 percent of the IMF credit unutilized.

The second phase of India's experience with MTNs, beginning about the mid-1980s, saw an emerging disjunction between the negotiating stance and domestic political and economic conditions. As mentioned in the previous section, the second half of the 1980s was characterized by improved economic performance accompanied by a sharp deterioration of macroeconomic balances and a sustained increase in external indebtedness. Moreover, this period was marked by unprecedented political uncertainty and loss of legitimacy of the state. The financial indiscipline and recourse to rampant populism eroded external confidence.[11]

Indian negotiators in the GATT, however, continued the tradition and sustained a leadership role.[12] India objected to the inclusion of services not so much because of its own competitive advantage as because of its aspiration to speak on behalf of developing countries. Opposition to inclusion of services was used primarily as a bargaining chip to ensure that issues of interest to developing countries remained on the table. India responded as a coalition player and as part of its objective of retaining the leadership role rather than acting on its own self-perceived or even attributable national concerns. This is especially true given India's marginal shares in global trade, the small share of foreign trade in its GDP, its negligible dependence on inflows of direct foreign investment and even concessional aid, and the predominantly import-substituting and regulatory policies it followed until the end of the 1980s.

During the course of the Uruguay Round, the developed countries and some of the developing countries perhaps discerned the dichotomy in holding a higher profile without the commensurate stake in global trade.

Moreover, India's political and economic weaknesses, particularly its increased vulnerability to foreign debt commitments, were emerging. Further, the United States and other developed countries were able to segregate India (and Brazil) from its peers. Consequently, India's position was effectively challenged in the prelaunch period. It is clear that Indian negotiators did not adjust to the new domestic conditions and did not acknowledge the changes in the international political climate that were rapidly eroding the advantages derived from maintaining a nonaligned stance between two rival economic formations, one of which was outside the GATT. Leadership of such a grouping could have been expected to yield far lower benefits and negotiating capital than it had done in the past. Because India failed to recognize these factors, it did not always go along with as large a group of developing countries as possible, even at the expense of compromising on some principled and crucial issues for developing countries.

India has since become aware of the need to bring its role in international trade negotiations in line with its changed domestic conditions and the new world order. This marks the beginning of the third phase in India's negotiating stance vis-à-vis the GATT and the IMF and World Bank. This latest phase is characterized by the onset of the payment crisis and the subsequent policy reforms. The country's top priority now is to set its own house in order. Policymakers finally see that India cannot hope to play the same leadership role among developing countries as in the past and that the benefits of such a role may not be commensurate with the costs. Moreover, other developing countries may not permit a domestically weak and internationally vulnerable India to take such leadership. Thus in MTNs India may be expected to pursue its own interests more vigorously and contribute to the negotiations in more constructive and yet less visible terms.

In negotiations with the IMF and the World Bank in 1992, India adopted a nonconfrontational stance. India has taken recourse to nearly $2.7 billion of exceptional financing from the IMF and the Bank together since the new regime entered office. This has helped it restore its foreign exchange reserves and rebuild confidence. There has already been a heated debate within parliament and outside on the country's acceptance of severe conditionalities from the IMF and the World Bank in order to secure credit from the upper tranche and under the SAL. Critics argue that national sovereignty has been compromised and that conditionalities represent a package of policies adverse to development objectives. Yet a number of Indian and non-Indian economists have advocated these policies; in general terms, a consensus had already begun to emerge around the time of the previous general elections. The IMF has drawn up the macroeconomic stabilization performance criteria it imposes under such loans, and the Bank has enumerated a number of trade and industrial policy reforms that are more microeconomic in their coverage. As expected, these have included the liberalization of the industrial and trade policy regimes. Most of the reforms the IMF and the Bank suggested had been announced by the government in advance of signing the agreements. To that extent economic independence and autonomy vis-à-vis the two financial institutions has so far been maintained.

THE PROSPECTS

The present government is committed to carrying on the process of macroeconomic stabilization and structural reforms. There are hardly any options left to overcome the payment crisis and establish a healthier current account position. Thus India's efforts to integrate its economy more fully and on a competitive basis with the world economy will continue with greater vigor. Its stakes in the preservation of the multilateral trading system are therefore likely to increase.

India's position in the multilateral trade negotiations will henceforth be more unambiguously inspired by clearly defined national interests. India thus may not take up positions on issues that do not directly concern it. In other cases, India's position may be expected to change as its interests change; for example, regarding foreign investment and services, India now wishes to pursue more aggressive and outward-looking policies.

Negotiators will certainly resist the bilateralization of essentially multilateral issues, such as TRIPs and TRIMs. These have been increasingly brought into the bilateral framework by the United States (see Chapter 3), a move Indian policymakers see as unfortunate. Yet India's sheer size and its international legitimacy and standing as the largest democratic polity will provide it with a degree of negotiating capital and freedom. Thus India can be expected to play a role commensurate with its economic size and position in the international order and one that can contribute to the achievement of its developmental objectives. It is to be hoped that there will be more direct and visible links between Indian positions in international trade negotiations and the country's own self-defined interests rather than the requirements of leadership. Indian negotiators should endeavor to reconcile the two while preserving the dominance of the former. This goal *can* be achieved.

NOTES

This chapter has benefited greatly from the comments of project participants, especially those of Diana Tussie and John Odell. The remaining weaknesses and errors are entirely mine. The views expressed here are strictly personal and do not necessarily represent that of the organization in which I am currently employed.

1. Even after the wide-ranging and deep changes announced in July 1991, Indian protection levels for its domestic industry through tariff and nontariff measures have remained the highest in the world. Openness toward foreign capital has increased significantly, but it still does not compare favorably with that in neighboring economies.

2. Events have completely overtaken the progress of the project. The first version of this chapter was started in early 1991. Since then three sets of major reforms have taken place, in July 1991, February 1992, and April 1992. The policy reversal means that India no longer stands apart from the trade openings in Latin America that are analyzed in this volume. Although differences in the level of protection remain, the trend is in the same direction.

3. See Chapter 11 for a description of the earlier confrontationist position India adopted as a leading member of the G10.

4. The rate of growth of the industrial sector during the 1950s, 1960s, and 1970s was 5.98 percent, 5.83 percent, and 3.79 percent respectively. This declining trend in industrial growth rate over the three decades was the prime cause for low growth of the economy.

5. This was amply demonstrated during the three bad monsoon and drought years of 1986–1988; the country did not need to import any food grains and no famine deaths were reported from any part of the country.

6. The growth estimates for the 1980s exclude two outlying years. The initial year 1979/80 is excluded as the growth rate was negative, and 1988/89 is excluded because it had an exceptionally high growth rate. With their inclusion, the growth performance would be even higher. See Nagraj, 1990.

7. The outflow continued at an average monthly rate of $120 million in July–September and then declined to $83 billion in October–December 1991. The outflow could be reversed only in January 1992. These details are taken from Government of India, 1992, 4–8.

8. The government clearly recognized that such excessive and open-ended protection would lead to a loss of competitiveness of Indian industry and also result in a welfare loss due to higher costs of industrial production. The early reports of the Tariff Commission, a statutory and autonomous government agency, on several industries (such as automobiles, textiles, etc.) are replete with warnings to this effect. The reports also tried to emphasize that the protection being afforded was temporary.

9. India, like Costa Rica (see Chapter 5), adopted reforms gradually and as a result of a ripe political consensus.

10. The sectors in which licensing requirements have been retained have security considerations or environmental hazards. Other than these, some sectors where import content is exceptionally high or sufficient capacity clearly exists in the economy have continued to be subject to licensing.

11. Authors of two of the papers written for an Indo-EC seminar in New Delhi in December 1986 pointed out the growing external indebtedness of the Indian economy and its vulnerability on this account. See Toye, 1989. Some leading Indian economists had also pointed toward the buildup of internal debt and the likely difficulties in mobilizing investment resources for the coming eighth five-year plan. See Bhattacharya and Mitra, 1989, and Patnaik, 1987. Thus to domestic observers, the emerging vulnerability of the Indian economy was already visible before the end of the 1980s.

12. For details of this position, see Chapter 11.

9

Bypassing Barriers: Lessons from the Asian NICs

DAVID GLOVER

This book relies on the comparative analysis of case studies to provide insights into the process of trade bargaining. The experience of the NICs of Asia is potentially a rich source of lessons for other countries. One of the questions a study of these nations should answer is, "Does the success of the Asian NICs with an export–oriented growth strategy result from an effective trade and industrial policy or also from an effective approach to trade bargaining?" The affirmative answer provided in this chapter weakens somewhat the argument that Asian export orientation occurred prior to the rise of trade barriers in developed countries and therefore could not be repeated by other countries today. The evidence shows that these countries faced significant trade barriers throughout their development but succeeded in circumventing them, in part through a successful bargaining strategy. The more relevant question for this project, then, is to what extent that bargaining strategy could be adopted by other countries.

This chapter approaches that question in three steps. First, it summarizes a study of the trade bargaining strategies of four Asian NICs done by David Yoffie (1983). Second, referring particularly to Korea, it highlights those features of the domestic political economy which made the chosen bargaining strategy feasible. Third, it offers some brief speculations on the extent to which those prerequisites exist in other countries. The last two sections are based on a slightly wider variety of sources than the first, but unlike the other chapters in this book, they are not based on primary research. Nor do I claim extensive knowledge of the subject; rather, I attempt to synthesize a small part of the vast literature on these countries. The value of this chapter, then, lies chiefly on its complementarity to the more thorough studies elsewhere in this volume.

TRADE BARGAINING

Yoffie's study examines the trade-bargaining experience of Japan, South Korea, Taiwan, and Hong Kong between 1955 and 1982. It draws conclusions based on an analysis of bargaining episodes in four sectors: textiles, footwear, color TVs, and automobiles. It is restricted to bilateral bargaining between individual NICs and the United States and focuses on one particular form of trade restriction, VERs.

In brief, the strategy employed by these countries could be called pragmatic, flexible adaptation in pursuit of long-term national gain. It is marked by a willingness to accept the inevitable, to roll with the punches, and to bargain for maximum flexibility in the application of trade restraints. Specifically, when faced with an impending trade restriction, the Asians pressed for VERs rather than tariffs and bargained to make those VERs as porous as possible. The NIC negotiators did not restrict themselves to bargaining over the overall level of quotas but also pressed to make the definition of products covered by VERs as vague and ambiguous as possible; to bargain over the rate of growth of quotas; to include the maximum degree of flexibility possible in the application of quotas (e.g., to allow countries to borrow against their quotas from future years); and to stall in the negotiation and application of quotas, allowing time for the base rate to increase and the economy to adapt to the incentives provided by the impending VERs. The aim is to negotiate a VER that is formally restrictive but in reality quite porous. This may satisfy the U.S. lobbies that pressed for trade restrictions in the first place while minimizing the damage to exporters. It is neither passive nor confrontational and serves to preserve a long-term relationship with the trading partner while maximizing the benefits within it.

By using a flexible bargaining strategy to maximize the exporter's room for maneuver within a VER, the NICs have created the opportunity to use a variety of methods to maintain or increase their export revenues. Since VERs are set in terms of unit volume rather than value, it is possible to sell higher-priced items in the same product category (e.g., luxury vehicles instead of economy cars) to raise prices for a good whose rate of growth is now restricted. Other responses have been to shift production into products not yet covered by VERs (e.g., trucks rather than cars); to shift into newly developed products (e.g., VCRs after TVs); to shift into unrestricted markets; and even to shift into different industries, as some Korean conglomerates have done. It is also possible to work within VERs by bringing forward quotas from future years. (If the country can move out of the restricted product, it may never need those future quotas.) It is also possible to get away with a certain amount of cheating. Finally, quotas provide incentives and time to diversify export markets.

The possibility of using these evasive measures highlights several of the advantages of VERs over tariffs. These go beyond the textbook advantage that revenue occurring from the restriction accrues to the exporter rather than the importing-country government. (In reality, this rent may be the object of bargaining between exporting and importing firms.) VERs are not only more porous than they appear, they also provide an incentive for innovation. They cause exporters to shift product lines faster and to diversify markets faster than they would have without an export restraint. The pressure to fully exploit the quota can induce rapid innovation before the productivity gains from current production methods have been exhausted: that is, it keeps the exporter on the steep portion of the learning curve. Yoffie argues that for these reasons VERs are not just preferable to a tariff for an exporter but are actually preferable to no trade restriction. (Obviously this would be a difficult argument to evaluate rigorously. Nor does Yoffie maintain that NIC governments were motivated by such a perception in negotiating VERs. It should also be pointed out that some of the incentive effects of VERs also apply to tariffs.)

A bargaining strategy such as that of the NICs has several prerequisites. First, the NICs were able to negotiate porous VERs because U.S. protectionism was relatively soft. U.S. trade negotiators were generally more liberal than the domestic interest groups to whom they responded. Their objectives were largely to placate those lobbies rather than provide completely effective barriers to imports, and VERs serve this purpose well. Second, NICs generally benefited from quite coherent governments with clear objectives and good interagency coordination. In the instances examined by Yoffie where such coherence was lacking, bargaining was generally unsuccessful. Third, NICs had clear priorities and a relatively narrow range of interests. They had targeted particular products and markets as being of key importance and devoted their best negotiators and technical support to agreements pertaining to those sectors. The United States, in contrast, had extremely diffuse interests in terms of trading partners, products, and nontrade geopolitical interests. In such circumstances, the apparently overwhelming superiority of the larger country in terms of negotiating resources can be reduced and even reversed. In many cases, relatively low-level U.S. bureaucrats were negotiating with high-level government officials from the NICs with abundant and specialized technical support.

POLITICAL ECONOMIC PREREQUISITES

This section highlights those aspects of political economy in the NICs which made possible the bargaining strategy described above. It assumes familiarity with the "revisionist" interpretation of Korean development promulgated by Wade, Westphal, Martin Bienefeld, and others, namely, that extensive state involvement rather than laissez-faire was key to Korea's success. Consequently, it does not attempt to provide a complete picture of Korea's trade and industrial policy, only those aspects of it that are relevant to bargaining. These can be considered prerequisites for the successful application of the strategy. The emphasis throughout is on Korea, though many observations are applicable to the other Asian NICs.

The bargaining strategy described above exploits loopholes in the coverage of VERs. Such loopholes are rare for standardized commodities but are much more common in manufactured goods, particularly those undergoing rapid technological change. This is the first prerequisite of the strategy.

More generally, the strategy requires flexibility in the economy in order to rapidly exploit temporary niches created through bargaining. This includes the ability quickly to shift product lines and markets, set up branch plants, upgrade products and identify new ones, switch between the export and domestic markets, and adjust pricing structures.

What permits such flexibility? Some authors (e.g., Caves and Uekusa, 1976) have emphasized the heavy reliance on subcontracting in Korea and Japan. Subcontracting allows large firms to avoid heavy investments in fixed capital for the production of components; components can instead be purchased to order from smaller firms. This allows quick changes of product lines (and compensates for the relative immobility of labor in parent firms in Japan). In Korea labor costs and labor immobility were minimized by denying unions the right to strike and by not legislating minimum wages.

A second general feature of NIC political economy that permitted effective bargaining was the existence of an autonomous, coherent state (Alam, 1989). The nature of the state's relationship with the private sector was important for managing the economy in such a way as to make the bargaining strategy feasible. The state saw its role as supporting and promoting the private sector rather than replacing it, "micromanaging" it, or excessively protecting it. Its leadership was exercised in building consensus with the private sector. Its autonomy was important in maintaining targeted protection for import-substituting industries for a limited period and resisting pressure for generalized and permanent protection. The state also limited import protection to industries that did or would in the near future export. This avoided the creation of an entrenched import substitution lobby geared exclusively toward the domestic market.

Korea's targeted approach—providing protection for a limited number of key industries—had general benefits for economic growth. It also facilitated success in bargaining. Scarce negotiating skills and technical backup could be concentrated on the targeted industries rather than spread thin. Targeting also made high rates of protection and subsidization less visible since they were concealed within a trade regime that was, on average, fairly neutral.

A relatively autonomous state could also afford to give a high degree of discretion to its officials in granting incentives to selected industries and firms. Discretionary measures increase the responsiveness and flexibility of targeting.

Other elements of NIC political economy relevant to a flexible bargaining strategy include a broad domestic market, a high savings rate, and an emphasis on education and the work ethic. In order to direct sales to domestic markets (e.g., at an early stage in an industry's development), the domestic market must have significant absorptive capacity. Such capacity appears to have been achieved not through high wages to a manufacturing labor aristocracy but through a broad-based market made possible by a relatively equal distribution of income. The latter was created by extensive land reform in an earlier period in Korea and Taiwan (Amsden, 1985). (That land reform also eliminated the landlord class, which might otherwise have impaired the state's autonomy; Jenkins, 1991.)

Complementing this absorptive capacity were policy measures that raised the public and private rates of saving (the former through fiscal reform, the latter through the creation of highly accessible savings institutions). This prevented the textbook situation of a flat income distribution's leading to a low private savings rate. With high domestic savings, foreign borrowing could be kept to reasonable levels.

Finally, the high value attached to education and work in East Asian culture is frequently cited. Its importance is difficult to assess empirically, but its intuitive appeal is hard to deny.

CAVEATS

Before turning to the implications of this analysis for other industrializing countries, it is important to qualify some of the observations made about NIC bargaining success in an earlier period. For one thing, some Korean observers have remarked that Yoffie's account ascribes more rationality and more success to Korean bargaining than it deserves. For example, much of the bargaining over color TVs is said to have been improvised; a small number of skilled negotiators were spread quite thin; and Korean industry has been less than enthusiastic about the bargaining achievements of its government representatives. It may well be that Yoffie describes NIC bargaining at its best, a level not always reached but one that shows the potential benefits available from an effective application of the strategy.

For another thing, much has changed since the 1960s. Protectionism has undeniably increased and become more sophisticated, and more countries are trying to penetrate the same markets. With 301 and Super 301, U.S. trade negotiators have more clout than they used to (Odell, 1985). There are now stronger quid pro quos for concessions to developing countries; Korea itself must bargain over its import regime just to maintain the status quo on exports. The end of the Cold War will reduce the geopolitical advantages that some countries have been able to exploit. The porosity of trade barriers is becoming harder to maintain as protectionist lobbies become more sophisticated and computers make cheating easier to detect. There are signs that decreasing returns to clever bilateral bargaining have led Korea to play a more active role in the Uruguay Round, even taking a leadership role on issues like antidumping that are important to it. Finally, success itself could make future bargaining more difficult. As the NICs effectively diversify their export markets and products, they may lose the ability to concentrate their bargaining resources in a few key areas.

It is difficult to know how important these caveats are or what their policy implications are. They could be read as support for export pessimism or inward-looking strategies; if so, it would be an ironic outcome of an examination of NIC export success! More sensibly, such caveats suggest some limits on how much one can expect from a single measure, such as bargaining strategy. They indicate that the stakes are now higher, the competition greater, and the barriers higher than in the past; better bargaining may become less of an option for moving ahead than a necessity to keep from falling behind. Acquiring greater flexibility and policy coherence may not produce the spectacular results it did twenty years ago, but the consequences of *not* acquiring them could be stagnation.

IMPLICATIONS FOR OTHER COUNTRIES

These features of political economy in the NICs appear to be prerequisites for the successful implementation of a bargaining strategy based on flexibility. If so, what are the implications? In what other countries do these conditions exist?

The number of developing economies in which this kind of flexibility exists is not large. Thailand comes to mind as a case in which continuous shifting into new products and new export markets has been successful, contributing to sustained GNP growth rates exceeding 10 percent. Outside of Asia, the examples are fewer. Latin American economies, for the most part, are not notably flexible for their level of development. In Latin America, in contrast to Africa, this lack of adaptability stems more from institutional factors than a reliance on a narrow export base or other structural factors. Furthermore, few countries have made the costly and directed investments in developing local technological capacity that made Korean flexibility and competitiveness possible.

For example, a long history of hyperinflation in Argentina and Brazil has generated extensive and persistent indexation, which has greatly reduced the flexibility of those economies. Those countries also have traditionally had highly institutionalized conflict between labor and capital over their respective shares of national income, related in a "chicken-and-egg" fashion to high inflation. This conflict has had the character of a zero-sum game, in contrast to Korea, where market-determined wages were the rule but significant real-wage increases occurred as the market wage rose. Many Latin countries, such as Colombia and Ecuador, also have inflexible regulations with respect to the establishment and dissolution of enterprises. This creates barriers to both entry and exit. In Ecuador, for example, the termination benefits to employees are so large that insolvent firms cannot afford to go bankrupt. In Colombia legal impediments to firing employees are so severe that many firms employ people only on short-term contracts, which are continuously renewed.

Nor do most Latin American governments exhibit the degree of coherence found in the Asian NICs. Jenkins (1991) notes a number of factors that have contributed to this difference. Landlords, industrialists, and workers were all too weak to challenge the authority of the state in the Asian countries. Foreign aid gave the state a source of finance independent of local interests at an early stage. And external military threats to Korea and Taiwan strengthened the impetus for state-directed industrialization to bolster military power. On the negative side, a multiplicity of government agencies, most captured by their private constituencies, has weakened the coherence of Latin American states.

Probably the most promising experiments with institutional reform to increase flexibility and coherence are taking place in Chile. One experiment is with *concertación* or consensus building: attempting to build a consensus about economic policy that recognizes the legitimate and interdependent interests of all sectors of society (see Chapter 5). Profit sharing is another experiment that by providing labor with incentives to improve overall firm performance, may lessen the zero-sum nature of worker-management bargaining. These reforms have been proposed in large part to prevent a resurgence of inflation, but they could well increase flexibility in ways beneficial to trade performance. Such approaches are certainly more attractive than the authoritarian measures used in many Asian NICs.

At the same time, the Korean experience shows that encouraging flexibility does not necessarily mean exclusive reliance on the market. The current wave of liberalization sweeping Latin America threatens to eliminate any scope for the sort of active, targeted industrial policy that has worked well in East Asia. The danger lies not only in the lack of policy space remaining but in the lack of intellectual investment in imaginative, pragmatic policies. While the Korean model may not be suitable everywhere, there is surely potential benefit from experimentation with policy mixes that suit the specificities of individual countries. Countries should perhaps devote some of their bargaining resources to the creation of such policy space. For example, they may well accept that the average level of tariffs should be low but bargain for a higher degree of tariff dispersion than current conventional wisdom would indicate. Such a policy regime would be consistent with the lessons of the Asian experience.

PART IV

COLLECTIVE RESPONSES

10

Holding the Balance: The Cairns Group in the Uruguay Round

DIANA TUSSIE

Agriculture has been the biggest failure in the entire trading system. The Cairns Group was established in 1986 as a coalition determined to remedy this failure and to make GATT play a role in the process of liberalizing trade. The mere establishment of the Group marked the emergence of an unprecedented type of partnership in international trade negotiations, one in which developed and developing countries crossed old boundaries and converged. In contrast to previous broad-based partnerships in the GATT, the Group retained its momentum and remained united throughout the Uruguay Round.

This chapter is an attempt to understand the factors that have sustained the cohesion of the coalition and the role it played in the Uruguay Round. It is an exercise in process rather than outcomes. It starts by describing the setting in which the negotiations evolved. In order to gauge the strengths and weaknesses of the coalition, the second section analyzes the trade interests of the members. Subsequently, the chapter traces the diplomatic history of the Group and describes how internal consensus was built. The last section offers some insights into the Group's input in the bargaining process and some lessons that can be extracted from the experience.

THE SETTING

It has always been accepted that international rules governing agricultural trade had to be different from those applied to manufactures. For one thing, agriculture is subject to vagaries of nature. For another, protection was considered legitimate for domestic political and economic reasons. Several special dispensations were included in the General Agreement allowing laxer treatment of agriculture. Subsidies are granted special treatment under Article 16; export subsidies are permitted provided they do not lead to a situation in which a country gains "more than an equitable share" of the world market. Definitions of *subsidy* as well as of *equitable share* are lacking.

Article 11 allows QRs on farm imports when these are "deemed necessary" for domestic support programs or for the removal of temporary surpluses of domestic production. These measures were not supposed to reduce imports relative to domestic production, but in practice this interpretation of Article 11 has never been implemented (Trela et al., 1986) and countries were able to justify all sorts of protectionist barriers.

These provisions were "largely tailor made to US requirements" (Eric Wyndham White quoted in Dam, 1970, 260), but as time passed it was to become increasingly clear that the tailor cut the cloth too fine. Since the days when the decisions on the broad treatment of agriculture under GATT were made, protectionism has made net agricultural imports more and more marginal in relation to domestic production and consumption. Moreover, by the end of the 1970s, except for oilseeds and cereal substitutes, on which a zero duty had been bound during the Dillon Round, the EC had turned from a net importer into the world's second biggest exporter of temperate agricultural products. The importance of this concession was largely unrecognized at the time. Under the CAP, grain prices increased in the EC and demand for imports of cereal substitutes rose rapidly. Total imports of oilseeds and oilseed meal more than doubled from 1975 to 1987. Unable to apply variable levies and the panoply of assistance in standard CAP programs, the EC subsidized processors for the purchase of imported soybeans, sunflower, manioc, and rapeseed.

The competition between the United States and the EC turned into an open subsidy war. By the early 1980s, the traditional U.S. surplus in farm trade had turned into a deficit, while two-thirds of the EC's budget was spent on supporting the CAP. The crisis that hit agricultural trade in 1982 was the worst since the 1930s, with prices for cereals falling by over 50 percent.[1]

Confronted with an increasing trade deficit, persistent oversupply, and the prospect of a continuing spiral of mutually self-inflicted damage, the United States took the initiative to put the discussion of a more rational regulation of agricultural trade at the center of the Uruguay Round. With its market share eroded and its access to the EC severely restricted, the United States turned into a forceful advocate of agricultural liberalization. Some half-hearted attempts to discuss the management of temperate agricultural products had been undertaken during the Kennedy and Tokyo rounds, but these ended in agreements to disagree. In fact, the agricultural trade negotiations of the Tokyo Round revolved around a series of efforts to negotiate international commodity agreements for the principal traded products: grains, meats, and dairy products. The Uruguay Round was the first time the issue acquired center-stage importance. Moreover, the mandate for the round was an ambitious one, going beyond GATT's traditional coverage; over and above border measures and trade competition, the external effects of domestic support were included on the agenda.

From its inception, as a crosscutting coalition of developed and developing countries, the Cairns Group advocated the need to reformulate the General Agreement to close its loopholes. Major changes regarding the special treatment of agriculture under the GATT had to be made. Agricultural negotiations in the Uruguay Round were about rules, and the first business of the Cairns Group was to ensure an appropriate mandate and to oversee the process of rule reform and rule making. This was its strategic role. The members of the Group both jointly and individually carried out intensive technical work in order to measure the extent of protection and to chart ways for incorporating agriculture into the GATT system.

Its second task was to reduce the impact of polarization between the EC and the United States. On one hand it was necessary to prod the EC out of the status quo and on the other to stop the United States from "fighting fire with fire".[2] Although the obstacle of access to major markets is significant, the gravest problem for the competitive status of the Cairns members is the explosion of export subsidies granted by the United States and the EC. To render multilateral negotiations possible some realism had to be injected into the United States' initial draconian stance, the so-called zero 2000 option that proposed to eliminate all forms of protection by the year 2000. Speedy dismantling of agricultural protectionism was politically unrealistic, but the Group was intent on assuring that the subsidy conflict was neither left unresolved nor that it was resolved bilaterally to the Group members' exclusion or neglect. The aim was to reach a multilateral solution in such a way that agriculture would be incorporated into new GATT disciplines over time.

The Uruguay Round, in contrast to previous rounds, operated in a leadership vacuum (see Chapter 1). The polarization in agriculture was a reflection of the changing balance of power, as was the new space for coalitions (Finlayson and Weston, 1990). In addition, the process of differentiation among developing countries themselves is today increasingly pronounced. For a long time under the GATT system, the interests of developing countries were largely convergent. As their economic structures have grown more complex and variegated, so have their trade interests. They have assembled more individualized agendas and placed different emphases on the issues involved. A new range of bargaining options has emerged allowing a selection of partners on an issue-specific basis.

The countries joining forces to form the Cairns Group were Argentina, Australia, Brazil, Canada, Chile, Colombia, Fiji,[3] Hungary,

Indonesia, Malaysia, New Zealand, the Philippines, Thailand, and Uruguay. The Group was led by Australia; Argentina, Brazil, Chile, Uruguay, and New Zealand were active militants at all times. From the outset, the Group was established as an issue-specific partnership; each member retained its autonomy in all other issues in the round. This is partly accounted for by the heterogeneous interests of the members, some of which will be outlined in the next section. But there are other reasons related to the bargaining context. First, the round's overall agenda was too complex to allow for the emergence of solid, across-the-board common interests. Second, the special features of agricultural policies covering narrowly defined commodities have led to negotiations' taking place on a sector basis. This feature was reinforced by the focus on rules, the talks concentrating on the definition of a framework under which to conduct negotiations, on the need to increase transparency and harmonization, and on the provision of a data base from which the more substantive negotiations on eventual reductions in levels of support could subsequently take place. The balancing of concessions either across commodities or more broadly between particular agricultural commodities and other products is a task for later stages.

TRADE INTERESTS:
PATTERNS OF COOPERATION AND CONFLICT

In the early 1960s the members of the Group taken together held one-third of the export market in cereals, oilseeds, meat, milk products, and sugar. A catalyst in the formation of the coalition was the steady decline in members' terms of trade and in the share of world markets that core countries of the Group have suffered. The share of the group fell from 32 percent to 24.5 percent of world trade in the period from 1964 to 1985. The share of the United States also declined from 26 percent to 18.5 percent (see Tables 10.1 and 10.2). Meanwhile, the EC's share grew from 0 to 10 percent of world trade, with the greatest hikes in wheat (from 0 to 15 percent of the world market), beef (from 0 to 28 percent) and dairy products (from 0 to 39 percent).[4]

Thus the Group's primary goal in its effort to dismantle protectionism is to overhaul the CAP. In this all members stand together, and they stand behind the United States, since by excluding its own deficiency payments to farmers and targeting export subsidies, the United States promoted a freer trade that puts the initial burden of adjustment on the EC's side.

Despite the Group's explicit common purpose—to incorporate farm trade into the multilateral framework—different countries have different overriding interests. Some of these can be inferred from the econometric

Table 10.1 Exports of Selected Agricultural Commodities (in millions of dollars)

	Maize		Rice		Wheat		Soybeans		Sugar		Meat		Dairy Products		Total	
	1964	1985	1964	1985	1964	1985	1964	1985	1964	1985	1964	1985	1964	1985	1964	1985
Argentina	168	765	—	33	242	1,146	—	582	6	27	327	247	13	18	756	2,818
Australia	—	9	8	94	405	2,232	—	—	175	444	267	1,148	97	302	952	4,229
Brazil	3	—	1	2	—	—	—	762	33	368	23	422	—	2	60	1,556
Canada	—	52	—	—	949	2,838	—	24	3	23	50	677	27	139	1,029	3,753
Colombia	—	2	—	12	—	—	—	—	3	37	—	18	—	—	3	67
Chile	—	—	—	—	—	—	—	—	—	—	—	2	—	1	—	5
Hungary	—	39	—	—	1	252	—	—	19	6	65	391	—	6	85	694
Indonesia	—	61	—	30	—	—	—	—	18	—	—	13	—	—	18	104
Malaysia	—	9	5	—	—	2	—	—	—	15	2	2	—	15	7	43
New Zealand	—	5	—	—	—	—	—	—	—	1	255	936	221	740	476	1,672
Philippines	—	—	—	—	—	—	—	—	177	168	—	—	—	3	177	171
Thailand	66	280	211	829	—	—	—	—	10	230	—	133	—	10	287	1,482
Uruguay	—	86	3	81	—	—	—	1	—	3	59	154	—	27	62	352
Cairns	237	1,308	228	1,081	1,597	6,470	—	1,369	444	1,322	1,048	4,133	358	1,263	3,912	16,946
EC[a]	178	1,799	32	562	220	3,439	—	25	451	1,221	737	10,072	543	8,055	2,161	25,173
United States	652	2,718	205	665	1,361	3,781	567	3,749	1	87	177	1,366	195	292	3,158	12,658
World	1,259	6,861	922	3,294	3,420	15,260	618	5,543	2,478	9,032	1,957	17,520	1,528	11,210	12,182	68,720

Sources: Food and Agriculture Organization (FAO), Yearbook, 1987 and 1989; UN, International Statistics Yearbook, vol. 2, 1988; UNCTAD, Commodity Yearbook, 1990; Villalobos, 1989.
Note: a. Figures include intra-EC trade.

Table 10.2 Market Shares in Selected Agricultural Commodities (in percentages)

	Maize		Rice		Wheat		Soybeans		Sugar		Meat		Dairy Products		Total	
	1964	1985	1964	1985	1964	1985	1964	1985	1964	1985	1964	1985	1964	1985	1964	1985
Argentina	13.34	11.15	—	1.00	7.08	7.51	—	10.50	—	0.30	16.71	1.41	0.85	0.16	6.21	4.10
Australia	—	0.13	0.87	2.85	11.84	14.63	—	—	7.06	4.92	13.64	6.55	6.35	2.69	7.81	6.15
Brazil	0.24	—	0.11	0.06	—	—	—	13.75	1.33	4.07	1.18	2.41	—	0.02	0.49	2.26
Canada	—	0.76	—	—	27.75	18.60	—	0.43	0.12	0.25	2.55	3.86	1.77	1.24	8.45	5.46
Colombia	—	0.03	—	0.36	—	—	—	—	0.12	0.41	—	0.10	—	—	0.02	0.10
Chile	—	—	—	—	—	—	—	—	—	—	—	0.01	—	0.01	0.00	0.01
Hungary	—	0.57	—	—	0.03	1.65	—	—	0.77	0.07	3.32	2.23	—	0.05	0.70	1.01
Indonesia	—	0.89	—	0.91	—	—	—	—	0.73	—	—	0.07	—	—	0.15	0.15
Malaysia	—	0.13	0.54	—	—	0.01	—	—	—	0.17	0.10	0.01	—	0.13	0.06	0.06
New Zealand	—	0.07	—	—	—	—	—	—	—	0.01	13.03	5.29	14.46	6.60	3.91	2.43
Philippines	—	—	—	—	—	—	—	—	7.14	1.86	—	—	—	0.03	1.45	0.25
Thailand	5.24	4.08	22.89	25.17	—	—	—	—	—	2.55	—	0.76	—	0.09	2.36	2.16
Uruguay	—	1.25	0.33	2.46	—	—	—	0.02	—	0.03	3.01	0.88	—	0.24	0.51	0.51
Cairns	18.82	19.06	24.73	32.82	46.70	42.40	—	24.70	17.92	14.64	53.55	23.59	23.43	11.27	32.11	24.66
EC[a]	14.14	26.22	3.47	17.06	6.43	22.54	—	0.45	18.20	13.52	37.66	57.49	35.54	71.86	17.74	36.63
United States	51.79	39.62	22.23	20.19	39.80	24.78	91.75	67.63	0.04	0.96	9.04	7.80	12.76	2.60	25.92	18.42
World	100.00	100.00	100.00	100.00	100.00	100.00	100.00	100.00	100.00	100.00	100.00	100.00	100.00	100.00	100.00	100.00

Sources: Food and Agriculture Organisation (FAO), Yearbook, 1987 and 1989; UN, International Statistics Yearbook, vol. 2, 1988; UNCTAD, Commodity Yearbook, 1990; Villalobos, 1989.

Note: a. Figures include intra-EC trade.

models compiled by the World Bank (1986). In all the projections, the major gainers in a liberalized grains market would be the United States followed by Australia, Canada, Argentina, New Zealand, Thailand, and Uruguay. Brazil, the Philippines, and Australia would receive major gains if the sugar programs in the United States and the EC were ended. In the case of beef, the biggest gainers would be Australia, Argentina, Brazil, and Uruguay (as well as the United States) if the beef markets in the EC and Japan should open to competition. However, Brazil and Argentina would have offsetting losses in feed grain exports. In the case of rice, Thailand would be the major gainer if Japan opened its market, but this gain would be affected if deficiency payments in the United States were retained.

Collective bargaining with the purpose of setting precise rules is a valuable instrument for countries interested in commodities such as rice and sugar, for which the major gains would not accrue to the big players with leverage in international negotiations. Without the support of the Group and without its emphasis on a rules-bound approach, such commodities may risk being excluded from the negotiating process. Sugar was a major export for the Philippines until the market collapsed in the 1980s, causing severe problems in one of the provinces. Likewise, Indonesia has a keen interest in developing the rice market, given that 70 percent of its population relies on rural incomes derived mostly from rice production.

Driven by a different motivation but with equal interest in clear, across-the-board rules are Australia, Argentina, Brazil, Thailand, and Uruguay. In all the scenarios they would be absolute gainers from liberalization; they have a keen interest in developing a framework for a generic rather than a commodity-by-commodity approach.

Differences in the urgency and the weight each country places on agricultural issues are related to the different degrees of export dependence. Argentina, with about 70 percent of its earnings coming from agricultural raw materials and food items, is the most dependent, followed by New Zealand, Colombia, Uruguay, and Thailand, for which agriculture accounts for more than half of their export earnings; in Australia this is 40 percent; in Chile 33 percent; in Hungary 24 percent; in Canada 16 percent. If tropicals are included, Brazil, Australia, and Canada are the major exporters of the Group, followed by Malaysia, Argentina, Thailand, Colombia, Indonesia, and New Zealand. Together they account for 70 percent of the Group's exports (see Tables 10.1 and 10.3).

However, the only net exporters of temperate farm goods are Australia, Argentina, Canada, Hungary, New Zealand, and Uruguay. But even among these, Canada is not typically a "fair-trading country."

Table 10.3   Exports of Selected Tropical Products, 1985 (in millions of dollars)

	Coffee	Rubber	Spices	Fresh and Dried Fruit	Tea	Palm Oil	Cocoa	Total
Argentina	—	—	—	135	40	—	—	175
Australia	—	—	1	117	1	—	—	119
Brazil	2,632	—	89	181	13	3	360	3,278
Canada	9	—	5	52	17	—	—	83
Colombia	1,801	—	—	157	—	—	6	1,964
Chile	—	—	—	372	—	—	—	372
Hungary	—	—	—	218	—	—	—	218
Indonesia	561	718	126	—	149	237	59	1,850
Malaysia	—	1190	61	48	1	1,591	165	3,056
New Zealand	—	—	—	28	—	—	—	28
Philippines	69	20	—	—	—	1	2	92
Thailand	32	499	11	188	1	6	—	737
Uruguay	—	—	—	—	—	—	—	0
Cairns	5,104	2427	293	1,496	222	1,838	592	11,972
United States	180	48	21	13	13	—	26	288
EC	693	23	159	254	254	114	179	1,422
World	13,714	2772	1,274	10,196	2,366	2,639	2,886	35,847

Sources: Food and Agriculture Organization (FAO), *Yearbook,* 1987; UN, *International Statistics Yearbook,* vol. 2, 1988; *UNCTAD, Commodity Yearbook,* 1990; Villalobos, 1989.

Although it does not subsidize its exports, it does intervene in the home market and implement import restrictions.

There is also the question of the differential damage each country has suffered in world markets, given that this issue in turn affects the priority granted to other issues in the round (see Chapter 1). New Zealand's share in its two main exports fell drastically: dairy products declined from 14.5 percent to 6.5 percent and meat from 13 percent to 5 percent. Australia's share in wheat grew by 4 percentage points, but it was badly hurt in beef, dairy products, and sugar. Brazil doubled its share in meat and sugar and increased its overall share by 2 percentage points, mainly because of the boom in soybeans and edible oils. Argentina also benefited from this boom but suffered great losses in meats, though its share of the maize and wheat market remained constant; as a consequence, its overall world market share declined slightly, as did Australia's. Canada was badly hurt in maize, with other shares remaining fairly constant (see Tables 10.1 and 10.2).

However, the crucial differences stem from two factors: first, the type of export of major concern to each country and, second, the position of each country in relation to the protection of its own market. It is true that three quarters of the total exports of the Group are food products. Yet there is an obvious rift splitting tropical from temperate goods, since the obstacles to market access confronting tropical goods are of a different nature altogether from those affecting temperate food items. For one thing, tropical products are not affected by the trade war between the EC and the United States. The tropical producers of the Group hold 30 percent of total world exports of these products.

The major concern of tropical producers is to use the multilateral system to bridge the gap that separates them from the ACP countries, which enjoy preferential access to the European market (see Chapter 2). Countries such as Colombia, Indonesia, and Malaysia, which have an immediate interest in tropicals and are today net importers of temperate zone products, joined the coalition in order to galvanize negotiations on freer access to the European market. Almost from the start, the issue was placed on the Group's agenda, and the United States, when it first tabled its farm proposal, conditioned its offer to results in agriculture. Brazil is more of a mixed case, since it has interests both in temperate and tropical products (Tables 10.3 and 10.4). In any case, according to the 1980 Valdés and Zietz study, liberalization in OECD countries would have raised prices for most tropical products above those of wheat, the most important agricultural import of these countries.

Chile stands apart: it neither exports tropical goods nor is victimized by the subsidy scramble. But Chile has an active interest in fruit, vegetables, and fishmeal (as well as in fish, minerals, and forest products, which have been negotiated separately in the natural resources group; see

Table 10.4   Market Shares in Selected Tropical Products, 1985 (in percentages)

	Coffee	Rubber	Spices	Fresh and Dried Fruit	Tea	Palm Oil	Cocoa	Total
Argentina	—	—	—	1.32	1.69	—	—	0.49
Australia	—	—	0.08	1.15	0.04	—	—	0.33
Brazil	19.19	—	6.99	1.78	0.55	0.11	12.47	9.14
Canada	0.07	—	0.39	0.51	0.72	—	—	0.23
Colombia	13.13	—	—	1.54	—	—	0.21	5.48
Chile	—	—	—	3.65	—	—	—	1.04
Hungary	—	—	—	2.14	—	—	—	0.61
Indonesia	4.09	25.90	9.89	—	6.30	8.98	2.04	5.16
Malaysia	—	42.93	4.79	0.47	0.04	60.29	5.72	8.53
New Zealand	—	—	—	0.27	—	—	—	0.08
Philippines	0.50	0.72	—	—	—	0.04	0.07	0.26
Thailand	0.23	18.00	0.86	1.84	0.04	0.23	—	2.06
Uruguay	—	—	—	—	—	—	—	0.0
Cairns	37.22	87.55	23.00	14.67	9.38	69.65	20.51	33.40
United States	1.31	1.73	1.65	—	0.55	0.00	0.90	0.80
EC	5.05	0.83	12.48	—	10.74	4.32	6.20	3.97
World	100.00	100.00	100.00	100.00	100.00	100.00	100.00	100.00

Sources: Food and Agriculture Organization (FAO), *Yearbook*, 1987; UN, *International Statistics Yearbook*, vol. 2, 1988; UNCTAD, *Commodity Yearbook*, 1990.

Chapter 1) and has pioneered resort to the GATT dispute settlement procedures to counter discrimination. Chile joined forces with the other Group members in part as a matter of principle.

The differences stemming from tropical versus temperate export products have had a centrifugal impact—albeit a mild one—in the bargaining process because of the predisposition of each country to look for different types of bilateral deals and even to place a different emphasis on the components of a multilateral framework. For tropical exporters, the major concern is to enlarge market access in developed countries; they are less concerned with the subsidy war in cereals, beef, and dairy products.

The second difference with a potential to drive a wedge in the Group arises from the degree of protection each country has allowed its own producers. This is more relevant than the country's net trade balance since it has a bearing on the country's stance on the shape of new rules and the modalities for incorporating agriculture into the GATT's framework. Not all members can lend unambivalent support to a blanket removal of all trade-distorting policies. Canada, in particular, is in a unique position. Despite being a net exporter, it is also a big food importer. Canada's farm sector on the east coast is heavily protected, while western grain and beef producers have suffered from distortions in international markets.

Canada stands very much apart in this respect because of its extensive supply management system, which has sheltered farmers from market forces. The price Canadian consumers pay for eggs is 20 percent above the world price; the price for milk is more than double the world price. Over 100 farm marketing boards operate at both the federal and provincial levels and cover poultry, eggs, milk, and other dairy products. The Canadian government is especially sensitive to the dairy lobby, almost half of which is concentrated in Quebec—which in turn has a disproportionate political influence in Ottawa. A GATT panel in 1989 upheld a U.S. complaint against the protection offered to this sector (in particular, import curbs on ice cream and yogurt).

The result is that Canada's stance about some of the initiatives of the Group has been selective and contradictory. (Higgot and Fenton Cooper, 1990). The five founders of the Group (Argentina, Australia, Brazil, New Zealand, and Uruguay) took Canada's split identity into consideration from the start and were somewhat ambivalent about inviting Canada to join. Some countries viewed Canada as a Trojan horse, believing it would undermine consensus on the need to regulate and reduce internal support programs, but in the end the argument that Canada would be able to establish more intimate links with the United States and would be able to make the Group's views better known in relevant U.S. quarters prevailed. In fact, Canada was a liaison with G7.

Nevertheless, the special treatment for supply-managed sectors opened a rift between Canada and the other members. The Group has, for example, opposed motions to eliminate GATT's Article 11.2c, which Canada would like reformulated so that Canadian import restrictions on dairy and poultry products do not run counter to it. Because of Canada's stiff opposition, Cairns was not able to incorporate a straightforward mention of this article in its program. Despite the widespread consensus that this was a major loophole in the trading disciplines, the Group went along with Canada's stance for the sake of unity. This was, however, a sensitive issue for Argentina, which steadily pressured for incorporation of this demand in subsequent meetings. A tangential reference to the issue was finally included in the meeting convened in Santiago prior to the July 1990 meeting of the Trade Negotiations Committee.

A rift similar in origin but more easily bridged has separated subsidizing and nonsubsidizing developing countries, with a spillover to the issue of special and differential (S&D) treatment. Brazil has been an active sponsor of S&D both for ideological reasons and economic interests, Brazil having traditionally subsidized wheat production. Brazil and Colombia have tabled a comprehensive proposal on S&D that included tying concessions by developing countries to concessions they receive from developed countries.

Thus S&D was the subject of some debate in the Group, especially between Brazil (where production as well as consumption has been subsidized) and neighboring Argentina. Brazil used to buy wheat mainly from Canada and the United States until the signing of the bilateral trade agreement with Argentina at the end of 1986. One of the protocols of the agreement was aimed at increasing wheat imports from Argentina to reach 2 million tons in 1991. Since then Brazilian purchases from Argentina have been on the increase, so Argentine opposition to the Brazilian stance was duly softened, and in the end Argentina gave in. A compromise solution granted developing countries a longer time period to adjust.

In any case recent research has shown that if liberalization were to be restricted to developed countries, Argentina would still benefit; in fact, it would be among the few winners in the developing world (Abreu, 1989). So S&D need not be a divisive issue. On the one hand, it can keep net exporters and net importers in the same boat; on the other, it can be used as a way of eliciting support from other net importing developing countries.

As a major importer of wheat, Brazil would be unfavorably affected by freer wheat trade because of higher international prices. But gains in relation to sugar and beef would more than compensate for Brazilian losses stemming from both higher wheat prices and falling soy exports. Because of the weight of soy exports, the net balance-of-payments effect of eliminating agricultural protectionism in developed countries would be favorable (see Chapter 7). (This would hold true as long as the EC does not increase the level of protection to cereal substitutes and thus rebalance the level of support in the EC.

At the other end of the spectrum, with an unambivalent and militant free trading attitude, is Argentina. Not only has it opposed S&D, it has also confronted Canada on the need to eliminate the loopholes of Article 11.2c and Thailand on the latter's proposed safeguards in the form of quantitative restrictions for currency fluctuations.

Both the Argentine private sector and the government have set the highest stakes on the Cairns Group (see Chapter 6) and have tried to use unilateral liberalization as a spearhead to prize open foreign markets. Argentina is the most dependent of the Group on farm exports for foreign currency, and its trade interests are much less diversified than those of other major net exporters (for instance, Canada, Brazil, or Australia, countries that were keener to view the round in all its complexities). If any one country in the world has a natural advantage in agriculture, it is Argentina. It has been squeezed out of the EC's market and badly hurt by the disposition of European surplus production in third markets. Of all the issues in the Uruguay Round Argentina's ammunition was therefore most sharply concentrated on agriculture.

WEAVING THE CONSENSUS

Cooperation is a delicate balance not always linked to short-term or narrow product interests. Moreover, trade shares show only a static picture that does not capture the potential of many members of the Group should distortions be reduced (e.g. Colombia's potential in beef or Indonesia's potential in rice exports). Higher prices in cases such as these would improve the profitability of crops and contribute to making food production more attractive in many countries.

In addition to requiring the definition and demarcation of a common purpose, a coalition develops in the context of a balance of power. Over the years agricultural exporters watched helplessly as agriculture fell deeper and deeper into disarray. At the disastrous 1982 GATT ministerial meeting, the United States and the EC began talks on how agriculture might be handled. The possibility that the usual escape route—agreement to disagree—would be used again precipitated a vehement display of anger from the Australian delegation. Impatient of diplomatic niceties, Australia initiated the first of a series of stormy walkouts.

Three years later, while the preparatory committee for a new round was in session, John Dawkins was made trade minister of the Australian Labour government, and he in turn named Alan Oxley as Australia's ambassador to GATT. The Australian delegation in Geneva was expanded from four to six. The idea that matters could no longer be left in the hands of the big two contenders gained momentum, and in Geneva the Australian team made contacts with those from Uruguay and New Zealand. Argentina, at the time an active member of the G10[5] and therefore making noises against the launching of a new round, was not at this stage formally approached.

At the initiative of Carlos Perez del Castillo of Uruguay, the first informal talks among fair-trading agricultural exporters were held in Montevideo in April 1986 while the preparatory committee for the Uruguay Round was still in session. Attended by delegates from Argentina, Australia, Brazil, New Zealand, and the host country, this exploratory meeting allowed delegates to sound out the idea of creating a wider coalition of farm exporters. Australia had already made contacts with the Thais, who hosted a July meeting in Pattaya to which the rest of the ASEAN countries were invited. A month later the group was invited to Cairns in northern Australia, where they agreed to work collectively at the Punta del Este meeting three weeks later. Three developed countries, nine developing countries, and one former centrally planned economy joined forces in an unprecedented type of partnership.

At Punta del Este the text on agriculture written by the Café au Lait Group (so called because it was led by Colombia and Switzerland) and supported by forty-seven countries met the objections of both the key Cairns countries and the EC.[6] Richard Lyng, then U.S. secretary of agriculture, gave the Group its official credentials on the occasion. According to an account of the events (Oxley, 1990), he refused to follow the tradition of settling differences privately with the EC and called for the Group's views. It was the Group's first public activity. The mandate for agriculture was thus settled before services and with the participation of the three interested parties. Brazil, as a member of both G10 and the Group of Cairns, played a key role. The Group was satisfied with what was considered an historic agreement to open negotiations to deal with domestic agricultural policies and the adverse trade effects of such policies. The Argentines, nevertheless, perhaps driven by a sense of betrayal, "reserved" on the section on agriculture requiring accurate time limits for the elimination of export subsidies, firmer commitments to standstill and rollback, and so on. This meant that they were not bound by its provisions and did not have to take it as a starting point when the round was opened. This was a time of reckoning in Argentine multilateral diplomacy; the country had recently broken away from G10 but at tne same time had signed a bilateral free trade agreement with Brazil, and both countries had pledged to coordinate their stances in GATT.

After this inaugural public presentation, back in Geneva throughout 1987 the Group went through a phase of introspection. Intensive work was needed to nurture the budding cooperation. The Group concentrated on building the bases for internal consensus, listing and defining their guiding principles: to seek ways of capturing all the different forms of protection as the ultimate goal of the long-term negotiations; to open up the process of gradual liberalization promptly; to implement immediate measures such as reduction of stocks to avoid greater disequilibria. The Group also acknowledged the need to accelerate the pace of negotiations on tropical products. Despite conventional wisdom, the countries hold a keen interest as much in temperate as in tropical products. (see Tables 10.1 and 10.3).

During this second phase, the Group gradually grew in stature. Oxley was recognized as a key personality with great capacity for leadership and conciliation. In June 1987, at the annual economic summit of the seven major economic powers in Venice, Canada put forward the point of view of the Cairns Group, and the final communiqué underlined the need to table negotiating proposals on agriculture by the end of the year. Proposals were in the offing and could be expected from the United States as well as Canada, but this decision meant that the EC and Japan had to come forward as well.

The coalition had been Australia's intellectual child, but gradually other countries were pulled to the center of the stage. Canada built the bridge with G7 while Argentina by then had become one of the most enthusiastic and militant members. In October 1987 the Group finished its first comprehensive proposal providing a link between the United States and the EC. A few weeks later the Australian prime minister, Bob Hawke, was due to address a special meeting of the GATT, and at the behest of the Argentine representative, Nestor Stancanelli, efforts were made so that he could speak in the name of the Group to announce the proposal. This was a turning point in the Group's history. It was evolving from an informal group into a formal coalition and as commitments to the Group's calling grew, initiatives were springing from other countries besides Australia. Argentina prodded the Group with bold initiatives, but a step such as this involved a major departure in Brazilian diplomacy. Up to that point, Brazil's guiding principle was South-South solidarity, and its participation in the Cairns Group was viewed with some ambivalence. The Brazilians had joined on the understanding that the Group would only be used to coordinate positions rather than to agree to joint positions. If Prime Minister Hawke was to speak in the name of the Group, Brazil had to address the issue of formal collaboration with developed countries. Paulo Tarso Flecha de Lima, deputy head of the Foreign Ministry and in charge of GATT issues, laid down the condition that the group would "support the principle that the special interests of developing countries would be recognised." (Oxley, 1990). These linked steps led to the further consolidation of the Group. It was gradually turning into the bargaining tool of more than one country; the mentors behind the Group included more than one personality. The Group was widening its agenda, encompassing more interests, and by making compromises among its members, it gained in stature and flexibility.[7] The internal bargaining about what the Group was meant to do and who was going to do what was finally bringing about results.

From that point onward, both Argentina and Brazil showed more readiness to take responsibilities within the Group, and each worked in different directions but with the common aim of strengthening the capacity of the Group. While Argentina operated as a vanguard, always pushing for tighter commitments, Brazil operated as a bridge with developing countries. Together with Colombia, it worked on ways in which S&D should operate in agricultural adjustment; with the support of ASEAN, the two countries tabled a joint proposal on the matter. The discussion over the issue elicited greater participation from the whole of ASEAN, which (except for Thailand) had kept a low profile up to that point. These were creative times, times of thinking, and the members grew closer and closer together, achieving a balance among all the members and their different priorities.

In 1988, preparing for the midterm review, the Group worked on a short-term package to lend force to the bargaining process and sustain the political commitment. This package aimed to close the gap between the EC's short-term concerns and the United States' longer-term focus. It included an immediate standstill on support policies and a 10 percent cut in 1989 and 1990 as a down payment for the longer-run commitments. An initial proposal that this cut be across the board was revised to take into account the Canadian position that each country be allowed to decide where to make cuts (Finlayson and Weston, 1990). In addition, the first stages of long-term reform should focus on increasing import access, lowering administered prices, maintaining controls on production, reducing acreage, and initiating stock disposal disciplines. In the context of more favorable treatment, developing countries would be exempted from contributing to the first steps to long-term reform of agriculture. The Group also worked on a framework for technical negotiations to define, control, and standardize the use of sanitary and phytosanitary measures.

Throughout 1988 the United States and the EC remained locked in their positions, hardly willing to negotiate. The United States stuck to complete liberalization, the EC to gradual reductions of support. Prior to the midterm review in Montreal, the Group met in Hungary to assess its options given the stalemate. It explored the idea that if no agreement were reached in agriculture, consensus to progress in the new areas should be withheld. Only Argentina, Brazil, Chile, Colombia, and Uruguay seemed likely to consider such a move. Just before the meeting, Leopoldo Tettamanti, Argentine ambassador to GATT, flew to Buenos Aires and met President Alfonsín. On his return to Geneva, Tettamanti informed a meeting of the Group that if the position on agriculture did not improve, Argentina would not support results in other areas of the round.

The Montreal session opened on December 5, 1988, presided by Ricardo Zerbino, the Uruguayan minister. Four days of tense arguing made it clear that neither the United States nor the EC was prepared to be sufficiently accommodating. When the Trade Negotiations Committee was convened to review overall progress in all the issues, the EC proposed that work on agriculture be continued in Geneva in the future. Argentina stood firmly against such an escape route, a replica of the agreement to disagree of previous rounds. Unable to find a compromise solution in the circumstances, Arthur Dunkel quickly adjourned the session and called Michael Duffy from Australia, Clayton Yeutter from the United States, and Paulo Tarso Flecha de Lima from Brazil to a private meeting. Brazil's conviction, however, was not softened, and Tarso then conceived the formula of putting the negotiations on hold. Duffy convened the Group of Cairns to inform it of the situation, but as had been expected, a joint approach could not be worked out. Argentina announced that with or without the Group, it would veto the results in other areas; Brazil supported the move; Colombia, Chile, and Uruguay followed.

The negotiations recommenced in Geneva in April 1989 under President Bush's new administration and a greater willingness for compromise. At a quiet meeting at the EC delegation, the United States, the EC, and Cairns, represented by Peter Field from the Australian Ministry for Trade Negotiations, agreed on a freeze on levels of protection and support with the long-term objective of "substantial progressive reductions." Although the exact pace and extent of reduction remained to be seen, the Latin members of Cairns, especially Argentina, were vindicated; without their principled stance, the Group would have lost its calling and credibility. Moreover, they became aware of their collective importance.

But internal discussions followed this agreement. On the one hand, the limits to a joint position had become known. On the other, as the negotiations advanced from principles to procedures and offers were expected, Canada's own limitations on freer trade in farm goods were surfacing. Canada tabled a paper proposing the use of a different measure for monitoring support and commitments to reform, the trade-distorting equivalent (TDE), instead of the one advocated by the Group, the producer subsidy equivalent (PSE), which captures intervention in the home market as well as in export markets. Its offer also included a revision of Article 11.2c in order to allow GATT to cover its quotas on dairy and poultry products and exempt them from tariffs.

By the end of 1989, the Group moved closer to the United States as a result of the EC's intransigence on using 1986 as a base year and not reforming its dual pricing system. Both Cairns and the United States singled out treatment of export subsidies, saying these ought to be frozen and then phased out altogether. But while the United States proposed a five-year period, Cairns proposed doubling the time limit, justifying the claim to greater flexibility. The EC, for its part, argued that export subsidies—albeit with tighter disciplines—should be allowed for the disposal of surpluses; in any case, as internal support was gradually cut back, the need for export subsidies would be reduced.

The Group also took up the United States' suggestion that NTBs to farm trade be converted into ad valorem tariffs and then reduced to low or zero levels over ten years or less. Tariffication would force the EC to scrap its variable import levies, the cornerstone of the CAP. The Group also adopted the traffic-light approach of the United States, with a red-amber-green categorization of domestic support measures. Policies are divided into those that cannot be permitted, those allowed only under GATT discipline, and those permitted.

As the Round began to draw in, the Group reconsidered bargaining tactics. The July 1990 meeting in Santiago accepted the program tabled by Art de Zeeuw, the Dutch chairman of the group handling agriculture, "as a framework for negotiations." Again Canada was given the task to send a firm message to the G7 summit in Houston to inject urgency into the negotiations. The Group called on the United States, the EC, and Japan to "meet their responsibilities and to make the contributions required of them." The Group also implicitly threatened to provoke a crisis in the negotiations by blocking action on all other matters until progress on agriculture was visible. The final declaration made an explicit reference linking the fate of liberalization and trade adjustment by LDCs to the evolution of reforms in agriculture.

Nonetheless, determination to block movement across the range of the round's issues never became firm at the joint level. Most members had serious misgivings and finally hesitated to carry out the threat made at Santiago. Neither Canada nor Australia was ever keen on using agriculture for cross-sectoral bargaining because of their interests in obtaining access in other groups as well. Canada, for instance (together with Japan, Sweden, and Switzerland), played a crucial role in drafting a financial services agreement, and Australia kept a sharp eye on the subsidies group. At the same time that Argentina was busy canvassing support for a walkout a few days before the Brussels meeting, Australia's trade negotiations minister, Neil Blewett, indicated that Australia was ready to compromise with the EC on the depth of the cuts in internal subsidies and export support payments; he further indicated that Australia saw "no point" in forcing a crisis (*Financial Times*, November 28, 1990). Canada's trade minister, John Crosbie, stressed that "the subject under discussion is too important" to take such a step (*Financial Times*, October 30, 1990). The ASEAN countries voiced their concern that the emphasis on agriculture had been unduly great.

Argentina remained a determined advocate of withholding consensus on the other issues if a positive result in agriculture were not obtained. After undertaking considerable trade adjustment and with virtually undiversified interests, Argentina has indeed tried to make use of brinkmanship tactics resorting to the broad reciprocity argument, and lobbied hard to get the Group as whole to do likewise. It was able to obtain lukewarm support only from the Latin American faction because of the feeling that without progress on agriculture there would be few incentives to make the concessions required of them in other areas (such as services and TRIPs). But even here convictions were not strong. Brazil, for example, became convinced of withdrawing from the round only by U.S. prodding after a visit by Yeutter a few weeks before the Brussels meeting.

Despite these differences, the marriage remained comfortable and convenient to all. Recognizing affinities yet accepting differences is what a marriage is about. When personalities mesh, the partners play different roles and shoulder their joint tasks. While Argentina, motivated by the urgency it felt over the issue, wanted to engineer a collapse of the talks, Australia and Canada were ready to accept a smaller package in agriculture involving only incremental change. The Group stood together nevertheless because a safe and comfortable average had been outlined, and if some countries (such as Argentina) were steadily moving one step ahead, others (such as Canada) slowed down the pace of demands. Argentina was a useful enfant terrible; Canada a bridge with G7, Brazil a bridge with developing countries; Australia the mentor, leader, and conciliator.

The efficacy of an alliance is closely related to its cohesiveness; its prospects are clearly improved if members are able to continue cooperating. The members of the Group were well aware of this. The Group's cohesiveness was put to the test at crucial points of the bargaining process, when it was forced to move from the level of agenda setting and proposal making (Hamilton and Whalley, 1989) to the nuts and bolts of bargaining. This happened first in Montreal and again in Brussels. The United States incited the Group to walk out of the Brussels meeting while the EC tried to exploit the potential split loyalties in the group by offering more generous terms on tropical products. Specifically, the EC proposed to eliminate tariffs on raw materials, to reduce duties on semiprocessed goods by 35 percent and to cut duties on processed goods by 50 percent. Products included were coffee, cocoa, tea, tropical fruits, spices, cut flowers, essential oils, rubber, and wood articles. This offer was coupled with another to restrict its original idea of rebalancing (reduction of the variable levy on grains in exchange for an increase in tariff protection on the products for which tariffs were bound at zero during the Dillon Round) just to corn gluten feed and citrus pellets—in other words, to exclude soybeans from a tariff hike. Brazil might also have been assuaged, but given the premature collapse of the negotiations, the solidarity of the Group was not at risk.

Nevertheless, the Group had not set out to be a coalition with a single negotiator at product level, such as the EC. It is not a customs union and therefore a wide range of disparities is bound to arise when bargaining across commodities emerges. The Group was meant to advance a common position on the agenda and the modalities for bargaining on one issue: agriculture.

INPUT INTO THE BARGAINING PROCESS: HOLDING THE BALANCE

"Alliances are a necessary function of the balance of power" (Booth, 1976). From this perspective, what was the impact of the Cairns Group on the evolution of the negotiations? To the United States' excessive zeal, Cairns could offer its moderation at appropriate times. The Group's action nonetheless underscores the role that coalitions can play in the bargaining process. Whatever leverage the Group may have had does not seem related to market shares but derived from joint action and from staying power.

Even though the United States first placed agriculture on the agenda and retained control over the overall dynamics, Cairns was able at certain points to catalyze change by bridging the gap in the extreme positions of the United States and the EC. This was clearly the Group's function in the first two years of the round, when the debate simply circled around the continuing U.S. insistence on long-term elimination of subsidies and Europe's refusal to accept such a draconian commitment. By introducing elements of flexibility into the polarized bargaining process, Cairns allowed movement toward an agreement not only to reduce protection over time but also to freeze existing levels of protection.

As the final stages of the round drew in, Cairns threw its weight to confront European intransigence over farm reform. The objective then was to add power to the U.S. side and apply unremitting pressure on the EC so as to isolate its farm lobby and force the pace of negotiations. In this sense the concerns of the coalition were dependent not merely on the perceived interest of the members but on the strategies of the major contenders as well.

Despite the different economic interests within the Group, the forces leading to cooperation were stronger than the forces leading to conflict.

The differences between developed and less-developed countries, or those between temperate and tropical producers, were less relevant than the Canadian interest in preserving its supply controls. The Group of Cairns proved to have staying power. "The foundation of cooperation is the durability of the relationship....Whether the players trust each other or not is less important in the long run than whether the conditions are ripe for them to build a stable pattern of cooperation with each other" (Axelrod, 1984).

Countries forming a partnership, such as the Cairns Group, are either seeking objectives for which their own resources are insufficient or are trying to lessen the costs of attaining an objective. This is achieved by becoming "a third key protagonist" (Higgott and Fenton Cooper, 1990) in the balance of power. In a polarized negotiation a third protagonist is called to tilt the given balance. This is in fact the strategy implemented by the Group in its struggle to reverse protectionism.

Speedy dismantling of protectionism in agriculture is politically unrealistic. But the initiation of a process of gradual reduction combined with an agreement to change domestic and trade policies does seem to offer some long-term prospect of eventually using multilateral negotiations to liberalize agriculture. A move toward the use of tariffs as the sole border instrument, the classification of domestic subsidies by their degree of trade distortion, and the reduction in export subsidies as domestic support levels fell would add up to a significant accomplishment (Josling et al., 1990). This is the type of agreement the United States and the EC can live with, and success must be measured against this standard. The Dunkel Draft, proposed at the end of December 1991, incorporated these measures and received the support of the Group (with the exception of Canada, which opposed the idea of tariffication).

How much of current progress in GATT talks can be attributed to the Cairns Group? It is difficult to draw a firm line between activism and influence. The Group's militancy ensured that the General Agreement was a framework for liberalizing trade, a bargaining forum. It is quite possible that without the Cairns Group, the idea of rebalancing protection might have provided the United States and the EC with an out, an excuse to accept the stalemate for want of any solutions.[8] The Cairns Group has kept up the pressure and the momentum. By hanging together and retaining a high profile throughout the round, its members made sure that agriculture would remain at the forefront of negotiations. Agriculture was the major bone of contention between the United States and the EC. Cairns campaigned to amplify the dimension of the problem. Bargaining over all forms of agricultural protection is now definitely on the agenda. The United States opened the road; Cairns provided the fuel for the journey. Yet over and above political campaigning, there is concrete evidence of the substantive contributions of the Group in the proposed Final Act for the Uruguay Round.

What are the lessons that can be extracted from the Group's experience? The members of the Group started out with a shared perception of the trade problem and a lack of power to do anything about it single-handedly. Every country was aware of the significant, identifiable gains that could be obtained if market distortions were reduced, but identifying the problem and the common purpose was just the first step. Cooperation had to nurtured, and this required not only the right personalities but also hard work. In this Australia played a key role, pulling all the countries together and providing the technical support and statistical background in order for the Group to make a substantial contribution to the Uruguay Round.

Both a sense of the Group's own importance and limited influence in affecting outcomes emerged in Montreal with the veto geared by the Latin American faction. The move proved that it was possible to block negotiations if agriculture remained doomed to failure or second-class status. Yet at the same time, power to disrupt and stall the negotiations was limited.

All efforts of cooperation involve a gradual process of confidence building and democratization in which other countries are brought in. A division of labor emerges, and tasks are shouldered by all members, who bring into the newly created relationship their particular interests. In the process of internal bargaining over what the coalition is about and who is going to do what, cohesion and commitment increase. Sustained commitment is a crucial ingredient of success. Here also the Group provided a lesson. Commitment in the Group was primarily at a ministerial level. This not only ensured the high profile of the Group's agitation but also the political willingness to carry out the proposal, even in the case of Canada, where some ambivalence could be expected.

Finally, the Cairns Group has shown that hybrid coalitions in which developing and developed countries mesh can play a significant part in trade bargaining. But whether developing countries should aim for this type of coalition or a purer form of developing-country coalition is not entirely certain.

NOTES

Research assistance by Cristina Simone and comments by Ricardo Ffrench Davis and project members are gratefully acknowledged. The following people were interviewed as part of the research for this chapter: Juan Manuel Cano, Mission of Colombia to GATT; Juan Agustín Figueroa, Ministry of Agriculture, Chile; Carmen Luz Guarda, Ministry of Foreign Relations, Chile; Rod Hall, Multilateral Trade Division, Australia; W. John Rigg, Embassy of Australia in

Argentina, P. Sadli, University of Indonesia; Antonio José Ferreira Simoes, Ministry of Foreign Relations, Brazil; Leopoldo Tettamanti, Ministry of Foreign Relations, Argentina; Francisco Thompson Flores, Ministry of Foreign Relations, Brazil.

1. This fall was also part of a broader drop in commodity prices; mining products fell even further, by 60 percent.

2. Interview with Ambassador Francisco Thompson Flores.

3. Fiji is not a member of the GATT, but it nevertheless joined the Group and attends ministerial meetings.

4. This draws on research done by Villalobos (1989).

5. See Chapter 11 for an account of this period.

6. Chapter 11 discusses the Punta del Este meeting in greater detail.

7. This disposition toward flexibility is exactly the opposite of that manifest in G10.

8. See Bradley MacDonald, 1990 for calculations that suggest the attraction of this option for the United States and the EC.

11

Developing-Country Coalitions in International Trade Negotiations

RAJIV KUMAR

The Uruguay Round has been a truly multilateral round of negotiations. The developing countries have played an active and important role at all stages, both individually and as members of various coalitions. These coalitions have varied in their composition, scope, and nature of contribution to the negotiations. This chapter reviews the experience of an umbrella coalition, namely, the G10 (the acronym derived from the number of original members), which emerged during the prelaunch period of the Uruguay Round. This historical review, along with an examination of other coalitions (including that of the G77 in UNCTAD), will provide insights into the possible future role developing-country coalitions can play in international trade and economic negotiations.

There have been earlier attempts at analyzing the role of such coalitions, notably those of Hamilton and Whalley (1988) and Kahler and Odell (1988). These earlier attempts were, however, undertaken soon after the Uruguay Round was launched and therefore did not cover the later experience of sectoral and general coalitions. Previous studies, including the contribution by Abreu (1990), did not look at the working of G77 or examine the feasibility of restructuring the coalition in view of the recent changes that have radically transformed the political and economic situations in developing countries. (see Chapters 1, 2, and 3).

This chapter begins with a comprehensive description of the experience of G10 in the Uruguay Round. It also tries to provide an overall assessment of this experience in terms of two criteria, the contribution of the G10 to the progress of negotiations in the round and the possible advantages or disadvantages it may have generated for its members and for developing countries as a group. The second section attempts an assessment of the role of the G10 in promoting developing-country interests and briefly reviews some other sectoral and mixed coalitions. The third section looks at various explanations put forward for the disbandment and demise of G10. The way forward into the future, as it emerges from the analysis of past experience, is discussed in the final section.

THE EXPERIENCE OF G10

It is important to locate the birth of G10 in its proper historical context. For more than two decades, an informal group has been operational among the developing contracting parties within GATT. The group has discussed the positions of individual developing countries[1] on specific issues being negotiated in GATT and tried to arrive at common positions wherever possible. Because the group did not insist on adoption of a unified position on all issues, it was not a formal coalition and was different from G77. Yet without being a coalition, the informal group had, until the culmination of the Tokyo Round, represented the position of developing contracting parties in the GATT fairly well.

The informal group was traditionally dominated by the big five: Argentina, Brazil, Egypt, India, and Yugoslavia. Other active members were Chile, Jamaica, Pakistan, Peru, and Uruguay. The major role of the big five stemmed partly from their political importance, derived from the absolute size of their individual economies and populations. It was reinforced by the position of leadership they enjoyed among the developing countries as evidenced in formations such as the nonaligned movement and G77. In effect a convention had evolved in GATT that no agreement could be finalized or seen to have global legitimacy and sanction until the big five were on board.[2] Successive U.S. administrations shared this perception, and the GATT secretariat effectively went out of its way on occasion to accommodate the views of these five countries.[3] The GATT convention of reaching agreement by consensus also contributed to the importance of the five. This role did not derive from their share in international trade, but (apart from the considerations mentioned above) the five could dominate the negotiations because of the skills of their negotiators in Geneva and the logical validity and appeal of their positions.[4]

The role of the informal group and the position of the big five continued unchanged until the ministerial meeting of 1982, at which the United States called for a new round with the inclusion of new issues, in particular, services and agriculture. The developing countries, achieving a fair degree of coordination, took a unified position that such a new round would be premature until the unfinished business of the Tokyo Round had been completed and the existing derogations from GATT were adequately addressed.

Pressures to launch the new round mounted relentlessly in following years. These were staved off, the unified position of developing countries remaining intact. Apparently, a core group of developing countries met regularly in the Colombian mission during 1985–1986.[5] By 1985, however, it was fairly clear that to argue further against the launching of a new round would be ineffective. This was also implicitly the view expressed in two papers discussed at the informal group meetings during this period.[6] The EC, Japan, and the United States (the three major powers) had become publicly committed to the new round, and some developing countries also supported the demand. Consequently, in July 1985 a senior officials group was proposed to work out the modality for the launch. The Brazilian delegation, presumably acting on behalf of the big five, opposed the measure. In response, the United States demanded that a vote rather than a consensus be used to reach a decision on holding a special session.[7] A postal ballot was in fact taken, although it will perhaps never be officially accepted. Nearly two-thirds of the contracting parties reportedly supported the demand for a special session of the contracting parties. This in effect was support for a new round; it demonstrated that almost half of the members of the informal group had moved away from the group's position. The United States and Japan recognized the importance of this signal, which conveyed to them that for the first time they could negotiate directly with the rest of the developing countries without the mediation of the big five, especially Brazil and India. The big five, for their part, ignored the signal.

By the beginning of the 1980s, the domination of the big five was beginning to be resented if not challenged within the informal group. ASEAN had come to adopt a harmonized position that was openly critical. The South Koreans had begun to talk of their largest share in international trade in relation to all other developing countries and demanded due weight to their views in the position of the informal group. The Andean Group had also become active and wanted a greater role in the group.[8] As a result, in the special session of the contracting parties in 1985, three distinct groups could be identified among the developing countries. The first was led by the five who were opposed to the inclusion of services in the new round. Their opposition had become stronger since 1982 as a result of work done in the meantime in the capitals that tended to show that any existing comparative advantage they had would be wiped out in case services came to be multilaterally negotiated.[9] The second group was made up of the enthusiasts for the new issues who had extended their support either for reasons of economic advantage or political considerations. The permanent members were Colombia, Chile, Jamaica, Korea, and Zaire. The third group consisted of countries that had an open view of the issue and would support the general position of developing countries.

An agreement to launch the new round had been reached in the November 1985 session of contracting parties. It clearly was not feasible to expect the informal group to build a unified position on the inclusion of services and other new issues. Yet the big five rapidly prepared a draft ministerial declaration on the basis of whatever papers were at that time available. They decided to undertake this task outside the GATT, not in the scope of the informal group.[11] Further, having decided to continue to oppose the inclusion of services and other new issues, the drafting group did not invite members who had openly supported the inclusion of services in the round.[12]

As prepared by the big five and supported by another five (who together came to constitute the G10), the draft did not contain any reference to negotiations on services,[13] only calling for a new round of trade negotiations on goods and other traditional GATT matters like the working rules. The ministerial declaration was presented as a fait accompli in the June 1986 meeting of the informal group. It was clear to all that the draft would be unacceptable to those members who had already declared their support for inclusion of services. One of the major reasons for presenting the draft in a finalized version was the support from the European Commission, whose ambassador, Tranh van Dihn, was known to work in close association at that stage with Paulo Batista Nogueira and S. P. Shukla, the chief negotiators from Brazil and India.[14] Soon afterwards, the EC delegation joined the Group working on the alternative draft in the EFTA building and thereby clearly withdrew whatever implicit support it may have demonstrated for the G10 position.

The so-called Enthusiasts Group objected to the draft and proposed that it be discussed more fully in the informal group at large, where amendments could be made. The G10 members apparently argued that such debate would serve no purpose, as the submission was not to be made on behalf of all developing countries but only on behalf of the signatories of the draft. The G10's stance created an unprecedented situation. It brought the operations of the informal group to a halt after which it never really regained momentum. Other members ostensibly resented the drafts, which surely violated the discipline of conventions and practices that had until then guided and tempered the working of developing-country delegations in the GATT. The breakup of the informal group was perhaps inevitable when in the meeting of the preparatory committee a few day later, Ambassador Felipe Jaramillo from Colombia made a statement regretting the action of the G10 and noting that this was the first time that such a development had taken place. In view of these events, amendments that would normally have been discussed in the informal group would be presented directly to the preparatory committee. The process of drafting the alternative declaration probably started immediately after, at the initiative of Ambassador Jaramillo. A group of about twenty developing countries soon got together and began discussion of a draft prepared by Ambassador Hill of Jamaica.

This initiative gathered immediate and substantial support among developing countries for several reasons. First, a number of delegations felt that by taking a rigid and uncompromising stand even on such issues as standstill and rollback, the G10 had created an impression that developing countries were not supportive of a new round even for trade in goods. This was not the position of the majority of the delegations, and they felt the need to take some concrete action to dispel any such impression. Second, the domination of the big five was, in any case, resented. This resentment was intensified by the manner in which negotiations were carried out in the 1985 special session that led to the decisions to establish the preparatory committee. It was widely felt that the entire package was decided upon by the so-called Tea Party Group in which the big five were involved and that had not pressed for a wider representation of developing countries.[15] Third, countries like Colombia and Thailand chafed at having their efforts to accede to the agreement on subsidies blocked by countries such as Brazil, India, and Egypt, who argued that it would create an unhealthy precedent if countries could accede only on the basis of an understanding. As a result, a Group of Twenty was formed that was able to attract more members to their position.

With the Swiss offering to work together with them, the Café au Lait group emerged. The drafting exercise also shifted to the EFTA building. On July 30, to the surprise of most contracting parties and especially the G10, an agreed draft prepared in the EFTA building and supported by about fifty delegations, was presented to the preparatory committee. The café au lait draft, as it came to be known after its principal sponsors, was transmitted to the Punta del Este meeting as the majority draft and one that had at least the tacit support of the secretariat.

The detailed description of the processes that led to the breakup of the informal group is necessary to understand that the G10 was not a fresh coalition, established to secure a greater leverage for the developing countries in the impending round. It came into being because some members of the informal group did not find it useful to adopt positions that would carry the whole group together. Given that later events showed that the majority of developing contracting parties went along with the inclusion of new issues and supported the draft presented by Colombia and Switzerland, the G10 could be said to have adopted an uncompromising position.

The G10 achieved its objective at least partially. The ministerial declaration at Punta del Este adopted a two-track negotiating strategy for the round. It clearly separated the negotiations on services from the GATT process. Further, all the issues of concern to developing countries were included, and the undertaking amounted to completion of the incomplete business of the Tokyo Round.[16] The Punta del Este declaration called upon the contracting parties to ensure that both sets of negotiations would strive to strengthen the developmental processes of developing countries. G10 could not, however, prevent the inclusion of TRIPs and TRIMs in the main round, where agriculture was also included.

After the launch of the Uruguay Round, G10 continued to attempt to hinder progress on the new issues in order to ensure instead that sufficient progress was made in negotiating groups dealing with traditional GATT issues, especially trade in goods and the working of GATT. At the same time, it tried to keep the demandeurs of the round from achieving GATT-supervised liberalization of service markets and multilateral supervision of enforcement mechanisms in intellectual property. Minus Argentina, which had moved away perceptibly (see Chapter 6), G10 pursued the tactic of preventing substantial negotiations both on services and other new issues, notably TRIPs.

G10 used four principal methods in its attempts to block progress in negotiations on services and TRIPs. First, it demanded that talks proceed only after definitional clarity was achieved, pointing out that such clarity was essential to determine the scope and coverage of negotiations. This was an enormous task, as until then practically no work had been done either on the definition and coverage of services or on the trade link in case of TRIPs and TRIMs. Second, G10 sought a clarification of the role that WIPO, other sectoral UN agencies, and other multilateral agencies that already existed in many of the services sectors would play in the context of the issues being negotiated in GATT. Third, G10 wanted to determine in advance whether the fundamental principles of GATT—the MFN provision, national treatment, reciprocity, and transparency—would be applicable in case of services. It also proposed to determine whether national sovereign control over developmental processes would be compromised by multilateral negotiations on TRIMs and TRIPs. Finally, G10 tried to secure assurances that the developmental processes of developing economies would be strengthened as contained in the Punta del Este declaration and that any links between the two tracks of negotiations would be avoided.

Despite or perhaps because of these tactics (see Chapter 1), there was considerable progress in the negotiations on services, as evidenced by the document transmitted by the president of the group to the Montreal review. In TRIPs, however, there was almost no agreement to negotiate until Montreal, as India continued to insist that WIPO was the appropriate forum for any such negotiations. By the time of the Montreal review, the G10 had effectively disintegrated. The United States had, as expected, brought tremendous pressure to bear upon some of the members by its use of Section 301 (see Chapter 3). Among the big five, Brazil and Egypt succumbed to U.S. pressure before the Montreal review.[17] Yugoslavia was marginalized because of its internal problems, which have since continued. India finally agreed to negotiate TRIPs in GATT in April

1989, having decided that India could play a more constructive role if it took full part in the round and in all the negotiating groups.[18] With India's change in thinking, G10 was disbanded.

G10: AN ASSESSMENT

Opinions on G10's role in the Uruguay Round and in promoting developing-country interests vary widely. Yet most negotiators and international civil servants in retrospect would agree that the group contributed positively to the round. It is clear that G10 was instrumental in bringing developing-country concerns to center stage. According to an observer who participated both as a country delegate and UN official, it was not easy to have the developing-country objectives included in a round that the developed countries initially wanted to devote almost exclusively to the new issues. He maintains that G10 had to act strongly and with sufficient doggedness to have the traditional issues included. On some occasions this may have given the impression that it opposed the round at large. If so, it was merely a negotiating stance. As mentioned earlier in the chapter, the content and format of the Punta del Este declaration are in some sense a testimony to the G10's efforts to include traditional issues.

The self-exclusion of the big five from the agenda-formation process meant that all developed-country demands were incorporated at the cost of making the negotiating agenda far too ambitious and thus unmanageable. This was perhaps the objective of the developed-member countries, who—having overloaded the agenda—could then determine the relative weight given specific issues and the progress on each during the negotiations.

The most important contribution of G10, though visible only in retrospect, was to raise fundamental questions with regard to negotiations on services in the early stages of the round. G10 had become practically service-centric in its approach during the early negotiating period, attempting to prevent progress until all its concerns were addressed. All contracting parties have since recognized the value of this insistence on forcing clarifications and gathering vast statistics. Similarly, the issues and questions the G10 raised in the context of TRIPs also helped to achieve the necessary conceptual and empirical clarity in a rather complex area of negotiations. Perhaps the fairest assessment of G10 came from a developed-country negotiator who said, "Although it is clear that G10 were operating in a vacuum of reality, they did contribute to the clarity and progress in the Round." Even if G10 was primarily blocking coalition, then, it did contribute positively to the round.

Another major—though indirect—contribution of G10 was that it made the Uruguay Round truly multilateral. For the first time in GATT history, developing countries played an important role in the progress of the MTNs, in part because G10 began the move in this direction. G10 fostered new negotiating abilities and skills among developing countries, perhaps unwittingly helping to dismantle the fairly long and almost complete domination of the big five. This is bound to have an impact on the negotiations in other fora, such as UNCTAD and other multilateral agencies. It may be seen as a loss of international stature for countries such as Brazil and India; the process has, however, reduced the disparity between the countries' shares in international trade and the negotiating leverage or status of contracting parties. This is surely a move in the right direction for the evolution of a multilateral trading system.

Against the above achievements, there were also some costs in the emergence and working of the G10. The first real cost was the breakdown of the informal group of developing countries, which could not be revived until July 1991. The utility of the informal group for pushing developing-country interests in GATT may be questioned. Yet it is clear that this was a functional formation and could, with some care and constructive contribution, be made steadily more effective. The fragmentation of developing-country negotiating strength has not been beneficial.

The second cost has been in terms of the impression created for a certain period that developing countries were not supportive of the MTNs per se. This impression gathered strength because of the early and consistent criticism of GATT. Yet the great majority of developing countries, including India and Brazil, are more than ever linked to the smooth and rule-bound working of the global trading system.

The third impact has been on the credibility and efficacy of GATT as an institution. G10 contributed to the undermining of this institution when it allowed the prelaunch negotiations to move out of GATT. It is in developing countries' interests to reinforce the GATT mechanism, in the absence of which they would have to contend with rampant bilateralism and a free-for-all in global trade markets (see Chapters 2 and 3).

The only other coalition made up exclusively of developing countries is a sectoral grouping in the area of textiles and garments, the International Textile and Clothing Bureau (ITCB), a coalition that has been in existence for most of the 1980s. ITCB has effectively represented the interests of major textile exporters along with those who have recently entered the textile trade. The bureau's success has so far been in formulating positions that have emphasized commonality of interests while maintaining flexibility in projecting the special concerns and requirements of the entrants and LDCs. The developed contracting parties have recognized the role of the ITCB in presenting a common set of positions that can form the basis of real negotiations.

The Uruguay Round has been unique in witnessing the evolution of hybrid coalitions of developing and developed countries that have continued to function over the entire duration of the round. Of these, the most active and formal has been the Cairns Group of major exporters of agricultural products.[19] The Café au Lait Group ceased to exist once the round was launched, but it was succeeded by the Hôtel de la Paix Group (the name referring to their first meeting place), a similarly informal coalition that serves the essential purpose of discussing individual positions to reach some kind of understanding before the issue is discussed formally in the various negotiating groups. None of the contracting parties attending the meetings of the group is bound to align its positions with the discussions in the group.

WHY DID THE G10 DISBAND?

A number of reasons explain the disbandment of the G10. First, the heterogeneity of developing countries is such that it undermines the continued survival of a coalition such as the G10 after the start of negotiations. According to this view, the coalition had served its objective by ensuring that issues of concern to developing nations were included in the agenda and its demise was a "natural event" once real negotiations had commenced. Second, the GATT (unlike UNCTAD) has not been a forum in which coalition bargaining is used. The only coalitions that emerge are flexible, temporary, and based on a specific and technical negotiating issue, and these cut across distinctions between developed and developing countries. Thus the G10, according to this view, would by convention not have any role in the GATT. Third, North-South issues or debates of that nature are not normally discussed in GATT; coalitions such as the G10 that are not issue-based or sectoral tend to wither away because their approach is essentially a North-South one.

A set of more empirical and contingent reasons relates to the operation of the group and of the dominant members within it: for example, the inability of the big five to carry along others because of their big-country behavior, the assumption (on the part of Brazil and India in particular) that they were leaders and representatives of other countries and the emergence of other negotiators in other developing countries who wanted to participate more actively in the negotiations.

The weakening of developing-country coalitions can also be witnessed in UNCTAD. The secretariat has been greatly involved in assisting developing-country delegations in formulating their positions in these MTNs. The collapse of G10 and divisions within developing countries in GATT have had an adverse effect on the working of G77 in UNCTAD. Global conditions have also undermined the traditional North-South dialogue on international economic order and on interlinking financial, trade, and services flows and their bearing on development objectives. With recent changes in Eastern Europe, the coalition of centrally planned economies, which operated as Group D in UNCTAD, has also disintegrated. Its presence had provided a counterpoint to the developed-country formation, the Group B, and permitted a greater negotiating space and leverage to G77. A number of developing countries, notably in Latin America, that had earlier followed import-substituting policies have adopted strong measures to open their economies and shift to greater integration with global commercial flows. This has increased their dependence on developed-country markets and led to an apparent weakening of their South-centric positions (see Chapters 4, 5, and 6). The weakening of oil prices almost continuously throughout the 1980s; the eight-year Iran-Iraq War; and the Gulf War, during which many developing countries aligned themselves with developed nations to push for the withdrawal of Iraqi forces from Kuwait have resulted in an erosion of G77's position as a negotiating coalition in UNCTAD.

It is also clear that G77 itself is now more heterogeneous in its perception of the role of markets and private agents in fostering the development process. The shared perception of the past—that of the predominant role of government in domestic economic activity and in securing an improved international environment for developing countries—has also changed markedly since the early 1980s. The more advanced developing countries have sharpened this heterogeneity by floating a smaller formation of G15, which broadly consists of five member countries from each of the three continents. In concentrating greater negotiating time and material resources on the worsening economic problems of LDCs, the developed countries have found a legitimate reason to shift the negotiating agenda away from traditional North-South issues. These factors have raised serious questions on the working of the G77 in its present form. Thus, even in UNCTAD, which has been the traditional home for coalition bargaining, the developing-country formation is under fairly severe pressure to change its objectives and modalities of operation. The process culminated in the 1992 UNCTAD held in Cartagena, Colombia.

There is an element of truth in all the reasons forwarded for the collapse of G10 in GATT and for the current existential problems G77 faces in UNCTAD. Yet these arguments provide only a partial explanation for the greater difficulties developing-country coalitions have recently experienced. Heterogeneity has, for example, always been a characteristic of developing countries and, moreover, has not prevented them from successfully operating sectoral coalitions or becoming members of hybrid groups in which the heterogeneity is even greater. The argument that GATT is not a forum for coalition bargaining is simply not tenable because formal and informal coalitions of developed countries—the Quadrilateral, the EFTA grouping, the Nordics coalition, and the EC, for example—have operated and continue to do so successfully in GATT.[20] Whether the negotiations take on a North-South nature depends on the issue being negotiated. G10, in its brief history, demonstrated both its ability and motivation to discuss each issue on its merit and within the established practices of GATT.

Four main structural factors account for the collapse of G10 and for the current strains in other developing-country coalitions. First, in recent times, there has been a dichotomy or a contradiction in the relative political and economic positions of various developing countries. In earlier years Argentina, Brazil, Egypt, India, and Yugoslavia had both the political and economic leadership among developing countries on account of their size in terms of population and domestic economy; their large and diversified industrial sectors, which preceded the development of such capacities in any other developing country; and their perceived capability to evolve an independent and competitive industrial structure. Over the years, however, the big five have clearly lost economic ground to other developing economies, which have grown at appreciably higher rates and whose industrial structures are visibly more diversified and certainly more internationally competitive. Politically, too, the big five have been seen to be more vulnerable both to internal and to external pressures than in earlier years (see Chapters 6 and 7). It is clear that even if the big five continue to be politically important, they cannot be expected to provide leadership in a situation in which their share of global trade and overall economic performance has steadily declined. New voices for developing countries in global commercial and economic issues must be heard, and the Uruguay Round has already become part of the transition.[21]

Second, the international environment has been radically transformed since the launch of the round. This transformation was obviously not expected by the developing economies, especially by the big five. With the end of the Cold War and of the intense rivalry between developed market economies and centrally planned economies, the developed economies have been able to press more strongly for complete reciprocity and to resist further extension or even continuation of existing preferential dispensations toward developing countries (see Chapters 1 and 3).[22] As mentioned earlier, other events have also contributed to the erosion in the developing-country bargaining position over the past few years. The end of the 1980s meant the end of the postcolonial era in international economic relations.

Third, the developed countries have finally got over the ideological problem of having to bear some additional and special responsibility for development. The Keynesian rationalization of this position, with its notion that growth in the developed economies was in danger of being brought to a halt in the absence of development in the Third World (the argument most eloquently put forward by the Brandt Commission), also worked itself out by the end of the previous decade. Any negotiating position based on these premises essentially became irrelevant for real bargaining.

Fourth, the negotiating position of developed countries has also been strengthened by the new growth opportunities opened up by the ongoing third technological revolution. This revolution (which has three dominant strands: microelectronics, new materials, and biotechnology) has forced developed economies to undertake massive restructuring that has left relatively lesser resources for transfer to developing economies. Further, the growth opportunities that have thus opened up have to that extent reduced the importance of developing-country markets. Competitive pressures generated by the new technologies have made the North much more self-centered and also self-contained, to the obvious disadvantage of developing countries. The new technologies have made it more difficult for any developing country to ignore the global division of labor. The costs of attempting to develop a self-sufficient and relatively "insulated" industrial structure in terms of efficiency and welfare losses are now prohibitive. Consequently, developing countries cannot afford not to integrate their economies into the global economy, dominated as it is by developed economies and their megacorporations. This has again transformed the context within which developing countries have to operate their coalitions and negotiate with developed market economies.

The above-mentioned four factors explain the problems developing-country coalitions face in successfully negotiating as a group to achieve a set of predetermined and shared objectives. They have found it more difficult to come to an understanding on issues of common interest in the transformed global conditions because they lack clear perspective on the nature of these changes and their impact either on domestic economic conditions or on the international negotiating environment. This shortcoming perhaps explains the relative inability of countries like Brazil, India, and other members of the G10 to anticipate the intensity of U.S. pressure on services and TRIPs and the extent of support for this demand among developed and developing contracting parties.[23] As the next section shows, with an adequate recognition of these factors, developing countries can establish a changed set of common objectives that will become the basis for successful coalitions in the future.

THE WAY FORWARD

Should the collapse of G10 and the near demise of G77 lead us to conclude that developing-country coalitions have lost relevance in multilateral trade and other economic negotiations? Have sectoral coalitions, the most formalized of which is the Organization of Petroleum Exporting Countries (OPEC), and hybrids such as Cairns instead taken precedence? Are there any objectives that can provide an agenda for developing-country coalitions?

Developing-country coalitions continue to be relevant for safeguarding and promoting the interests of developing economies. In doing so they will also contribute to the improvement of the multilateral trading environment. The essential condition for a resurgence of developing-country coalitions is the awareness that developing countries are now more interested partners in safeguarding and reinforcing a multilateral and rule-based trading environment (see Chapter 1). Developing countries should see themselves and should be seen as the principal defenders and supporters of the GATT and the proposed MTO, which provide the institutional basis for the multilateral trading system. The direct lesson from the experience of the Uruguay Round and of the working of G10 in the prelaunch period is that developing countries should never permit or be party to any process that results in the negotiations' moving out of GATT, as they did during the time of agenda formation in the Uruguay Round.

The second condition for such a resurgence is acknowledgment that the North-South paradigm for international negotiations is passé. Developing countries will need to share the responsibility toward the seriously affected economies more equitably, even if this means that some of the newly industrialized and large developing countries must give up their claims to preferential and differential treatment. The "North" within the South will have to be recognized in order for the coalition of developing countries to reclaim the morally superior and hegemonic positions they occupied during the 1960s and 1970s in the context of international economic relations. Some suitable criteria need to be devised to allocate the responsibility toward the LDCs and for graduation of some developing countries out of S&D treatment.

The third condition is resolution of the contradiction that the coalition has not operated according to the relative economic and trade strengths of individual developing countries. On occasion, positions have been unrelated or even opposed to the actual interests of the developing countries as a whole. Developing economies that have a greater share in global commerce and economic output should be expected to assume the role of principal representatives of developing countries in MTNs and other economic negotiations.

Once these three conditions are fulfilled, developing-country coalitions will rediscover their basis for participation in international negotiations. The coalition's usefulness and indeed its raison d'être will, however, be dependent upon the adoption of a common agenda.

The agenda should focus on five issues. First, the strengthening of the existing institutions that govern the working of the multilateral trading system and the improvement in the economic and trading conditions of the LDCs should be explored. A developing-country coalition will do well seriously to consider the initiatives it can launch in these two areas and the resources it can commit to them.

Second, the creation of an MTO should be made a priority. This would also imply that the coalition would continue to press for rectification of derogations from the existing protocols and conventions and exceptions to general multilateral principles and practices. These departures should not be carried over to the new organization, so that it enjoys the highest legitimacy and jurisdiction in its activities. The run-up for the creation of an MTO may also include the review of the persistent use of the balance-of-payment argument as a condition for continued nonapplication of multilaterally agreed protocols in the case of both developed and developing countries.

Third, developing countries will need to ask for a complete rollback of existing protectionist measures, both tariff and nontariff and both by developed and (over a longer time period) developing countries. The gray-area measures, VERs, and orderly market arrangements may be made into specific targets of negotiating practice in coming years and as a run-up to the formation of an MTO.

Fourth, developing countries may now call for a completion of the negotiations on trade in services. This would require that apart from the agreements reached so far in this area, there should be substantial negotiations on freer mobility of different factors of production, including both capital and labor, and a greater role of multilateral international institutions in monitoring and regulating operations of large service corporations. This is especially important in the context of building up the required confidence in developing countries that liberalization on services trade will not be detrimental to their development goals.

Fifth and finally, the coalition should take up environmental concerns, which have become critical for some developing countries. Developing countries must devote their attention to and support inquiries into environmental aspects of international trade in goods, services, and technology. Some critical issues relate to exports that may have been restricted in their country of origin, relocation of industrial capacity, and export of technology already known to be ecologically unsound.

Developing countries should not abandon their coalitions. Hybrids may be tried out, but the extent to which these can help developing countries achieve objectives that may be at some variance with the goals of developed-country partners is yet unclear. The above-mentioned conditions of a new basis for the establishment of developing-country coalitions as well as the set of common objectives that provide their raison d'être will contribute to their restrengthening. Such coalitions have served a useful purpose in the past, and their current difficulties simply reflect a period of transition during which the role and nature of operations must be redefined. Once this redefinition is achieved, developing-country coalitions may be expected to act as an effective instrument both for developing countries and for improving the working of the multilateral trading system at large.

NOTES

This chapter relies on extensive interviews and has benefited from the comments received of the participants in this project. The views expressed here do not necessarily reflect those of the organization in which I am currently employed.

1. Preference for developing countries is normally for developing-country contracting parties in the GATT.

2. This was despite the clear understanding among all contracting parties that GATT had served primarily as a mechanism first to resolve European–North American trade problems and latterly to tackle trade-related issues among the trio of super economic powers, the United States, the EC, and Japan.

3. At one stage the GATT secretariat, in particular the director general, was criticized for allowing the big five to be overrepresented in the informal consultation process known in GATT parlance as green room consultations. This criticism was first voiced in the rather trying period preceding the launch of the round.

4. As one of the principal negotiators from one of the Nordic countries stated, "Once inside a negotiating room, trade shares are not important. What comes into play is the extent to which positions have been worked out, how specialized knowledge is brought to bear upon the negotiations, and the skill of the individual negotiator."

5. According to the memory of one of the chief negotiators, the core group consisted of Argentina, Brazil, Colombia, Egypt, India, Singapore, Uruguay, Tanzania, and Yugoslavia.

6. One of these papers was prepared by the so-called whole group of the developing countries and the other by a group of twenty-five to thirty developing-country contracting parties.

7. This was unprecedented in terms of GATT conventions but not contrary to GATT rules, which permit such a vote.

8. It is reported that Ambassador Hill of Jamaica had on two occasions complained of the tendency on the part of the "big few" to evolve common positions and to take the positions of the others for granted. The big five denied this charge and maintained that the numbers were kept small to facilitate drafting and that these position papers were always open to discussion and change.

9. The validity of this position was questioned even in the capitals of some developing countries. In the case of India, for example, a number of people (and some studies) argued that India could benefit from liberalization in certain sectors and needed to undertake a detailed cost benefit exercise before concluding anything on the country's comparative advantages.

10. It seems that a resolution had been adopted at the 1984 meeting of African trade ministers to support the demand for inclusion of services in the new round. The Africans' view would have been known to all contracting parties.

11. This meeting seems to have been held at the Indian mission at the invitation of the Indian chief negotiator.

12. Some of the other delegations that had been invited went to a few meetings and then dropped out because their brief was not to take an openly negative stand on the issue of services. Once it was clear that G10 was committed to exclusion of services, they abstained and were later active in the Group of Twenty, which was established at the initiative of the Uruguayan and Colombian delegations led by Ambassadors Lacarte and Jaramillo, respectively.

13. The ten that constituted the G10 were Argentina, Brazil, Cuba, Egypt, India, Nicaragua, Nigeria, Peru, Tanzania, and Yugoslavia. Argentina was effectively to break away from the group within two months of its formation when it presented its own compromise draft on the ministerial declaration toward the end of July 1986 (see Chapter 6).

14. The EC, too, as was borne out later, played the game of keeping all its options open until the very end and could well have encouraged the G10 to go ahead with its draft on goods negotiations.

15. The group was so called because it started when the U.S. delegation invited the "more important" delegations to a tea party. Both Abreu (Chapter 7) and Tussie (Chapter 6) report the heavy pressures, many of them "debt-fed," that negotiators felt at the time.

16. It is reported that the idea of the two-track negotiating authority came from the Colombian delegation, which suggested it at the plenary session on the first day of the Punta del Este meeting.

17. Brazil, threatened with the use of 301 in 1988 (see Chapter 7), signed a bilateral agreement in return for the lifting of the ban on GSP exports to the U.S. markets. Egypt was also brought around, with only some pressure on aid. Yugoslavia was beset with grave internal economic and political troubles that have made it a marginal negotiator since the end of 1988.

18. It is perhaps important to note that this change came about coincidentally with a change of the chief negotiator in Geneva and also of senior officials in the administrative ministry in Delhi. Some observers regarded it as India's retreat in the face of an impending U.S. threat to name it to the Super 301 list. In my view India took action not to try to prevent a U.S. move but as a consequence of a shift in negotiating strategy. The United States did not in fact take India off the 301 list. In April 1992 the United States, still unhappy with India's stand on patent protection in drugs and pharmaceuticals, banned GSP imports from India.

19. For details and an evaluation of the Cairns Group, see Chapter 10. For an analysis of the Indian change in strategy, see Chapter 8.

20. The Quadrilateral is an informal grouping of the four major economic powers, namely, the United States, the EC, Japan, and Canada. It is used regularly to inform the members of others' positions and to reconcile them to the extent possible. Similarly, the EFTA countries maintain regular though informal contact for similar purposes. The Nordics have a more formal arrangement whereby each Nordic country represents the others in a number of negotiations, the distribution of subjects having been decided upon earlier through mutual consultations. This division of work, backed up by contracts in the capitals, has proved cost effective and beneficial. The savings in resources this strategy achieves would be most welcome for developing countries. Finally, there is the EC as represented by the European Commission. This is obviously more than a coalition. Yet it may be

noted that the Commission has to arrive at consensual positions among members who are fairly heterogeneous and have vastly varying interests at times. This has become even more true with the recent expansion of the EC.

21. This transition in leadership also happens among developed countries, as is clear from the transition from the UK to the United States after World War II and the emergence of Germany and Japan as the principal economic players within the OECD. Although the United States has maintained its leadership for the moment, it has been unable to force its will on the multilateral system in the same manner as in the earlier rounds. (see Chapter 3).

22. The United States has led this move for graduation and complete reciprocity because of intense competitive pressure from Germany and Japan in an increasing number of industrial sectors. The attempt therefore to prize open developing-country markets can assuage domestic public opinion. It may also see developing-country markets as better hunting grounds for its corporations, which have lost substantial ground to Japanese and German firms.

23. The analogy could be drawn with the conditions immediately after World War II, when the negotiations for the International Trade Organization and subsequently for tariff reductions under the GATT were launched. Not many of the countries understood the implications of the newly emerging mass-production technologies for international trade in goods. As a result, some chose to abstain from GATT, and others effectively ignored the essence of multilateral tariff protocols even while participating in MTNs.

PART V
CONCLUSIONS

12

Developing Countries in World Trade: Implications for Bargaining

DAVID GLOVER & DIANA TUSSIE

The rules of the game in international economic relations have changed dramatically since the early 1980s. In the course of this process, the heterogeneity among developing countries has become more prominent. As the case studies have shown, despite a general move toward more open trade regimes, bargaining behavior is increasingly diversified.

In this chapter we analyze the effects of the new external environment on the objectives and bargaining power of developing countries. We then describes the tactics countries choose to promote their interests in the world trading system. These include the preferred combination of bi-, pluri-, and multilateral bargaining; the formation of coalitions; and the deployment of negotiating and technical skill. Finally, we offer an assessment of the results achieved through bargaining, some speculation on the future of the world trading system, and policy recommendations.

EXTERNAL INFLUENCES ON BARGAINING BEHAVIOR

The multilateral negotiations in the GATT have always been the bedrock of world trade policy. The Uruguay Round was launched in the late 1980s with an ambitious and complex agenda. It was of particular concern to developing countries. A major endeavor in itself, the round coincided with their own trade policy adjustment. The subsequent deadlock in the negotiations added a further sense of frustration (and urgency) to trade relations in general. Negotiations evolved against the backdrop of new regional initiatives and indebtedness (or, more precisely, a widespread balance-of-payments crisis). How did these developments affect the bargaining options and stances of the countries in question? What were the debt-trade links?

In the first instance, it is worth emphasizing that no amount of trade liberalization could have solved the debt problem. Laird and Nogués

(1989) calculated that full MFN trade liberalization by the United States, EC, and Japan could have increased the yearly exports of the group of seventeen highly indebted countries by only $6.5 billion, equivalent to less than 14 percent of their total annual service. There is also a geographical divergence. North American banks were mostly exposed to the larger countries in Latin America, while the largest volumes of imports from developing countries come from Asia. In short, trade alone was not the way out of debt, even for the banks.

Financial distress has had a strongly negative effect on the trade-bargaining options of developing countries, as examples from Brazil and Argentina illustrate. The terms under which a number of life-saving bridging loans were granted were not only financial ones; in many instances, changes in trade policy were responses to financial pressures (see Chapters 6 and 7). When the weight of debt servicing is substantial, this is not surprising.

The indirect effect of debt—structural adjustment programs to ensure repayment—was also serious. The policy process has changed, with the weight of finance ministries in overall policy formulation increasing dramatically. Policy-based lending was initially important to induce countries to liberalize, although many countries have by now internalized that advice. Mexico and Argentina, for example, continue to take decisive strides toward more open trade regimes, regardless of conditionality (see Chapters 4 and 10). The import-substitution strategy has been swept aside, and a new set of intellectual convictions reigns, especially throughout Latin America. Perhaps as much as conditionality, World Bank and IMF research and writing contributed to the shift in intellectual fashion. In some instances, the Bank and the Fund have acted as an external technocratic lobby to counteract the resistance of domestic lobby groups. In others, such as India and Costa Rica, governments blended the need to meet conditionalities with the need to build a consensus over the course of adjustment (see Chapters 5 and 8).

In general, then, indebtedness increased vulnerability and reduced the bargaining options of developing countries. Their power to gain market access has been greatly impaired precisely when they need it most: when liberalization has made these economies more export-dependent. Because their trade liberalization has not been part of an internationally coordinated exercise, their plight is compounded. While the removal of trade barriers could not in itself have resolved the debt problem, the persistent bias against them imposes costs as well as limits on greater outward orientation. As all of our case studies show, bargaining efforts have focused on short-term market access to the detriment of longer-term systemic or development goals.

In this situation of limited economic leverage, it would be tempting to use geopolitical advantages to secure more favorable treatment. Here, too, however, leverage has decreased with the end of the Cold War. The traditional advantage of strategically situated or nonaligned countries is fast disappearing, as the case studies of Costa Rica and India indicate. There will probably continue to be opportunities for some countries to use specific issues—such as drug traffic, refugees, or illegal immigration—to their advantage. These opportunities are likely to be episodic and available to few countries, however, and are counterbalanced by leverage exerted by industrialized countries on human rights, democracy, and so on.

In any case, the great "systemic" issue of East-West conflict around which countries could plan stable, long-term strategies has passed. The only issue on the horizon that has major bargaining potential is the environment. Here some developing countries do have possibilities to hold industrialized countries hostage, for example, by refusing to curtail carbon or chlorofluorocarbon (CFC) emissions in return for trade concessions. Even here, however, bargaining will be very tricky, given the high degree of ecological interdependence involved.

UNILATERAL, BILATERAL, OR MULTILATERAL?

The redefinition of global bargaining arrangements currently under way (see Chapters 1–3) poses further challenges. The emerging regional fragmentation of the trading system and the deadlock of the Uruguay Round have led some countries to place their hopes for smoother, more secure, and predictable market access in subglobal rather than the system-wide arenas. A credible (and substantial) offer, however, may materialize only for selected countries, and it forces crucial strategic decisions on whether to move faster in bilateral instead of multilateral trade negotiations.

In this situation, a key tactical choice for any country is how to make use of uni-, bi-, and multilateral openings to produce a desired outcome. When tariffs are very high, there are real economic gains to unilateral liberalization. This is a desirable trade policy for one's own good and therefore not a real bargaining chip. Yet once trade barriers are cut back to reasonable levels, the additional efficiency gains become marginal. It is at this stage, when further reductions will mean a diminished impact on efficiency, that the design of a bargaining strategy is essential.

The uni-, bi-, and multilateral components of trade strategy are not independent and must fit into a coherent whole. Not all combinations are possible or compatible with other options like coalition formation or regional common markets. Costa Rica's liberalization and accession to the GATT, for example, had repercussions on the CACM and preempted regional coordination.

Mexico has combined the uni-, bi-, and multilateral elements sooner, more deliberately, and more effectively than most (Chapter 4). The credibility of unilateral liberalization was subsequently anchored by two further steps, accession to the GATT and the creation of an FTA with the United States (and Canada).[1] Mexico needed results quickly to maintain domestic support for its sweeping reforms. Moreover, 70 percent of the country's exports were to the United States; why not concentrate bargaining resources there? The FTA was seen as a direct and efficient way to address specific problems, as well as a complement to the results expected to accrue to all countries from a successful Uruguay Round. The FTA negotiations were facilitated by prior unilateral liberalization, which demonstrated Mexico's "seriousness," and by GATT accession, which provided principles and a legal framework that could be invoked during the discussions.

Canada's approach has been similar in some respects. It entered an FTA with its largest trading partner largely as a defensive measure, not so much to increase market access, which was already fairly good, but to prevent the latter from deteriorating in the face of increasing U.S. protectionism. What began as a series of sectoral discussions became economy-wide in order to allow more trade-offs and facilitate an agreement. The disadvantage was that as the scope of the negotiations increased, it encompassed issues, particularly subsidies, on which the chances of a favorable outcome were better in the GATT. In the end, there was no agreement on subsidies, only a dispute settlement mechanism to verify that the letter of existing U.S. law was being applied.

Some aspects of the free trade negotiations were of differing importance to Mexico and Canada. The former had already opened its doors to foreign competition through unilateral liberalization; it hoped that an FTA would stimulate flows of private investment by increasing confidence and reducing barriers to investment from the United States. The Canadian government and officials, in contrast, believed their country needed a strong dose of import liberalization to improve its international competitiveness. Beyond these differences, however, lies an important commonality: the role of an FTA to lock in an initial program of economic liberalization by raising the costs of reversal to subsequent governments. Furthermore, the expectation of a stake in the U.S. market creates converts to the cause.

Playing the uni-, bi-, and multilateral cards skillfully can have benefits, but it is not always possible for countries to direct the issues they wish to the most favorable forum. In addition, bilateral negotiations subject a country to a different and generally tougher set of rules than the GATT. The threat of sanctions exposes a country's domestic politics to the bargaining process in a way that multilateral ones generally do not. These problems were illustrated by the United States' (GATT-illegal) use of

Super 301 against Brazil (see Chapter 7) and the threat pending on Argentina (see Chapter 6). To enforce intellectual property rights the USTR made exporters of a variety of products aware that they would lose access to U.S. markets if their governments failed to be accommodating. In such a hostage-taking game, the United States can drive a wedge between import-competing and exporting interests and create articulate and influential lobbyists for its own cause among the latter. This threat of cross-sectoral retaliation can so far only be implemented bilaterally because, until the Uruguay Round is completed, it is not permitted under the GATT. Brazil, on whom sanctions were in fact finally imposed, took its case to the GATT. However, driven by financial pressures, it also had to come to terms with U.S. bilateral demands. The threat of sanctions has operated as ad hoc conditionality.

Finally, there are fallacies of composition at work. While early entrants to an FTA, like Mexico and Canada, will enjoy some trade diversion benefits, these will be diluted as other countries join. The lessons derived from previous phases of the project are applicable. As in debt rescheduling, firstcomers may get immediate and tangible advantages, but these are quickly eroded since they will also serve as precedents for potential entrants waiting on the sidelines. Separate, noncooperative action makes dividends short-lived (Tussie, 1988).

The transaction costs of negotiating an FTA may appear to be small (especially if the disadvantages will accrue all the same via policy-based lending and/or Section 301 of U.S. trade legislation). Yet a world trading system consisting of a hodgepodge of such agreements would be extremely cumbersome. In the Western Hemisphere there is danger of a hub-and-spoke agreement, whereby the United States has free access to all countries in the region but these do not enjoy free trade with each other. Not only is more secure or open access not guaranteed; there may be a higher price to pay than in the GATT (see Chapter 3). It is here that the GATT stalemate has created a dangerous situation. It diverts efforts into bilateral bargaining for urgently needed market access. Each FTA negotiated separately can entail a higher cost than might be necessary. The GATT is further marginalized and with it a world trading system based on nondiscrimination.

COALITIONS

Faced by deterioration in their traditional sources of bargaining power, some countries have explored the advantages that might be derived from coalitions. Three such coalitions are described in this book: the Cairns Group, the Group of 10,[2] and regional coalitions such as the Central American initiatives. The G10 was the most traditional of the three in that it took up issues along the North-South divide (see Chapter 11). Informally led by India and Brazil, it emphasized traditional issues, insisted on their inclusion in the Uruguay Round, and opposed the introduction of new issues. Its inability to hold together can be attributed to bargaining errors, in particular, a lack of willingness to compromise among its members. Negotiation is persuasion, and in this the G10 failed.

It is likely, however, that without the G10, the old issues would have received less attention than they did. The two interpretations are not necessarily contradictory; both are consistent with evidence from many of the case studies that, in current circumstances, developing countries do better by participating and advancing issues than by attempting to block them. In bilateral negotiations, the strongest evidence comes from the Asian NIC experience; in multilateral fora, it can be found in the results of the Cairns coalition.

The Cairns Group brought together a set of developed and developing countries that shared common (though not identical) interests in a single issue: agriculture. G10, by contrast, was exclusive to developing countries but represented them on a variety of issues. By late 1992 the Uruguay Round had not concluded mainly because of the lack of agreement on agriculture; this makes an assessment of the Cairns Group's achievements difficult. Still, it is fairly clear that Cairns played an important role in keeping the negotiations over agriculture alive. The Group did a great deal of useful technical and preparatory work, and many points of agreement can be traced back to earlier texts prepared by Cairns. This is perhaps its most important contribution. This is in contrast to G10, which formulated many positions and questions but did little or no technical backup. Negotiators often depended on the quality of their rhetoric rather than on adequately researched economic arguments. In part, this reflected G10's emphasis on blocking rather than influencing developments.

Cairns's more fundamental difference from G10 is that it comprised developed and developing countries with a shared interest. As such, it played a useful role as a miniforum in which issues could be debated and proposals floated before being introduced into more difficult negotiations in wider fora. It sought movement rather than defense. The formation of other such groups could be beneficial. A focus on more narrowly defined ends may be more helpful than acting exclusively through grand coalitions based on hazy, nonbinding economic foundations. The new approach may also be better suited to the growing heterogenity within the South.

If so, why did a hybrid coalition similar to Cairns not arise around other issues, such as services? The context was clearly different. For one thing, in services the space was initially occupied by G10; its subsequent breakdown left little incentive for a nonblocking coalition to emerge out of its rubble. The polarization in agriculture created both the need and the space for moderation. In services the situation was never so clearly polarized. In fact, the complexity and opaqueness of the issues in services were probably the most important factors affecting the evolution of the negotiations. Brazil and India, as leaders of G10, were not merely intent on delaying the process. Although it could not provide technical knowledge as did the Cairns Group, G10 did show a genuine desire to clarify obscure matters. The reversal of positions in services as negotiations evolved, with the United States backtracking from its original forcefulness (see Chapters 1 and 11), vindicates the G10 contention that the United States did not really know what it wanted, or could offer, when it first raised the issue. Once liberated from the need to adopt adversarial positions and freed from the East-West paradigm, developing country coalitions have a new role to play. It is not certain, however, that such coalitions will extend to the entire community of developing countries or be confined to smaller units depending on the special issues involved.

BARGAINING SKILL

Whatever its strategy or tactics, a country's skill in employing them will have a bearing on the outcome. In general, a country's stock of competent negotiators will be related in an approximate fashion to its size and level of economic development. This is not a particularly interesting observation, however, or one that offers much in the way of policy guidance. More interesting are indications from our study that it is not so much the stock of human capital that matters but the effectiveness with which it is employed. Furthermore, recent developments in the world trading system have on balance made it more difficult for developing countries to apply their skills effectively.

The experience of the Asian NICs provides an illustration (see Chapter 9). The trade success of these countries made them subject to permanent negotiation for market access. With a clear idea of where their interests lay, they have concentrated on product bargaining. Having well-defined objectives gives countries an advantage over opponents who are less decisive and makes it easier to concentrate resources in the key areas.

Today, however, it is much more difficult for countries to define their interests clearly. Several influences come into play. First, the new issues introduced during the Uruguay Round (services, investment, and intellectual property) are uncertain and complex; the implications of change in these fields are being clarified only after years of study and negotiation. Second, the addition of the new issues, complexity aside, increases the total number of issues on the table and makes it harder for small countries to follow them all. Third, development itself brings complexity. As Korea diversifies its export products and markets, for example, it finds it harder to concentrate its bargaining resources in a few areas. As the agenda expands so do the opportunities for friction. It is difficult today to be a single-issue country. Argentina discovered this when, in spite of its efforts to concentrate on agriculture, it was drawn into bilateral disputes over intellectual property (see Chapter 6).

The complexity of the new issues has also led to changes in the locus of responsibility for trade bargaining. Traditionally, most countries have assigned this function to foreign affairs ministries, which spoke in the "national interest." As the interests of the nation, and even those of particular sectors within it, become less clear, and as the issues become more technical, input from other ministries is required. Decentralization may improve the quality of decisionmaking, but it can also slow down the process and reduce coherence. Moreover, it presents a wider range of targets for lobbying by other countries, as the Brazilian case illustrates (see Chapter 7). In Brazil, as in most countries, the Finance Ministry has greatly increased its say in trade negotiations, as financial variables become important determinants of trade policies. The U.S. Treasury has, on occasion, applied pressure to the Brazilian Finance Ministry to persuade Foreign Affairs to change its positions on subjects important to the United States. Such bilateral influences affected multilateral stances.

More generally, the Uruguay Round has seen developing countries begin to play an active and pragmatic role, participating in discussions rather than blocking them (see Chapter 1). This approach is much more demanding; being a demandeur requires clear objectives and the technical skills to participate usefully in problem-solving negotiations. The need for skills increases the advantage of a relatively developed country; the need for coherence may actually decrease it. Countries with complex economies and societies like Brazil have found it difficult to define their objectives and set priorities among them during this round. As a result, they have not achieved as many successes as their stock of skilled negotiators would lead one to expect.

Several side issues could be noted here. When multilateral bargaining could be broadly articulated by the grand coalition of developing countries, it was not necessary for each country to follow every issue and attend all meetings. Nor was it necessary to have large teams in the capitals do extensive backup research and provide adequate instructions on all issues. Today, as interests among developing countries become increasingly differentiated, more efforts must be made at the country level. To participate effectively countries must acquire detailed knowledge of the system and appropriate technical skills.

Finally, even countries with large pools of able negotiators may not be well equipped to participate effectively in today's trade negotiations if they are experienced only in the old-style negotiations. The skills needed to demand access and to gain the maximum benefit from a willingness to liberalize are quite different from those used to resist liberalization.

How one deals with this problem is difficult to say. Replacing the old negotiators with new ones may well be necessary. But as Mexico discovered when the Salinas government did this, the approach carries with it a serious loss of continuity and knowledge. The Canadian government faced a similar problem in implementing its FTA with the United States. After the agreement was signed, the Department of External Affairs reassigned the assistant chief negotiators to other duties, effectively leaving it to the Americans to "explain" what was intended when a given clause was drafted. If a change of negotiators is necessary, a sensible approach may be to retain some of the old negotiators as advisers to the new team, at least during the transition period.

New skills will also be required as developing countries move into new, narrowly defined coalitions. In old-style negotiations, diplomats receive credit for defending their country's policies. In times of coalition building, new propositions must be sold, and diplomats must move from warfare positioning to more creative and positive proposals. Australia realized early on that persuasion was required to promote the Group of Cairns and appointed the right diplomats for the task. Although negotiations could not bring about major change, skilled handling could give structure to the ongoing process.

RESULTS

What results have developing countries achieved with the bargaining strategies they have chosen? The question is hard to answer for at least two reasons. First, it is difficult to specify the counterfactual: what would have happened if a different strategy had been followed? The problem is compounded in multilateral negotiations, where any one country's actions contribute only partially to the outcome. Second, any ex post facto assessment enjoys the advantage of hindsight. Strategies that now appear to be wrong could not necessarily have been so identified at the time. Still, while criticism based on hindsight is not "fair," it can be useful if it provides lessons for future action. It is in this spirit that the following observations are offered.

Developing countries exercised considerable leverage at the time of the prelaunch period of the Uruguay Round, even though they did not present a united front. Some quietly followed Brazil and India, while others joined the smaller developed countries. In the negotiations they were able to work out the framework for the round as a whole (see Chapter 11). When negotiations involve drawing a mandate, consensus is required. At this point the process is a positive-sum one, not a matter of clear-cut victory and defeat. In order to reach consensus, every party must receive something within the framework.

Market access negotiations are essentially a competitive game in which the language of gains and losses, mercantilism and reciprocity prevails. In the Uruguay Round a remarkable shift of attitude occurred as the Round progressed and countries moved from principled declarations toward pragmatic and constructive participation. The results of this phase still remain to be seen.

The difficulty of reaching agreement in the Uruguay Round has been a disappointment to all participants in the negotiations, so the lack of major breakthroughs by developing countries should not be judged harshly. In agriculture, the results are still inconclusive. As mentioned earlier, the Cairns Group expanded the terrain of possible agreement. A similar observation can be made about the ITCB (see Chapter 11). In services, developing countries (within and outside the G10) achieved significant improvements in the tentative agreement by participating creatively in the latter stages of the negotiations. For example, a draft section prepared by a Latin American group was eventually incorporated into the accord; one would not have predicted this from the positions developing countries took early in the round. More generally, developing countries learned a great deal about this issue and are today much better able to define and defend their interests with respect to services than they were five years ago.

Developing countries have been very accommodating, as is reflected by the broad acceptance of the Dunkel Draft proposed at the end of 1991. The draft does have a number of elements to benefit developing countries: the gradual phasing out of the MFA, clearer safeguard mechanisms, and disciplines for ADDs and CVDs. Panel decisions will be binding unless rejected by consensus (instead of adopted by consensus, as before). Many countries had conceived the round to be mainly a means of containment of "aggressive unilateralism" (see the Introduction and Chapter 1) as expressed in Section 301 of the U.S. trade law. As part of the accord on a speedier and more efficient dispute settlement mechanism the United States has pledged to exhaust the new GATT procedures before resorting to Section 301. It has not, however, agreed to give up unilateral measures altogether. The U.S. insistence on maintaining GATT-illegal domestic legislation is a demonstration of its half-hearted commitment to a multilaterally determined rule of law.

Overall, the expected outcome of the round demands substantial concessions from developing countries, namely, the harmonization of intellectual property rights, acceptance of stricter disciplines on subsidies, a generalized erosion of special and differential treatment, and, within this, tighter disciplines on QRs for balance-of-payments reasons

(Article 18b). It is not altogether clear that the willingness to undertake greater policy commitments will be translated into firmer market access.

Has bilateral bargaining succeeded for the countries willing to try it? Here the conclusions are mixed. For the Asian NICs, product-by-product bargaining has maintained market access (see Chapter 9). However, there are signs that the strategy has diminishing returns as the United States reduces the porosity of its trade barriers. This has precipitated active participation in multilateral rulemaking to govern CVDs and ADDs during the Uruguay Round.

So far, Mexico is the only developing country to negotiate a comprehensive trade deal with the United States. If it succeeds in providing a defense against increased protection and arbitrary applications of sanctions, it will have achieved important gains. However, the Canadian experience suggests that even a dispute settlement mechanism is no guarantee against ad hoc protectionism in sensitive sectors. Again, though, all countries are not Mexico, and others trying to negotiate similar FTAs will not necessarily have Mexico's leverage. Moreover, the price to pay in terms of accommodation in trade (and nontrade) matters may be higher (see Chapter 3).

Brazil and Argentina have had to face the United States bilaterally under financial distress and the threat of sanctions (see Chapters 6 and 7). This allowed the United States to create allies among exporters and to exert leverage over multilateral bank loans. The availability of a wider range of sanctions and rewards (including financial ones) is one of the reasons the United States has preferred to push its trade demands toward these countries bilaterally rather than in the GATT.

In addition to bargaining multilaterally and bilaterally, countries have also liberalized their trade regimes unilaterally. What results have countries achieved in "bargaining by not bargaining"? Have they received credit or counterconcessions for previous unilateral actions? This was one of the principal questions posed in the early stages of this project: Are countries giving their bargaining chips away when they unilaterally liberalize? Would they do better to hold onto them and demand concessions in return?

When protection is very high, liberalizing only in return for concessions is pointless. First, there are efficiency gains to be had. Second, if the country is small, the initial liberalization will have little weight and elicit little response. Third, the question is academic if the country lacks the ability to withhold liberalization because of external conditionality or internal political conditions.

The lack of significant offers in multilateral market access may simply reflect the state of play. Many countries have lowered their applied tariff levels substantially but have withheld commitment to those levels in GATT as a last bargaining chip, that is, they have not bound the new tariffs or have offered to make bindings above the applied rates. This resistance to bind applied rates has brought scarce dividends—except rewards reaped bilaterally for cases such as Mexico and Costa Rica (see Chapters 4 and 5). "Credit" in GATT is given depending on the level at which tariffs are bound, not the level at which they are applied.

In most cases, external financial pressures (i.e., balance-of-payments vulnerability and Bank/Fund conditionality) will ensure that tariff levels remain low. Conditionality may not be as binding as a formal GATT commitment but in practice the distinction is irrelevant: the general trend toward lower tariffs (despite possible ebbs and flows) is quasi permanent (see Chapter 7). The difference, of course, is that conditionality is in theory of much shorter duration than a GATT binding and it brings with it immediate financial relief. In any case, it is clear that some form of binding will be required to secure even the possibility of receiving credit. Standards applied to developing countries have become stricter and more consistent in this respect in recent years, as seen in the conditions of accession for Mexico and Costa Rica.

In the meantime, some rewards have been collected elsewhere. There are indications that Mexico received some bilateral credit from its unilateral liberalization, for example, through the lowering of some NTBs and increases in some quotas from the United States following devaluation. It could also be argued that liberalizers like Argentina have been quite clever in obtaining World Bank loans, protesting about conditionality while carrying out trade policy reforms that they would have implemented voluntarily in any case.

On the whole, however, one must conclude that liberalizing in the hope of receiving credit has not been a particularly successful tactic, if governments ever saw it as one. In trade, as in debt bargaining, good behavior is rarely rewarded (Griffith-Jones, 1988). Compensation for good behavior should not enter into a negotiator's calculations. With unilateral liberalization, virtue is its own reward.

THE FUTURE

Global bargaining arrangements are at a crossroads. The decline in confidence in the GATT as its agenda becomes overloaded and agreements more elusive is tilting the balance in favor of bilateral and regional arrangements. While individual countries may be able to strike some good deals, the effects on a rules-based trading system and the interests of the least developed countries within it are likely to be negative.

Are there forces in play that might arrest this trend? Few are obvious. An important one would be an interest by the large industrial countries in preserving the GATT, but this interest does not appear strong. The GATT was once useful to the U.S. executive branch in dealing with a protection-ist Congress. But the reduced effectiveness of the GATT has lessened this advantage at the same time that Congress has assumed a greater say in trade (see Chapter 3). The motives behind U.S. trade policy have also become more nakedly economic, and fewer countries can expect favor-able treatment for geopolitical reasons, as the Mexican and Costa Rican cases illustrate.

The degree of protectionism is also disturbing. Without a decline in the discrimination against developing countries, their export-oriented strategies are less rewarding and may ultimately be less sustainable. Liberalizers will receive only the benefits coming from the import side (e.g., on prices and competition). Larger devaluations or lower export prices will be needed to achieve a given degree of export earnings, putting further strain on adjusting economies.

The emerging pattern of trade management also contains disturbing elements. One is the extension of the "level playing field" into areas hitherto subject to domestic discretion. These include protection of cul-tural industries, workers' rights, the environment, technological policies, savings rates, and so on. Another source of concern is the per-versity of protectionism. Protection in industrialized countries continues to shelter declining industries, while the freedom to protect infant industries in developing countries is increasingly restricted. The trend is disturbing not only for North-South income distribution but for the long-run growth and efficiency of the world economy. It is unlikely that Japanese or Korean industry could have developed under the restric-tions being promoted today; the benefits forgone from industries and countries that fail to develop in the future will be invisible but their loss no less important.

One source of optimism lies in the spread of unilateral liberalization. Neighboring countries, which are natural trading partners, will be drawn together as they liberalize. This opens up new market opportunities; it also allows the strengthening of coalitions for joint bargaining in third markets. As the case of the CACM shows, this is an incremental process. Brazil and Argentina together with neighboring Uruguay and Paraguay have formed Mercosur with similar objectives. A new agenda for South-South cooperation and trade is now on the table.

POLICY RECOMMENDATIONS

The studies in this volume have important implications for the trade-bar-gaining strategies of developing countries. These are relevant for both objectives (What should countries bargain for?) and methods (How should they bargain?).

Countries that attempt to bargain over trade today do so in an increasingly tough environment. Developed countries suffer from aid fatigue and are less willing to offer nonreciprocal preferential treatment to developing countries. The postcolonial ties between Britain and the Caribbean or France and Francophone Africa, which provided some trade preferences, are also weakening as the EC consolidates (see Chapter 2). The end of the Cold War removes opportunities for nonaligned countries to play off one superpower against another.

Such an environment calls for agility and pragmatism in choosing both goals and tactics. Emphasis should be placed on issues of concrete benefit, such as obtaining contractual market access commitments, dispute settlement mechanisms, and the like. Measures that reduce uncertainty and thereby encourage investment are likely to be of more benefit than preferential treatment that can be revoked when the bargaining gets tough (as in the Argentine dispute with the United States).

The experience of the Asian NICs also indicates the risks in unilaterally adopting extreme and indiscriminate versions of trade liberalization. NIC success in export-oriented industrialization has resulted in part from selective, targeted government intervention. Although average levels of protection have not been high, subsidies for targeted industries have been significant. There is a danger that the scope for selective, temporary protection of this type will be eliminated, to the particular detriment of late developers. Developing countries that have the political and administrative capacity to apply such a strategy should bargain for the flexibility to apply it. In negotiating policy loans with the World Bank, for example, countries might accept low average tariffs but insist on the right to retain some dispersion. Similarly, tariff bindings in the GATT should not be unreasonably low, and a gap should be retained between applied and bound rates, for bargaining as well as for industrial policy considerations. Countries may at some point need to increase tariffs given that they have agreed to restrain their right to apply QRs for balance-of-payments reasons (under Article 18b). If tariffs are bound at across-the-board low levels, a cumbersome process of renegotiation would have to be reopened with all affected parties. Indeed, the laboriousness of the process might lead to increased lending from the Bank and the IMF to finance disequilibria.

Pragmatism should also be applied in choosing bargaining tactics. The NIC strategy of rolling with the punches—maintaining long-term relationships with valued trade partners while working at the margins to delay, evade, or adapt to specific sanctions—has been extremely effective for those with the skills to apply it. The trend toward active and constructive participation (as opposed to blocking) in MTNs has also shown concrete results, for example, in services and to some extent in agriculture. Helping to draft agreements, mediate in conflicts, and carry out technical work gives countries more opportunities to influence events than they would get by distancing themselves from the proceedings. An extension of this approach is "technocratic bargaining" (Odell, 1988). In this approach, a negotiator uses knowledge of an opponent's interests, internal politics, and legal/technical constraints to put forward acceptable solutions that the opponent might not have thought of. (The policy recommendation derived from this project's previous phase—that tax and banking regulations in creditor countries be modified in specific ways to encourage debt relief—is an example; see Rodríguez and Griffith-Jones, 1992). Such an approach is particularly suitable for countries that may lack economic weight but have skilled personnel and clear objectives.

There may also be a role for more minifora like the Cairns Group that bring together a variety of countries with an interest in a single issue. While it is difficult to form such groups around complex issues, the very act of creating them and beginning to think out loud about them can be useful. The recently formed interministerial committee of the OECD on trade and environment appears to be achieving some success in this regard.

With respect to the optimal mix of bilateral and multilateral bargaining, the conclusions are less clear. Countries can obviously achieve short-term benefits by pursuing a relatively quick and efficient route to agreement. Such bargaining will continue and increase unless the GATT becomes significantly more effective. The down side of course, is that numerous bilateral agreements will further reduce the importance of the GATT and the resources that countries devote to it, accelerating the downward spiral. It is naive to expect that larger countries will abandon bilateral bargaining, but they might at least be aware of the potential danger and be advised not to pursue this route to the exclusion of others. The "plurilateralist" alternative—the negotiation of agreements among a medium-sized group of countries—can avoid the transaction costs of very large multilateral negotiations while offsetting some of the bargaining power of a single large country.

The authors of this volume have in some cases provided advice for specific countries. Kumar applauds India's recent pragmatism and suggests it be continued and extended; India should no longer attempt to represent the Third World and should instead use its many skilled and experienced negotiators to work out multilateral agreements. Rodríguez recommends that Costa Rica not overemphasize bilateral bargaining and recognize the benefits that could be achieved by forging a common position on some issues with the rest of Central America. Weston cautions Latin America against putting too many eggs in the U.S. basket, emphasizing trade relations with a possibly declining power to the exclusion of global opportunities. Griffith-Jones invites international financial agencies to develop a methodology for an ex post facto evaluation of the trade diversion effects of European integration. This would counteract the information disadvantage of developing countries and would give them a base on which to make a claim for compensation when their market access is eroded.

An urgent issue is the potential fallacy of composition created by simultaneous policy changes. Economists have long warned that the widespread adoption of export-oriented policies by developing countries, especially in manufactures, could saturate world markets, or at least the tolerance of protectionist lobbies. To date there has been no recognition of this problem in country-specific trade liberalization programs, but many of the pressures on the multilateral trading system and the increased resort to regional solutions are responses to this problem. As in other areas of adjustment, measures solely directed at developing countries under the aegis of the World Bank and IMF are incomplete. A global solution is needed.

Finally, the project has some lessons for small countries, whose bargaining prospects are the dimmest. The interests of countries in the South are diverging. Many countries that are industrializing and/or striking good bilateral deals with countries in the North see little common interest with the smallest and least developed. (Some even aspire to OECD membership.) But coalitions of the poorest alone will have negligible economic weight. (The forty-two least developed countries account for only one-third of 1 percent of world exports: UN, 1990.) Their political weight has also diminished with the end of the Cold War. Shortages of technicians and negotiators make technocratic bilateral bargaining difficult as well.

The smallest and poorest countries will thus see their interests best served by a world trading system based more on rules and less on power and skills. They should have much to gain from pooling talent and establishing an efficient division of labor allows them to make technically credible contributions to negotiations about rules. (Donor agencies should recognize the high potential payoff from research, training, and advisory services in this field.) The composition of these coalitions might vary with specific issues, sometimes involving developed countries (like the Cairns Group) or a broad spectrum of countries in the South.

For although the smallest and poorest have the most to gain from a rules-based trading system, the benefits are more general. Without the certainty that rules provide, investment and adaptation are discouraged at a time when they are badly needed. And while small countries may benefit most from rules, the burden of maintaining an open multilateral trading system cannot be borne mainly by its weakest members. To reverse the disturbing trends we have described, countries will need to make a genuine commitment to multilateralism.

NOTES

This chapter reflects contributions from all the case study authors, offered during the project's workshops, as well as those provided by Patrick Low, John Odell, Jeffrey Schott, and Susan Strange. Valuable comments on an earlier draft were provided by Manuel Agosin, Gerald Helleiner, and John Whalley.

1. Although these negotiations are in theory trilateral, in practice they have remained bilateral.

2. This G10 should not, of course, be confused with the better-known and more influential G10 that comprises the most important economies and operates in the context of the World Bank and the IMF.

Acronyms

ACP	African, Caribbean, and Pacific countries
ADD	antidumping duty
AID	Agency for International Development
ASEAN	Association of Southeast Asian Nations
CACM	Central American Common Market
CADEXCO	Chamber of Exporters of Costa Rica
CAP	Common Agricultural Policy
CARIBCAN	Canadian Program for Cooperation with the Commonwealth Caribbean
CBI	Caribbean Basin Initiative
CFF	Compensatory Financing Facility
CINDE	Coalición de Iniciativas de Desarrollo
CUSFTA	Canadian–U.S. Free Trade Agreement
CVD	countervailing duty
EAI	Enterprise for the Americas Initiative
EC	European Community
ECLAC	Economic Commission for Latin America and the Caribbean
ECU	European currency unit
EEA	European Economic Area
EFTA	European Free Trade Association
ERM	Exchange Rate Mechanism (of the European Monetary System)
ERP	effective rate of protection
ESF	Economic Support Fund
FDI	foreign direct investment
FTA	free trade agreement
GATS	General Agreement on Trade in Services
GATT	General Agreement on Tariffs and Trade
GDP	gross domestic product

GNP	gross national product
GSP	Generalized System of Preferences
IMF	International Monetary Fund
ITAC	International Trade Advisory Committee
ITCB	International Textile and Clothing Bureau
LAIA	Latin American Integration Association
LDC	less-developed country
LIBOR	London Inter-Bank Offered Rate
MFA	Multifiber Arrangement
MFN	most-favored nation
MTN	multilateral trade negotiation
MTO	multilateral trade organization
NAFTA	North American Free Trade Agreement
NGOs	nongovernmental organizations
NIC	newly industrializing country
NRBP	natural resource–based product
NTB	nontariff barrier
OECD	Organization for Economic Cooperation and Development
OPEC	Organization of Petroleum Exporting Countries
PECE	Economic Solidarity Pact
PFI	private foreign investment
PMA	Pharmaceutical Manufacturers Association
PROFIEX	promotion of exports program
PSE	producer subsidy equivalent
QR	quantitative restriction
S&D	special and differential
SAGIT	Sectoral Advisory Group on International Trade
SAL	structural adjustment loan
SCEAIT	Standing Committee on External Affairs and International Trade
SEA	Single European Act
SELA	Latin American Economic System
SEM	Single European Market
SII	Structural Impediments Initiative
TDE	trade-distorting equivalent
TPL	trade policy loan
TRIM	trade-related investment measure
TRIP	trade-related intellectual property
UNCTAD	United Nations Conference on Trade and Development
USTR	U.S. Trade Representative
VER	voluntary export restraint
WIPO	World Intellectual Property Organization

Bibliography

Abreu, M. de Paiva, "Argentina and Brazil During the 1930s: The Impact of British and American International Economic Policies," in R. Thorp (editor), *Latin America in the 1930s: The Role of the Periphery in World Crisis,* Macmillan, London, 1984.

———, "O Brasil e o GATT," draft prepared for the project "60 Anos de Política Externa Brasileira," Rio de Janeiro, 1991.

———, "Developing Countries and the Uruguay Round of Trade Negotiations," in *Proceedings of the World Bank Annual Conference on Development Economics,* Washington, D.C., 1989.

Abreu, M. de Paiva, and Fritsch, W., "Obstacles to Brazilian Export Growth and the Present Multilateral Trade Negotiations," in J. Whalley (editor), *Developing Countries and the Global Trading System,* vol. 2: *Country Studies,* Macmillan, London, 1989.

Ahluwalia, J., *Industrial Growth in India—Stagnation Since the Mid-Sixties,* Oxford University Press, New Delhi, 1985.

Aicardi, M., and Tussie, D., "La Argentina ante la Nueva Ronda del GATT," *América Latina Internacional,* vol. 3, no. 10, 1986.

Alam, M. Shahid, "The South Korean "Miracle": Examining the Mix of Government and Markets," *Journal of Developing Areas,* no. 23, January 1989.

Alizadeh, P., and Griffith-Jones, S., "European Integration and Its Implications for LDCs," *Pensamiento Iberoamericano,* no. 20, 1991.

Amsden, A., "The State and Taiwan's Economic Development," in P. Evans et al. (editors), *Bringing the State Back In,* Cambridge University Press, New York, 1985.

Anderson, K., and Tyers, R., "How Developing Countries Could Gain from Agricultural Trade Liberalization in the Uruguay Round," in I. Goldin and O. Knudsen (editors), *Agricultural Trade Liberalization,* OECD World Bank, Paris, 1990.

Argentina, Secretaria de Industria y Comercio Exterior, *Boletín de Comercio Exterior,* various issues.

Axelrod, R., *The Evolution of Cooperation,* Basic Books, New York, 1984.

Baker, J., Speech to the National Cotton Council, February 2, 1988.

Banco Central de Costa Rica, "El programa de ajuste estructural y la política comercial de Costa Rica durante las décadas del setenta y del ochenta y perspectivas para la década del noventa," *Comentarios sobre asuntos económicos,* no. 93, 1991.

Banco de México, *Informe Anual 1987,* Mexico: Banco de Mexico, 1988.

Baumann, R., and Moreira, H., "Os incentivos às exportaçöes brasileiras de produtos manufaturados—1969/85," *Pesquisa e Planejamento Econômico,* vol. 17, no. 2, August 1987.

Bennett, B. T., "Las relaciones comerciales recientes entre México y Estados Unidos: Resultados positivos y mayor cooperación," in Roett (editor), *México y Estados Unidos: El manejo de la relación,* Siglo Veintiuno Editores, Mexico, 1989.

Berlinski, J., "La protección efectiva de actividades seleccionadas de la industria manufacturera argentina," Ministerio de Economía, Buenos Aires, 1978.

———, "Trade Policies in Argentina: 1964–1988," mimeo, Buenos Aires, 1989.

Bhagwati, J., *The World Trading System at Risk,* Harvester Wheatsheaf, Hemel Hempstead, 1991.

Bhagwati, J., and Patrick, H. (editors), *Aggressive Unilateralism: America's 301 Trade Policy and the World Trading System,* University of Michigan Press, Ann Arbor, 1990.

Bhattacharya, B. B., and Mitra, A., "Industry-Agriculture Growth Rates: Widening of Disparity—An Explanation," *Economic and Political Weekly,* August 1989.

Blanco, H., Mexican Senate Hearings, May 11, 1990.

Booth, K., "Alliances," in J. Baylis, K. Booth, J. Garnet, and P. Williams, *Contemporary Strategy: Theories and Policies,* Croom Helm, London, 1976.

Bouzas, R., "United States–Latin American Trade Relations: Issues in the 1980s and Prospects for the 1990s," in J. Hartlyn, L. Shoultz, and A. Varas (editors), *United States–Latin American Relations in the 1990s: Beyond the Inter-American System,* University of North Carolina Press, Chapel Hill, 1992

Bouzas, R., and Keifman, S., *Política comercial y tendencias recientes del comercio exterior en la Argentina (1976–1985),* Facultad Latinoamericana de Ciencias Sociales (FLACSO), September 1987.

Brown, D. K., Deardorff, A. V. and Stern, R. M. "A North American Free Trade Agreement: Analytical Issues and Computational Assessment," paper presented at a conference on North American Free Trade: Economic and Political Implications, Washington, D.C., June 1991.

Bueno, G., "Las opciones de negociación comercial de México," in G. Vega Cánovas (editor), *México ante el libre comercio con América del Norte,* El Colegio de México, Mexico, 1991.

Cámara de Exportadores de Costa Rica (CADEXCO), "La adhesión de Costa Rica al GATT," San José, 1990.

Carneiro, D. D. and Modiano, E. M., "Ajuste externo e desequilíbrio interno," in M. de Paiva Abreu (editor), *A ordem do progresso. Cem anos de política econômica republicana 1889–1989,* Campus, Rio de Janeiro, 1990.

Castillo, C. M., "La crisis internacional de la deuda: La experiencia de Costa Rica," in R. Ffrench-Davis and R. Feinberg (editors),. *Más allá de la crisis de la deuda: bases para un nuevo enfoque,* Corporación de Investigaciones Económicas para Latinoamérica (CIEPLAN), Santiago, 1987.

Caves, R., and Uekusa, M., *Industrial Organization in Japan,* Brookings Institution, Washington, D.C., 1976.

Central Bank of Brazil, *Brazil Economic Program: Internal and External Adjustment,* Brasília, several issues.

Coes, D. V., "Brazil," in D. Papageorgiou, M. Michaely, and A. M. Choksi (editors), *Liberalizing Foreign Trade,* vol. 4: *The Experience of Brazil, Colombia, and Peru,* Blackwell, Oxford, 1991.

Cox, D., and Harris, R., "North American Free Trade and Its Implications for Canada: Results from a CGE Model of North American Trade," mimeo, Simon Fraser University, 1991.

Curtis, J., "Which Way: Canadian Trade Policy in a Changing World Economy," in J. Whalley (editor), *Canada and the Multilateral Trading System*, University of Toronto Press, Toronto, 1985.

Dam, K., *The GATT: Law and International Economic Organization*, University of Chicago Press, Chicago, 1970.

Davenport, M., "The Charybdis of Anti-Dumping: A New Form of EC Industrial Policy?" Royal Institute of International Affairs, Discussion Paper No. 22, London, 1988.

Davenport, M., and Page, S., *Europe: 1992 and the Developing Countries*, Overseas Development Institute, London, 1991.

de las Carreras, A., "La próxima rueda del GATT en el área de las carnes," Fundación Cámara de Consignatarios de Ganado, Buenos Aires, 1985.

del Castillo, G., "El proteccionismo estadounidense en la era de Reagan," *Comercio Exterior*, vol. 37, no. 11, November 1987.

de Lima, M. R. S., "The Political Economy of Brazilian Foreign Policy: Nuclear Energy, Trade, and Itaipu," Ph.D. dissertation, Vanderbilt University, 1986.

de Villalobos, R., *La Argentina y la discusión sobre la reforma del comercio agrícola mundial en el GATT*, Centro de Economía Internacional, Buenos Aires, 1988.

Destler, I. M., and Odell, J., *Anti-protection: Changing Forces in US Trade Politics*, Institute for International Economics, Washington, D.C., 1987.

Doern, G., "The Department of Industry, Science and Technology: Is There Industrial Policy After Free Trade?", in K. Graham (editor), *How Ottawa Spends 1990–91: Tracking the Second Agenda*, Carleton University Press, Ottawa, 1990.

Economic Council of Canada, *Managing Adjustment: Policies for Trade–Sensitive Industries*, Ottawa, 1988.

——, *Au courant*, vol. 11, no. 2, 1990.

Eden, L., and Molot, M., "From Silent Integration to Strategic Alliance: The Political Economy of North American Free Trade," paper presented in a joint session of the annual meetings of the Canadian Economics Association and the Canadian Political Science Association on "Canada-US-Mexico Free Trade," June 1991.

"Entendimiento en materia de comercio e inversión," *Comercio Exterior*, vol. 37, no. 11, November 1987.

Erzan, R., and Yeats, A., "Prospects for US–Latin American Free Trade Areas: Empirical Evidence Concerning the View from the South," mimeo, World Bank, Washington, D.C., 1991.

Federation of Private Organizations of Central America and Panama (FEDEPRICAP), "Informe de la visita de la delegación de FEDEPRICAP, a Washington D.C. el miércoles 20 y 21 de noviembre de 1991, y reunión con la Embajadora Comercial de los Estados Unidos Carla Hills," mimeo, San José, 1991.

Finger, J. M., "That Old GATT Magic No More Casts Its Spell (How the Uruguay Round Failed)", *Journal of World Trade*, vol. 25, no. 2, April 1991.

Finger, J. M., and Murray, T., "Policing Unfair Imports: The US Example," *Journal of World Trade*, vol. 24, no. 4, August 1990.

Finlayson, J., and Weston, A., *Middle Powers in the International System: The GATT, Middle Powers and the Uruguay Round*, North-South Institute, Ottawa, 1990.

Fritsch, W., "Escolhas estratégicas em face do plano Bush," mimeo, Rio de Janeiro, 1990.

Fritsch, W., and Franco, G., "The Progress of Trade and Industrial Policy Reform in Brazil," in *Pensamiento Iberoamericano,* no. 21, 1992.

General Agreement on Tariffs and Trade (GATT), *Annual Report,* Geneva, 1991.

———, *Basic Instruments and Selected Documents,* 14th Supplement, Geneva, 1966.

———, *International Trade,* various issues.

———, *Trade Policies for a Better Future* (also called the Leutwiler Report), Geneva, 1985.

———, *Trade Policy Review Mechanism: Canada,* Geneva, 1990a.

———, *Trade Policy Review Mechanism: United States 1989,* Geneva, 1990b.

———, Committee on Subsidies and Countervailing Measures and Committee on Anti-Dumping Practices, tables, Geneva, 1986.

Griffith-Jones, S. (editor), *Managing World Debt,* Harvester Wheatsheaf, Hemel Hempstead, 1988.

Gurría, A., "La restructuración de la deuda: El caso de México," in S. Griffith–Jones (editor), *Deuda externa, renegociación y ajuste en América Latina,* Fondo de Cultura Económica, Mexico, 1988.

Hamilton, C., and Whalley, J., "Coalitions in the Uruguay Round" *Weltwirtschaftliches Archiv,* vol. 125, no. 3, 1989.

Hart, Michael, *A North American Free Trade Agreement, The Strategic Implications for Canada,* Centre for Trade Policy and Law, and the Institute for Research on Public Policy, Ottawa, 1990.

Helleiner, G., "Consideraciones sobre un Area de Libre Comercio entre Estados Unidos y México. Experiencias de la integración económica entre socios desiguales," in G. Vega Cánovas (editor), *México ante el libre comercio con América del Norte,* El Colegio de México, Mexico, 1991.

Hernández, H., "Vicisitudes en el comercio entre México y Estados Unidos," in *Medio siglo de financiamiento y promoción del comercio exterior de México,* Banco Nacional de Comercio Exterior and El Colegio de Mexico, Mexico, 1987.

Herrera, C., "Costa Rica's Experience with Trade Policy Reform Since 1983," in M. Agosin, and D. Tussie (editors), *Trading Places: New Dimensions in Trade Policy and Development,* Macmillan, 1992.

———, "Las negociaciones de Costa Rica en el marco del GATT," *Comentarios sobre asuntos económicos,* no. 86, Banco Central de Costa Rica, 1990.

Higgott, R., and Fenton Cooper, A., "Middle Power Leadership and Coalition Building: Australia, the Cairns Group, and the Uruguay Round of Trade Negotiations," *International Organization,* vol. 44, no. 4, 1990.

Hudec, R., *Developing Countries in the GATT Legal System,* Trade Policy Research Centre, London, 1987.

Hufbauer Gary, and Schott, Jeffrey, *Prospects for a North American Free Trade Agreement,* Institute for International Economics, Washington, D.C., 1992.

Hurrell, A., and Felder, E., "The US–Brazilian Informatics Dispute," mimeo, Johns Hopkins University, Baltimore, 1988.

India, Government of, *Economic Survey,* New Delhi, 1992.

Instituto de Pesquisas Economicas e Analise (IPEA/CEPAL), *Protecionismo das Comunidades Européias contra as exportações brasileiras,* Brasília, 1985a.

———, *Relações comerciais entre o Brasil e os Estados Unidos,* Brasília, 1985b.

Ize, A., "Trade Liberalization, Stabilization and Growth: Some Notes on the Mexican Experience," IMF Working Paper, Washington, D.C., March 1990.

Jenkins, R., "The Political Economy of Industrialization: A Comparison of Latin

America and East Asian Newly Industrializing Countries," *Development and Change*, vol. 22, 1991.

Josling, T., Tangerman, S., and Warley, T. K., "Still Time to Rescue a Worthwhile Agreement," *Financial Times*, November 16, 1990.

Kadar, B., *Symposium of Reforms in Foreign Economic Relations of Eastern Europe and Soviet Union*, Geneva, 1990.

Kahler, M., and Odell, J., "Developing Country Coalition-Building and International Trade Negotiations," in J. Whalley (editor), *Rules, Power and Credibility*, Centre for the Study of International Economic Relations, University of Western Ontario, 1988.

Kelkar, V. L., and Kumar, R., "Industrial Growth in the Eighties: Emerging Policy Issues," Economic and Political Weekly, New Delhi, January 1990.

Kelkar, V. L., Kumar, R., and Nangia, R., "India's Industrial Economy: Policies, Performance and Reforms," mimeo submitted to the Asian Development Bank, New Delhi, 1990.

Kuttner, R., *Managed Trade and Economic Sovereignty*, Economic Policy Institute, Washington, D.C., 1989.

Laird, S., and Nogués, J., "Trade Policies and the Highly Indebted Countries," *World Bank Economic Review*, vol. 3, no. 2, May 1989.

Lawrence, R. Z., and Schultze, C. L. (editors), *An American Trade Strategy: Options for the 1990s*, Brookings Institution, Washington, D.C., 1990.

Lee, Y. S., Hadwiger, D. F., and Lee, C., "Agricultural Policy Making Under International Pressures: The Case of Korea," *Food Policy*, vol. 15, no. 5, 1990.

Lustig, N., "Bordering on Partnership: The U.S.–Mexico Free Trade Agreement," Brookings Discussion Papers, Washington, D.C.: Brookings Institution, 1991.

MacDonald, B., "Agricultural Negotiations in the Uruguay Round," *The World Economy*, vol. 13, no. 3, 1990.

Maciel, G. A., "Brazil's Proposals for the Reform of the GATT System," *The World Economy*, vol. 1, no. 2, 1978.

Magun, S., "The Role of Trade in North American Integration," paper presented at the Canadian Economics Association annual meeting, 1991.

Magun, S., et al., "Open Borders: An Assessment of the Canada–US Free Trade Agreement," Economic Council of Canada, Discussion Paper No. 344, Ottawa, 1988.

Malpica de Lamadrid, L., *¿Qué es el GATT?* Grijalbo, Mexico, 1985.

Modiano, E., "A ópera dos três cruzados: 1985–1989," in M. de Paiva Abreu (editor), *A ordem do progresso: Cem anos de política econômica republicana, 1889–1989*, Campus, Rio de Janeiro, 1990.

Molina, I., "La renovación del Sistema Generalizado de Preferencias arancelarias y sus implicaciones para México," M. García y Griego and G. Vega Cánovas (editors), *México–Estados Unidos 1984*, El Colegio de México, Mexico, 1985.

Morici, P., *Meeting the Competitive Challenge: Canada and the United States in the Global Economy*, National Planning Association, Washington, D.C., 1991.

Nagraj, R., "Growth Rate of India's GDP, 1950–51 to 1987–88," *Economic and Political Weekly*, New Delhi, June 1990.

Nogués, J., "Notas sobre los casos de aranceles compensatorios de Estados Unidos en contra de México," *Estudios económicos*, El Colegio de México, vol. 1 no. 2, July 1986.

———, "Notes on Patents, Distortions and Development," World Bank, Working Papers Series 315, Washington, D.C., January 1990.

Odell, J., "From London to Bretton Woods: Sources of Change in Bargaining Strategies and Outcomes," *Journal of Public Policy*, vol. 8, nos. 3 and 4, 1988.

———, "The Outcomes of International Trade Conflicts: The US and South Korea, 1960–1981," *International Studies Quarterly,* no. 29, 1985.

Olea, M. A., "Las negociaciones comerciales y la inserción de México en la economía internacional," mimeo, Mexico 1990a.

———, "Las negociaciones de adhesión de México al GATT," *Foro Internacional,* vol. 30, no. 3, January–March, 1990b.

Ortega, A., "El sistema anti-dumping mexicano: Factor crítico de la apertura comercial," *Comercio Exterior,* vol. 39, no. 3, March 1989.

Ostry, S., "Anti-Dumping: The Tip of the Iceberg," in M. Trebilcock and R. York (editors), *Fair Exchange: Reforming Trade Remedy Laws,* Policy Study No. 11, C. D. Howe Institute, Toronto, 1990a.

———, *Governments and Corporations in a Shrinking World: Trade and Innovation Policies in the United States, Europe and Japan,* Council on Foreign Relations Press, New York, 1990b.

Oxley, A., *The Challenge of Free Trade,* Harvester Wheatsheaf, Hemel Hempstead, 1990.

Patnaik, P., "Recent Growth Experience of the Indian Economy: Some Comments," *Economic and Political Weekly,* New Delhi, May 1987.

Pérez, W., "From Globalization to Regionalization: The Mexican Case," OECD Development Center, Technical Papers No. 24, Paris, 1990.

Rakesh, M., and Aggarwal, V., "Commands and Controls: Planning for Industrial Development, 1951–1990," paper presented to the Conference on Indicative Planning, Washington, D.C., 1990.

Rodríguez, E., "Costa Rica: A Quest for Survival," in S. Griffith-Jones (editor), *Managing World Debt,* Harvester Wheatsheaf, Hemel Hempstead, 1988.

———, "A Path in the Maze: Costa Rica, Cross-conditionality and Development," in E. Rodríguez, and S. Griffith-Jones (editors), *Cross-conditionality, Banking Regulations and Third World Debt,* Macmillan, London, 1992.

Rodríguez, E., and Griffith-Jones, S. (editors), *Cross-conditionality, Banking Regulations and Third World Debt,* Macmillan, London, 1992.

Rodrik, D., "Trade Policies and Development: Some New Issues," Centre for Economic Policy Research Discussion Paper Series No. 447, London, 1990.

Sachs, J., "Trade and Exchange Rate Policies in Growth Oriented Adjustment Programs," World Bank and IMF, Symposium on Growth Oriented Adjustment Programs, Washington, D.C., mimeo, 1987.

Schott, J., *Free Trade Areas and US Trade Policy,* Institute for International Economics, Washington, D.C., 1989.

Sistema Económico Latinoamericano (SELA), *Estudios de casos en las diferencias comerciales entre Estados Unidos y América Latina,* Caracas, 1987.

Standing Committee on External Affairs and International Trade, *North American Free Trade,* House of Commons, Ottawa, January 1991.

———, *Securing Our Global Future: Canada's Stake in the Unfinished Business of Third World Debt,* House of Commons, Ottawa, June 1990.

Stone, F., *Canada, the GATT and the International Trade System,* Montreal, Institute for Research on Public Policy, 1984.

Sturzenegger, A., "Price Discrimination in the Pampas: The Political-Economy of an Anti-Dutch Disease," World Bank, mimeo, Washington, D.C., 1988.

Ten Kate, A., "Trade Liberalization and Economic Stabalization: Lessons of Experience," *World Development* vol. 20, no. 5, Pergamon Press, Oxford, 1991.

Ten Kate, A., and De Mateo, F., "Apertura comercial y estructura de la protección en México," *Comercio Exterior,* vol. 39, no. 4, April 1989.

Toye, J., "Indo-European Cooperation in an Interdependent World," mimeo, New Delhi, 1989.

Trebilcock, M., and York, R., (editors), *Fair Exchange: Reforming Trade Remedy Laws,* Policy Study No. 11, C. D. Howe Institute, Toronto, 1990.

Trejos, J. D., and Elizalde, M. L., "Costa Rica: La distribución del ingreso y acceso a los programas de carácter social," Universidad de Costa Rica, Working Paper No. 90, San José, 1985.

Trela, I. and Whalley, J., "Bilateral Liberalization in Quota Restricted Items: US and Mexico in Textiles and Steel," paper presented at a conference on "North American Free Trade: Economic and Political Implications," Washington, D.C., June 1991.

———, "Do Developing Countries Lose from the MFA?" Department of Economics, University of Western Ontario, Working Paper No. 8804C, London, Ontario, 1988.

Trela, I., Whalley, J., and Wigle, R., "International Trade in Agriculture: Domestic Policies, Trade Conflicts and Negotiating Options," Centre for the Study of International Economic Relations, University of Western Ontario, Working Paper No. 8618C, 1986.

Tussie, D., "The Coordination of Latin American Debtors: What Is the Logic Behind the Story?" in S. Griffith-Jones (editor), *Managing World Debt,* Harvester Wheatsheaf, Hemel Hempstead, 1988.

Tussie, D., and Botzman, M., "Sweet Entanglement: Argentina and the World Bank Under the Baker Plan," in E. Rodríguez and S. Griffith-Jones (editors), *Cross-conditionality, Banking Regulations and Third World Debt,* Macmillan, London, 1992.

Twentieth Century Fund, Task Force on the Future of American Trade Policy, *The Free Trade Debate,* Priority Press Publications, New York, 1989.

Tyson, D. L., "Managed Trade: Making the Best of the Second Best," in R. Lawrence, and C. Schultze, (editors), *An American Trade Strategy: Options for the 1990s,* Brookings Institution, Washington, D.C., 1990.

United Nations, *Handbook of International Trade and Development Statistics,* several issues.

———, *International Trade Statistics Yearbook,* New York, 1988 and 1990.

———, *Monthly Bulletin of Statistics,* several issues.

———, *Trade and Development Report,* Geneva, 1989, 1990, and 1991.

———, *Yearbook,* New York, 1987 and 1989.

———, Conference on Trade and Development (UNCTAD), *Commodity Yearbook,* Geneva, 1990.

———, Economic Commission for Latin America and the Caribbean (ECLAC), "Latin American and Caribbean Lobbying for International Trade in Washington, D.C.," mimeo, Washington, D.C., June 1990.

U.S. Department of Commerce, *U.S. Trade Performance in 1988,* U.S. Government Printing Office, Washington, D.C., 1989.

———, International Trade Administration, *Caribbean Basin Investment Survey,* U.S. Government Printing Office, Washington, D.C., 1988.

Valdés, A., and Zietz, J., *Agricultural Protection in OECD Countries: Its Cost to LDCs,* International Food Policy Research Institute, Washington, D.C., 1980.

Vega Cánovas, G., "El entendimiento sobre subsidios e impuestos compensatorios entre México y Estados Unidos; implicaciones económicas y políticas," in G. Székely (editor), *México–Estados Unidos, 1985,* El Colegio de México, Mexico, 1986.

———, "Comercio bilateral: Sin redes protectoras," *Nexos,* no. 143, November 1989a.

———, "Prospects for Mexico–U.S. Trade Relations in an Era of Economic Crisis and Restructuring," paper presented at the Fifth International Congress of the

Latin American Studies Association, 1989b.

———, (editor), *México ante el libre comercio con América del Norte,"* El Colegio de México, Mexico, 1991.

Whalley, J. (editor) *Canada and the Multilateral Trading System,* University of Toronto Press, Toronto, 1985.

Windham, G. R., *International Trade and the Tokyo Round Negotiation,* Princeton University Press, Princeton, 1986.

Witker, J., "Códigos de conducta internacional del GATT suscritos por México," Universidad Nacional Autónoma de México, México 1988.

Wonnacott, R., "US Hub-and-Spoke Bilaterals and the Multilateral Trading System," Commentary 23, C. D. Howe Institute, Toronto, 1990.

World Bank, *Argentina: Industrial Sector Study,* Washington, D.C., 1987.

———, *Report and Recommendation of the President on a Proposed Second Trade Policy Loan to the Republic of Argentina,* Washington, D.C., October 1988.

———, "Trade Policy in Brazil: The Case for Reform," mimeo, Washington, D.C., 1989.

———, *World Development Report,* Washington, D.C., several numbers.

Yoffie, D. B., *Power and Protectionism: Strategies of the Newly Industrialized Countries,* Columbia University Press, New York, 1983.

Zabludovsky, J., "Trade Liberalization and Macroeconomic Adjustment," in D. S. Brothers and A. Wick, (editors), *Mexico's Search for a New Development Strategy,* Westview Press, Boulder, 1990.

The Contributors

DIANA TUSSIE is a senior research fellow at the Facultad Latinoamericana de Ciencias Sociales in Buenos Aires, where she also heads the Masters' Program in International Relations. She has been an advisor to the Argentine Ministry for the Economy and the Ministry of Foreign Affairs. She is consultant to several international organizations, such as UNCTAD, UNDP, IDB, and SELA. Her publications include *Latin America in the World Economy, The Less Developed Countries and the World Trading System: a Challenge to the GATT,* and *Trade and Growth: New Dilemmas in Trade Policy* (with Manuel Agosin).

DAVID GLOVER is director of the Economic, Trade and Technology Program at the International Development Research Centre in Ottawa, Canada. Dr. Glover is the author of a number of journal articles on trade, agricultural policy, and structural adjustment; and coauthor of *Small Farmers, Big Business: Contract Farming and Rural Development.*

MARCELO DE PAIVA ABREU is presently a professor of economics at the Catholic University of Rio de Janeiro, where he is also the director of the Department of Economics. He has been visiting professor at Universitá degli Studi di Modena, at the University of Illinois, and at the University of Cambridge. His recent publications include *O Brazil e o GATT: 1947–1991;* and *The Nicaraguan Trade Regimes: Past, Present and Prospects.* He edited *A Ordem do Progresso: Cem Anos de Política Económica Republicana, 1889–1989.* He has been an occasional consultant to the Ford Foundation, SELA, the South Commission, the World Bank, UNDP, the Brazilian Planning Secretariat, and the Brazilian Ministry of Foreign Affairs.

STEPHANY GRIFFITH-JONES is a fellow of the Institute of Development Studies at the University of Sussex. She previously worked at the Central Bank of Chile and Barclays Bank International in the United Kingdom. She has been a consultant to several international organisations, including the World Bank, the Commonwealth Secretariat, the European Commission, UNCTAD, and UNICEF. She has recently edited *Managing World Debt,* and she is coeditor of *Cross Conditionality, Banking Regulations and Third World Debt.*

ALEJANDRO JARA is a lawyer and member of Chile's foreign service. He was Chile's representative to the GATT in the mid-1980s and is currently director for trade negotiations for Sistema Economico Latino Americano (SELA).

RAJIV KUMAR is an economic advisor to the Ministry of Finance in India. He has been a consultant to the government of India and a professor at the Indian Institute of Foreign Trade. He has also been a consultant to international organizations such as the World Bank and the Asian Development Bank.

ENNIO RODRÍGUEZ is project coordinator, Investment Programme for Central America, while working for the Economic Commission for Latin America and the Caribbean. He is former minister of external finance and debt of Costa Rica and former adviser both to the minister of planning and economic policy and to the minister of agrarian development. He is coeditor of *Cross Conditionality, Banking Regulations and Third World Debt.*

CLAUDIA SCHATAN is an economics affairs officer at the Economic Commission for Latin America and the Caribbean. She has been a visiting lecturer at the Economics Department of the University of Connecticut, at Brown University, and at the University of California. She has been a researcher and lecturer at Centro de Investigación y Docencia Económica in Mexico. Her recent publications include *México–Estados Unidos: La Integración Macroeconónomica,* coedited with Darryl McLeod and Cassio Luiselli; and *Exports and Employment Generation in Mexico.*

ANN WESTON is presently with the North–South Institute, Ottawa. Before that she worked as a research officer with the Overseas Development Institute in London. She is author, with Vincent Cable and L. C. Jain, of *The Commerce of Culture: the Experience of Indian Handicrafts;* with Vincent Cable and Adrian Hewitt of *The EEC's Generalised System of Preferences—Evaluation and Proposals for Reform;* and, with Vincent Cable, of *South Asia's Exports to the EEC: Obstacles and Opportunities.*

Index

About the Book

The external conditions faced by developing countries have changed dramatically in the 1980s and 1990s. This book analyzes the effects of those changes on the LDCs' bargaining positions and power, the tactics they have chosen to promote their interests in the world trading system, and the results they have achieved.

Within a comparative framework, the authors examine the implications for the LDCs of developments in the North, the responses of countries in Latin America and Asia, and the evolution and effectiveness of collective bargaining strategies. They also speculate on the future of the world trading system.